Coleridge and the Conservative Imagination

The Conservative Imagination

*No man was ever yet a great poet,
without being at the same time
a profound philosopher.*

—Samuel Taylor Coleridge (1772–1834)
Biographia Literaria (1817) chap. 15

Coleridge and the Conservative Imagination

by
ALAN P. R. GREGORY

Mercer University Press
Macon, Georgia USA
2003

ISBN 0-86554-801-3   MUP/H605

Coleridge and the Conservative Imagination
Copyright ©2002
Mercer University Press, Macon, Georgia USA
All rights reserved
Printed in the United States of America

The paper used in this publication meets the minimum requirements
of American National Standard for Information Sciences—
Permanence of Paper for Printed Library Materials,
ANSI Z39.48-1984.

Library of Congress Cataloging-in-Publication Data

Gregory, Alan P. R., 1955–
Coleridge and the conservative imagination / by Alan P. R. Gregory.
   p. cm.
Includes bibliographical references and index.
ISBN 0-86554-801-3 (alk. paper)
1. Coleridge, Samuel Taylor, 1772–1834—Criticism and interpretation.
2. Conservatism—England—History—19th century.
3. Coleridge, Samuel Taylor, 1772–1834—Philosophy.
4. Coleridge, Samuel Taylor, 1772–1834—Religion..
5. Conservatism in literature.
6. Philosophy in literature.
7. Religion in literature.
I. Title.
PR4482.G74 2003
821'.7—dc21
                                                    2003005085

Contents

Preface vii

Acknowledgments x

1. Coleridge among the Conservatives 1

   Radical Imaginings 1
   Among the Conservatives 10
   The Later Political Writings 27

2. Philosophical Psychology and Conservative Politics ... 39

   Prologue: Does Fortune Favor Fools? 39
   Identification and the Goals of Rhetoric 42
   Imagination and the Renewal of the Mind 51

3. Imagination and the Wisdom of History 71

   Historical Method: Knowledge as Power 71
   The Scriptures: History as Prophecy 96

4. Social Conflict and the Balance of the Mind 119

   Imagination and the Extremes of Revolution 119
   Reason and the Critique of Commerce 143

5. Social Criticism and the Religious Imagination 167

   True Religion and Proper Interests 167
   Stifling the Imagination 179

6. The Conservative Imagination:
   Culture, Nature, and Grace 197

   The Secularization of Political Argument 197
   Beyond Utility: Church, State, and the Higher Reason 208
   Prophetic Relations: The Ordering of Nature and Culture .. 233
   The World's "Befriending Opposite" 241
   The Imagination 255

7. Conclusion 259

   Bibliography 267

   Indexes 281
      Name Index 281
      Subject Index 283

Preface

At an early stage of my research, I was asked why anyone should bother with Coleridge either as a theologian or a political theorist. Since I was, at that moment, suffering a job interview, I thought more was called for than a shrug and a winning smile. My slightly desperate stab was to suggest that Coleridge mounted an important critique of reductionist explanations of human society and moral agency. Looking back now, I am slightly surprised to find that my frantic intuition was a rather happy one. The attack on reductionism is an important theme of this book and I will follow it through several contexts, including Coleridge's defense of the will against associationism, his criticisms of Enlightenment historiography, his discussion of the inadequacies of political economy, and the Trinitarian arguments against monism.

Ultimately, the roots of this critical theme are, for Coleridge, theological. There is no grasping the range or inner dynamic of Coleridge's thought without appreciating his religious vision. Whilst there have been some excellent discussions of Coleridgean theology, it remains the case that explorations of his politics, as indeed general discussions of his thought, remain insufficiently attentive to his theological commitments. Furthermore, Coleridge is, as we shall see, poorly served if he is treated broadly as a "religious thinker."[1] The material of Coleridge's mature thought is shamelessly that of Christian doctrine, in particular, that of a Trinitarian understanding of God. His theory of the imagination is a theological theory and his politics, in a sense we shall describe later, a theological politics.

The theology, however, is mediated through a philosophical psychology that expounds what it means for a human being to be made in the *imago Dei*. In the late-eighteenth and early nineteenth centuries,

---

[1]This is a weakness of Rosemary Ashton's in many respects very illuminating treatment of Coleridge and his work. See, in particular, her treatment of *Aids to Reflection* in Rosemary Ashton, *The Life of Samuel Taylor Coleridge* (Oxford: Blackwell Publishers, 1996) 361-65.

theories of mind accompany and generate political vision. One of the purposes of this book is to show how, in the case of Coleridge, an account of reason and understanding, imagination, emotion, and sense is foundational for a political theory. The argument of the following chapters may be stated fairly simply. The conceptual underpinnings of Coleridge's political theory in his "conservative years" are provided by a philosophical psychology, a doctrine of the mind that has, I will argue, a remarkable range of implication. Within this psychology, the imagination, among the powers of the mind, is decisive for the human calling. So essential is Coleridge's theory of the imagination to his politics, his ethics, and his religion that, even when in his later writings explicit reference to the imagination dwindles almost to nothing, the *activity* named by "imagination" remains crucial.

Philosophical-psychology, then, is the unifying center of this book. From that center, we will move out toward politics and society and eventually toward the doctrine of the Triune God. We will also attend to Coleridge's interest in establishing himself as a public educator, advisor, sage, and man of letters to government ministers, young intellectuals, future statesmen, and, generally, the "higher and middle classes."[2] Here too, his theory of the mind proves crucial for interpreting his rhetorical and pedagogical strategies.

Another broad purpose of this book is to contribute to the historical examination of early British conservatism. Coleridge is counted among the conservatives in the succession of Burke, and reckoned with Wordsworth and Southey as a traitor to youthful radicalism: "A dainty dish to set before the King / Or Regent, who admires such kind of food."[3] I hope my interpretation of Coleridge's mature politics will make it clear that his is a distinctive voice in the conservative tradition. The "conservative imagination," as I have called it, because of the way in which Coleridge understands the imagination, has some disconcerting, disruptive implications for certain conservative convictions or, perhaps better, complacencies. This phrase, "the conservative imagination," focuses, I believe, the disturbing, unsettling quality that John Stuart Mill recognized as a feature

---

[2]The "middle classes" appear as the addressees of *A Lay Sermon*. A third "sermon" written to "to the Lower and Laboring Classes" was projected but never written. It might well have been tellingly peculiar.

[3]Byron, *Don Juan*, Dedication, 11-12.

of Coleridge's conservatism. At the risk of oxymoron, Coleridge introduces us to a decidedly restless example of conservative thought.

Before we turn, therefore, to Coleridge's theory of the imagination together with the account of mind to which it belongs, the first chapter considers the origins of modern conservatism. Some British radical writings of the 1790s, including those of Coleridge, provide the context for examining Edmund Burke's response to the French Revolution. With the aid of the concept of "identification," chapter 2 introduces the philosophical psychology and its formative role in Coleridge's rhetoric. An argument as to the theological character of the theory of the imagination prepares for the discussion of historiography and biblical symbolism in the third chapter.

At this point, I begin direct consideration of Coleridge's political writings, analyzing his critique of the spiritual economy of the French Revolution and, also in chapter 4, of the commercial economy of Britain. In both cases, we will find the analysis of reason, understanding, and imagination undergirding the critical attack. Chapter 5 takes up the proposals Coleridge makes as to the place of religion in society and shows how "religion" in both its social and individual aspects assumes functions Coleridge has, elsewhere, accorded the imagination. At this stage my focus is on *A Lay Sermon* and to some extent *The Friend* of 1818 which leaves *On the Constitution of Church and State*—in which Coleridge describes the famous "clerisy"—for the final chapter. I read the latter work as a response to a secularization of political discourse during the early nineteenth century. The theological and Trinitarian context of *Church and State* is obscured when commentators, as is generally the case, give short shrift to Coleridge's discussion of the Christian church and ignore the, admittedly somewhat eccentric, material Coleridge appended to the treatise. Taking these less-regarded passages seriously suggests that the discussion of the Trinity found in the manuscripts of the "Opus Maximum" is the embracing context for reading *Church and State*. That, as we shall see, makes for a reading of the relationship between "National" and Christian church more nuanced than it generally receives. I conclude by returning again to the theme of reductionism and to Coleridge's concern with the mystery of "personality." That, as Coleridge might say, is the "final landing place" for our reflections.

Acknowledgments

Much gratitude is due many. I was introduced to Coleridge as theologian and political theorist whilst a graduate student at Emory University. David Pacini made that introduction and Walt Reed accompanied my initial research with kindness, insight, and generous hours. Jon Gunnemann, Brooks Holifield, Roberta Bondi, and Rebecca Chop were admirable teachers and fellow student Jan Heller listened and listened. The long and circuitous route from research to more research to book would never have reached its end without the encouragement and suggestions of Lisa Moore from the University of Texas.

I have spent great energy annoying librarians. Rob Cogswell and Mikail McIntosh-Doty of the Episcopal Theological Seminary of the Southwest library, though, have belied every curmudgeonly thought I ever harbored concerning their profession, and to their names must be added that of Linda Oliver of Victoria College, Toronto, who trusted me with precious things.

I have learnt a good deal from colleagues and friends, especially Graham Davidson, Bill Green, Tom Garza, Elizabeth Richmond-Garza, and, for many years, Richard Buck. Dusty McDonald, Titus Presler, and John Bennett Waters mobilized support for this project from the Episcopal Seminary of the Southwest, where it is my privilege to teach. Barkley Thompson weighed into the vagaries of my footnotes and the oddities of my hybrid part-American, part-British style and has rendered me strangely consistent. Eleanor Gregory and Jim Flowers drove themselves near witless working on the indexes, and Edd Rowell was a patient, kind, and eagle-eyed editor.

Grief, though, would have struck this entire enterprise without the affection of my children, Eleanor, Damian, and Camilla, and my son-in-law, Chris: they have all endured much. Above all, my gratitude goes to my wife, Suzy, whose price is quite beyond words, let alone rubies, and who, loving me more than I deserve, agrees to live where daffodils do not grow and the temperature hits 106°. To her, this book is dedicated.

1

Coleridge among the Conservatives

Tous les établissemens en France couronnent le malheur du peuple: pour le rendre heureux il faut le renouveler; changer ses idées; changer ses loix; changer ses moeurs; . . . changer les hommes; changer les choses; changer les mots; . . . tout détruire; oui, tout détruire; puisque tout est à recrèer.
—M. Rabaud de St. Etienne, National Assembly

As in most questions of state, there is a middle. There is something else than the mere alternative of absolute destruction, or unreformed existence. . . . I cannot conceive how any man can have brought himself to that pitch of presumption, to consider his country as nothing but carte blanche, upon which he may scribble whatever he pleases.
—Edmund Burke, *Reflections on the Revolution in France*

Radical Imaginings

As a political ideology, rather than just a settled preference for keeping things the way they are, Conservatism is modern. British Conservatism begins in the 1790s, preeminently with Edmund Burke's *Reflections on the Revolution in France*, written in protest against French revolutionaries and English radicals, the politics of "reason" and the "rights of man." The classic Conservative text, then, is an argument in reaction, a polemic, the targets of which inform Burke's claims, rhetorical strategies, and political vision. To appreciate Burke's *Reflections*, therefore, prefatory to seeking Coleridge's distinctive contribution to early Conservatism, we must begin with the radicals and, among them, with Coleridge himself, in his early twenties.

In 1795, William Hodgson was sentenced to two years in Newgate for tagging his Britannic majesty with an unflattering comparison to a German hog butcher. While in prison, Hodgson completed *The Commonwealth of Reason*, a treatise that would be mercilessly dull if it were not so unintentionally comic. Hodgson offers a plan for the rights of citizens and the procedures of politics in an impeccably rational state. The fount of political evil, according to his argument, is "power long continued in the same individual" and the only way to prevent the political arteries thus hardening into a state of corruption is to make every position of power "revolutionary or rotative."[1] Hodgson proposes, therefore, a democratic republic with very regular elections, short terms of office, and restrictions upon reelection. The electoral structure is laid out with the simplicity of strict numbers, the country divided into regions of 25,000 electors apiece. "Simplicity," though, a common ideal in radical texts, designs a bureaucratic hell. The finance committee, for instance, which holds the purse strings of government, consists of twelve members, four of whom lose their jobs every month to be replaced by novices elected from the national house of representatives. Responsible for inspection of all "roads, buildings, canals, and rivers" as well as everything to do with money, this hapless finance committee is further forbidden to execute any decision whatsoever without a majority vote in the national assembly.[2]

Social evil originates with inequalities of wealth. Hodgson provides, therefore, for redistribution of property, through the abolition of entailed estates and primogeniture and the end of such exclusive privileges as those preserved, for instance, by the game laws.[3] Hodgson does not suggest how this rational order is achieved but he does insist on the importance of education for its maintenance. Again, a recurring theme in radical texts of the period is that of a sociopolitical fall. There is no taint of original sin, human beings coming "equal and free" from the "hands of nature," formed for benevolence and reason. Misery is consequent upon society and politics. The sorry condition of the present is accounted for in a variety of ways: the "demon of property" and its corrupting display; the establishment of social distinctions not based on virtue alone; or the slowly tightening grip of despotism.[4] In each case, there is a

---

[1]William Hodgson, "The Commonwealth of Reason" (1795), in *Utopias of the British Enlightenment*, ed. Gregory Claeys (Cambridge UK: Cambridge University Press, 1994) 201.

[2]Hodgson, "The Commonwealth of Reason," 225.

[3]Hodgson, "The Commonwealth of Reason," 203-205.

[4]For the "demon of property," see Mary Wollstonecraft, *The Vindications: The Rights of Men; The Rights of Women*, ed. D. L. Macdonald and Kathleen

historical occlusion of the natural good of humanity. According to Hodgson, democracy is the original and beneficent political condition into which corruption entered by a gradual relaxation of the electoral process, allowing for an eventual monopoly of power. Such a monopoly persists owing to the "ignorance and credulity" of the people, an ignorance cultivated by "despots, priests, and usurpers." From this derives the importance of education in the commonwealth of reason. By contrast, conservative ideology is rooted, as we shall see, in a less sanguine view of the individual and a more optimistic reading of previous history. For the conservative, hope is held out from the past, for the radical it is suspended from the future.

While William Hodgson was building constitutions in Newgate, Coleridge was blowing his "Baby Trumpet of Sedition" in Bristol.[5] The "Lectures on Revealed Religion," delivered at the Assembly Coffeehouse, in May and June of 1795, fall, in part, along with Hodgson's *Commonwealth of Reason*, into the genre of utopian writings. Coleridge's utopia, sketched out principally in the second and sixth lectures, has some significant differences from Hodgson's, principally concerning religion. Beyond the familiar conspiracy theory of priesthood and the tyranny of ignorance, Hodgson shows small interest in religion and religious conviction has almost no significance in his rational utopia. It is a "matter of opinion," that, within the bounds of the negative definition of liberty, should be "as free as the circumambient air."[6] For Coleridge, however, religion is central and its importance remains a constant throughout his political writings, receiving reinterpretation across the dramatic changes in his politics and in his theology. In the 1790s, he endorsed the vital role of Christianity for a radical vision of social change, defying other radicals such as Holcroft and Godwin who, rejected or, much like Hodgson,

---

Scherf (New York: Broadview Press, 1997) 38.

[5]On Coleridge's early politics, see Rosemary Ashton, *The Life of Samuel Taylor Coleridge* (Oxford: Blackwell Publishers, 1996) pt. 1; Richard Holmes, *Coleridge: Early Visions* (London: Hodder & Stoughton, 1989) chaps. 4 and 5; John T. Miller, *Ideology and Enlightenment: the Political and Social Thought of Samuel Taylor Coleridge* (New York: Garland Publishing, 1987) chaps. 1–3; Nicholas Roe, *Wordsworth and Coleridge: the Radical Years* (Oxford: Clarendon Press, 1988).

[6]Hodgson, "Commonwealth of Reason," 217.

marginalized religion.[7] Later, the conservative Coleridge, writing in the context of a political discourse grown increasingly secular, continues to develop a theological politics and, from that perspective, to argue for the social and political significance of religion.[8]

Opposing Godwin, Coleridge contends that religion "appears to offer the only means universally *efficient*" for that "general Illumination [which] should precede Revolution." The goal of a final but historically distant perfection is not sufficient to wean the burdened poor from dulling their minds in immediate satisfactions. A nearer power is required than "the perfectness of future Men, and that power is religion:

> "Go, preach the GOSPEL to the Poor." By its Simplicity it will meet their comprehension, by its Benevolence soften their affections, by its Precepts it will direct their conduct, by the vastness of its Motives ensure their obedience.[9]

Religion, therefore, provides the means for that transformation of consciousness without which change is but change of masters. Furthermore, according to the "Lectures on Revealed Religion," religion also provides the model that elevates us above present corruption, enabling recognition of our sorry historical captivity as well as preparing us for that social perfection at which "thinking and disinterested Patriots" are to aim.[10]

The model offered us by revelation is the "Jewish Constitution," as given to Israel by God through the mediation of Moses. Coleridge's

---

[7]Holcroft is, most probably, the "professing patriot" referred to in the second of the 1795 "Lectures on Revealed Religion," and Coleridge has William Godwin much in mind, both positively and negatively, throughout the political sections of these lectures.

[8]See below, chap. 5.

[9]"Conciones ad Populum, Introductory Address," LPR 43-45. The lecture was given in February 1795. Unlike the "Lectures on Revealed Religion," this was published, together with its companion lecture "On the Present War." They were less likely to provoke accusations of sedition. Coleridge has in mind the closing sentences of William Godwin's *Enquiry Concerning Political Justice* ed. I. Kramnick (London: Penguin Books, 1976) 794-95. The same passage is approvingly cited in Northmore's *Memoirs of Planetes* (see below, 7).

[10]Samuel Taylor Coleridge, *Lectures 1795: On Politics and Religion*, ed. Lewis Patton and Peter Mann, vol. 1 of *The Collected Works of Samuel Taylor Coleridge* (Princeton NJ: Princeton University Press, 1971) 12.

strategy is partly apologetic and, here, too, he probably has Godwinian anarchy in his sights.[11] He interprets the Old Testament as a vital source of political wisdom, something we shall still find Coleridge attempting, albeit in very different terms, in *The Statesman's Manual* of 1816. The 1795 lectures offer the Mosaic order as a qualified utopia, qualified because of its anticipatory relationship to Christianity and because of the limitations of those for whom it was designed.[12] Nevertheless, articulated within a scheme of progressive revelation, the Jewish Constitution is, set against present corruption, a utopian model and one which shares important features with Hodgson's commonwealth. In both cases, the root evils that afflict contemporary societies are monopolies on power and inequalities of wealth. The Mosaic order provided for a division of the country into agricultural units of twenty-five acres for each man.[13] The ban on usury and the cancellation of debts every sixth year resisted any tendency toward the alienation of property and thus unequal ownership. If these proved insufficient, the Jubilee, every fifty years, restored all lands to their original equality of distribution. In this way, the Jubilee fulfilled the requirement of all Constitutions, that they "be frequently brought back to their first principles."[14] Acknowledging, therefore, that "Property is Power and equal Property equal Power," the Jewish Constitution guarded itself against that disproportionate accumulation to which "we are indebted for nine-tenths of our Vices and Miseries."[15]

The Pentateuch presents Israel as a theocracy provided with a legal code that, given its divine legislator, hardly admits of repeal or addition. Coleridge, therefore, has to work hard to come up with some suitably democratic elements in the Hebrews' "federal Republic."[16] He does his best, though, drawing his hearers' attention to the solemn assent given by "each individual" to this social order in which no human being was another's superior and each member was directly and equally the subject

---

[11]Coleridge, *On Politics and Religion*, lxviii-ix.

[12]Coleridge, *On Politics and Religion*, 115-16, 139-41.

[13]Coleridge derives his description of the Jewish Constitution largely from Moses Lowman, *A Dissertation of the Civil Government of the Hebrews* (1740), see Coleridge, *On Politics and Religion*, 122.

[14]Coleridge, *On Politics and Religion*, 125.

[15]Coleridge, *On Politics and Religion*, 125, 127.

[16]Coleridge, *On Politics and Religion*, 125.

of God. Democratic procedures, too, guard against that other fateful corruption: power monopolized. The 24,000 members of the Hebrew militia serve also as the nation's representative assembly. This body, though, is entirely changed each month as another 2,000 from each tribe come up for duty. Since everyone has a turn, there is no need, of course, for elections. Finally, as in Hodgson's commonwealth, the assembly's right of decision is limited and "when any point of more than common importance was proposed, the twelve tribes met and enacted it personally."[17]

The ideal, theocratic republicanism of the Mosaic law does not survive the weakness of Israel. Coleridge, too, has his story of historical decline. In his case, though, the biblical narratives upon which it is based have a muting effect upon the anthropological optimism typical of radical writings. The paradigmatic political disaster is Israel's desire for a king "like unto the nations."[18] The Israelites, "weary of independence," spurn the liberty that is their birthright and the gift of God. They are therefore guilty of "the foulest [crime] of which human nature is capable."[19] Unlike the reductionist histories we find, for instance, in Wollstonecraft or Hodgson, Coleridge's account of political enslavement is informed by the awkward particulars of a specific narrative. Israel's struggle with idolatry and the notion of a chosen people redeemed from the darkness of the nations disturb, if they do not eliminate, conviction of this-worldly human perfectibility. There is no acknowledgement of original sin in the "Lectures on Revealed Religion," though as early as 1798, Coleridge was prepared to admit the doctrine; nevertheless, even in these lectures, his anthropology engages themes less optimistic than those found among "British Jacobins," Painites, and Godwinians. Thus, we find somewhat Augustinian hints of the threat the passions pose to the path of human progress.

The Jewish Constitution is both utopian and preparatory, equal property being still a compromise with human weakness. Coleridge's defense of revealed religion finds its climax, therefore, in the mission and teaching of Jesus and in the social prospect he opens for humanity. "Uni-

---

[17]Coleridge, *On Politics and Religion*, 130. Coleridge also notes that the Hebrews possessed a "senate" of seventy elders with advisory powers and a "judge" who functioned as president.

[18]First Sam. 8:1-6.

[19]Coleridge, *On Politics and Religion*, 133.

versal Equality," Coleridge argues, "is the Object of the Messiah."[20] On the basis of the Sermon on the Mount and the Matthean story of the rich youth seeking salvation, Coleridge represents Jesus inveighing against any and all forms of personal wealth.[21] This is the advance upon, the radicalization of, the Jewish Constitution. Not just equal property but no property, the abolition of ownership.[22] In his views on property, Coleridge outradicalizes most of the radicals. While these lectures are frequently critical of William Godwin's *Enquiry Concerning Political Justice*, Coleridge's attack upon the institution of government as corrupting and his analysis of the deleterious effects of property are both indebted to this text. Godwin, however, advocates the equalization of wealth and preserves the "sacred right of property." Coleridge, on the other hand, projects its ultimate abolition, claiming that equalization is both impractical as well as failing to root out the evil which lies in ownership itself. Again, by contrast, the Godwinian Thomas Northmore, whose description of the utopian republic of Makar was published in the same year as Coleridge's lectures, retains private property for his ideal society. He also defends the domestic and international benefits of commerce, an institution that, at this stage of his career, Coleridge judges with special fierceness.[23]

---

[20]Ibid., 218.

[21]Matt. 6:25-33; 19:16-24. "Now it is absurd to suppose that Jesus meant any particular sum by Riches. Wealth is a comparative Word. . . . If we understand by Riches comparative Wealth the meaning is clear and conveys a sublime Truth. That as long as anyone possesses more than another, Luxury, Envy, Rapine, Government & Priesthood will be the necessary consequence, and prevent the Kingdom of God." Coleridge, *On Politics and Religion*, 227.

[22]Coleridge's critique of property ownership was also, of course, the inspiration for his—and Southey's—scheme, proposed in 1794, for a "Pantisocratic" community in America. Property was to have no place under the terms of the Pantisocracy.

[23]Thomas Northmore, "The Memoirs of Planetes" (1795), in *Utopias of the British Enlightenment*, 189-90: "Commerce is of greater advantage to mankind than the opposers of commerce are aware of. The sciences of navigation and astronomy are advanced by commerce. The happiness of man in a moral view is likewise increased thereby, inasmuch as the laws, manners, customs, and improvements of nations, are thus made known to each other." For Coleridge's condemnation of commercial activity, see Coleridge, *On Politics and Religion*, 223-26: "Commerce then is useless except to continue Imposture and oppression"

Among the advocates, then, for political reform during the 1790s, there is a trajectory of ideas that involve the prospect of a thoroughgoing restructuring of British politics and society. Inspired in particular by Paine's *Rights of Man*, this radical tradition went beyond calls for parliamentary reform to advocate forms of democratic republicanism.[24] Where others appealed to the ancient benefits of the English constitution, here present woes are judged according to the inalienable rights of man, rights Coleridge claims would be evident, were it not for priestcraft, to all honest readers of the Bible.[25]

A revolutionary song published in 1791, asks "Shall Britons the Chorus of Liberty hear / With a cold and insensible mind?"[26] By the mid-1790s, the answer was a resounding "No" though not in the form hoped for by the anonymous songwriter. The overwhelming majority of Britons stirred into action by the revolutionary events in France and by reform demands at home, refused to "contend for the Rights of Mankind." Instead, they signed resolutions supporting king and constitution, burnt effigies of Tom Paine, and joined loyalist associations.[27] Conservative treatises, tracts, sermons, and speeches drew on lengthy traditions of political argument, just as did the radical and reform writings they attacked.[28] Revolution in France, however, served as a lens that focused

---

(223-24).

[24] Political ideas of this kind, despite the influence of Paine and the fears of loyalists, informed the demands of reform societies only to a limited extent, even when sympathetic to the French revolution. The London Corresponding Society, for instance, strenuously rejected the charge of republicanism and insisted that they called for Parliamentary reform involving universal suffrage and annual parliaments. John Stevenson, "Popular Radicalism and Popular Protest, 1789–1815," in *Britain and the French Revolution, 1789–1815*, ed. H. T. Dickinson (London: Macmillan Education, 1989) 72-74.

[25] Coleridge, *On Politics and Religion*, 208.

[26] "The Trumpet of Liberty," *Norfolk Chronicle*, 16 July 1791. Reprinted in *The New Oxford Book of Romantic Period Verse*, ed. Jerome McGann (Oxford: Oxford University Press, 1993) 79.

[27] H. T. Dickinson, "Popular Conservatism and Militant Loyalism, 1789–1815," in *Britain and the French Revolution*, 103-25; Frank O'Gorman, *The Long Eighteenth Century: British Political and Social History, 1688–1832* (London: Arnold Books, 1997).

[28] *Britain and the French Revolution*, 73, 104-109.

both radical and conservative discourse and, in the case of the latter, reaction to revolution instituted an ideological tradition at least as important and influential as political radicalism. Loyalist associations, conservative newspapers, and popular tracts mediated to a receptive population elements of an ideology that had found its paradigmatic statement in Burke's *Reflections on the Revolution in France*.[29]

Village Politics, one of the most widely distributed of Hannah More's "Cheap Repository Tracts," stages a dialogue between a blacksmith, Jack Anvil, and Tom Hod, a mason who is muddling his mind and poisoning his morals with reading Paine's *Rights of Man*."[30] More employs traditional themes concerning the duties of obedience, the providential disposition and value of social inequality, and the blessings of being English. She also, however, introduces popularized arguments from Burke, noting the necessary imperfections of politics, castigating the folly of utopianism and of trust in the "new made," and summarizing "French *liberty*" as an assault on property and the right "to murder more men in one night, than ever their poor king did in his whole life."[31] Her loyal representative from the forge offers a distinctively Burkean allegory for the logic of constitutional history, preservation, and reform:

> When Sir John married, my lady, who is a little fantastical and likes to do everything like the French, begged him to pull down yonder fine old castle and build it up in her frippery way. "No," says Sir John; "what! shall I pull down this noble building, raised by the wisdom of my noble ancestors; which outstood the civil wars, and only underwent a little

---

[29] Burke, though, was not the only contributor to the development of early Conservative ideology, see P. Schofield, "Conservatism in the Late-Eighteenth Century," *Historical Journal* 29 (1986): 601-22.

[30] *Village Politics* was first printed in 1793. By 1798, some two million of the various "Cheap Repository Tracts" had been printed. It is uncertain just how many tracts were read by their intended recipients. The scale of conservative literature, however, is startling: two million of the Cheap Repository Tracts were distributed between 1795 and 1798 and there is no reason to think they were appreciated solely for their suitability as toilet paper.

[31] Hannah More, "Village Politics, Addressed to All the Mechanics, Journeymen, and Laborers in Great Britain. By Will Chip, a Country Carpenter," *The Complete Works of Hannah More*, vol 1 (New York: Harper & Brothers Publishers, 1855) 367.

needful repair at the Revolution; a castle which all my neighbors come to take a pattern by—shall I pull it all down, I say, only because there may be a dark closet, or an awkward passage, or an inconvenient room or two in it? Our ancestors took time for what they did. They understood foundation work; no running up your little slight lath-and-plaster buildings, which are up in a day and down in a night." . . . the castle was let stand . . . tho' there may be a trifling fault or two . . . so now and then they mend a little thing, and they'll go on mending, I dare say, as they have leisure, to the end of the chapter.[32]

Propagandists for social contentment and patriotic loyalism deployed a considerable range of arguments and rhetorical strategies. Describing Hannah More, therefore, as "Burke for beginners," is clearly an exaggeration. Nevertheless, events in France, particularly after the September massacres of 1792, secured Burke's arguments an authority such that they informed popular loyalism with themes and strategies that, transforming the discourse of traditional allegiance, constituted a new ideology: conservatism.

Among the Conservatives

Burke's classic analysis of the early stages of the French revolution was occasioned by the "very extraordinary miscellaneous sermon" preached by Richard Price on 4 November 1789 and then included in the proceedings of the Revolution Society along with that association's congratulatory address to the National Assembly in Paris.[33] The "revolution" of the society's name and which is the ostensible object of Price's celebratory address is the "Glorious Revolution" of 1688 which ended the reign of James II. Recent events in France, however, provide the energetic center of the sermon and the subject of its peroration in which Price celebrates "THIRTY MILLIONS of people, indignant and resolute . . . demanding liberty with an irresistible voice; their king led in triumph."[34] This is not,

---

[32]Ibid., 361.

[33]Edmund Burke, *Reflections of the Revolution in France*, ed. Conor Cruise O'Brien (London: Penguin Books, 1968) 85-94; quotation at p. 93.

[34]Richard Price, *A Discourse on the Love of our Country, delivered on Nov. 4th 1789 at the Meeting House in Old Jewry, to the Society for the Revolution in Great Britain* (London: Edward E. Powars, 1790) 40.

as such, a republican sermon but Price rereads the English revolution in the light of the French in such a way as to make legitimate monarchy depend upon the will of the people. It is this reading of the constitution, according to which the English have the right to frame their own government, choose their own governors, and to "cashier them for misconduct," that drew Burke's fury.[35]

During the course of the 1790s, regicide, the Terror, and war with France, together with the pressure of loyalist enthusiasm and legislation against sedition changed attitudes among radical writers toward the French revolution. Hodgson, Northmore, and Coleridge, for instance, all write, with respect to the revolution, as chastened radicals. Hodgson is silent about the genesis of his rational commonwealth; Northmore urges that revolutionary change need not involve violence; and Coleridge insists that pantisocratic equality is "not to be procured by the tumultuous uprising of an indignant multitude."[36] This shift, however, occurs within a continuity of radical concern: the need for a restructuring of society based upon "reason" and those "rights of men" that are prior to all historical formations and by which all societies must be measured. This need arises from a social and political corruption that renders the past all but useless as a positive guide. To the extent to which human beings are freed from the past that is tyranny, are they released for a future that, even when not envisaged as this-worldly perfection, nevertheless, inaugurates at present unimaginable possibilities.[37] It is this claim, within this ideological trajectory, that provokes the most distinctive objections of conservatism and over against which early nineteenth century British conservative thought appears most sharply.

Conservatism, then, begins with suspicion. Burke takes vigorous issue with the notion that social life and its political governance can be subject to a radical, "rational" remaking. His suspicion of this proposal arises

---

[35]Price, *Discourse*, 30. The passage to which Burke takes especial exception is: "First: The right to liberty of conscience in religious matters, Secondly: The right to resist power when abused; Thirdly: the right to chuse our own governors; to cashier them for misconduct; and to frame a government for ourselves. On these three principles, and more especially the last, was the Revolution founded."

[36]Northmore, "Memoirs of Planetes," 170-72; Coleridge, *On Politics and Religion*, 218.

[37]Wollstonecraft, *Vindication*, 65-66.

only partly from his understanding of the decisions and initiatives of the French National Assembly. More profoundly, it derives from a particular view of history and of those accumulations of human experience that are institutions, laws, customs, and discourses. In order to appreciate Coleridge's conservatism as both appropriating and differing from that of Burke, it is necessary to consider the latter's understanding of history: of social institutions and established practices as constituted over time. Thereafter, we will turn briefly to Burke's views on the individual as a member, not just of a "society," but, by virtue of that, as belonging also to such communities as family, religion, school, region, and town.

A British subject, Burke argues, is a beneficiary of the past, receiving as "an entailed inheritance," institutions of law and government together with the liberties they provide and protect. Such institutions are "artificial," existing by virtue of the efforts of one "whose prerogative it is, to be in a great degree a creature of his own making."[38] The transient thoughts, decisions, and actions of human beings take form in social structures that transcend them both in their endurance and in the benefits that are constituted for future generations. The relationship between the intentions of agents at a certain point in time, acting with particular desires and limited understanding, and relatively permanent institutional forms, is complex and frequently indirect:

> The real effects of moral causes are not always immediate; but that which in the first instance is prejudicial may be excellent in its remoter operation; and its excellence may arise even from the ill effects it produces in the beginning. The reverse also happens; and very plausible schemes, with very pleasing commencements, have often shameful and lamentable conclusions.[39]

Radical writings often project the past so as to constrain present action: the past is an unworkable past, its significance drained to the force of a negative, a demand for thoroughgoing change, whether the process of that change be conceived as brief or lengthy. Burke also seeks to constrain action through his account of the past, to map out real as opposed to illusory or destructive possibilities. The "conservative past" is present with an unforgiving weight of contemporary benefit and

---

[38] Burke, *Reflections*, 189.
[39] Ibid., 152.

complex actuality. The innovator who promises good from untried schemes does so against forms of law, government, and common life, that, though inevitably imperfect, are nevertheless already the source of good, already sustain social life, gift liberties, secure rights, offer an object for hope, loyalty, and love, and provide a sphere for moral and religious action. Furthermore, all this so dwarfs "the fallible and feeble contrivances of our reason" that while its problems make improvement a duty, its complex history damns innovation as a horror of presumption.

Burke, then, recognizes that human beings are the makers of their political environment. Constitutional history is the history of a human labor. The radicals, too, as we've seen, hold out this agency as vocation and promise. If we attend to Burke's rhetoric, however, we notice that while he affirms human making, he does so in order to reabsorb and secure it through an identification with the natural.[40] We hold "our government and our privileges" as an inherited gift and trust, this policy appearing to Burke as "the result of profound reflection." He then pointedly corrects himself, it is "rather the happy effect of following nature, *which is wisdom without reflection, and above it.*"[41] In the process of history, human understanding serves a wisdom that is "without reflection," and human work is absorbed in the growth of institutions constituted in an analogy with nature:

> Our political system is placed in a just correspondence and symmetry with the order of the world, and with the mode of existence decreed to a permanent body composed of transitory parts; wherein, by the disposition of a stupendous wisdom, moulding together the great mysterious incorporation of the human race, the whole, at one time, is never old, or middle-aged, or young, but in condition of unchangeable constancy, moves on through the varied tenour of perpetual decay, fall, renovation, and progression.[42]

---

[40]The importance of the concept of "identification" for understanding rhetoric is discussed in chap. 2 below.

[41]Burke, *Reflections*, 118; my emphasis.

[42]Ibid., 120.

The wise statesman marks the lesson and "preserves the method of nature in the conduct of the state."⁴³ Human beings are indeed makers of themselves but the ordering, if they make rightly, is "decreed."

The history that gifts us our political environment, an environment formative of rights and duties, hopes and loyalties, eludes our comprehension. This is partly owing to the limited perspective of human beings whose reason is constrained by a particular point in time. It is also because of the unpredictable elements in the process itself whereby human intentions have unintended consequence and accidents stabilize as benefits. The political lesson that follows from this is that the constitution possesses the mystery of organism, not the clarity of a controllable machine. Thus, actual rights, as opposed to the abstract "rights of men," do not admit of a clear and simple listing but are "in a sort of *middle*, incapable of definition, but not impossible to be discerned."⁴⁴ "Improvement," therefore, which is necessary given the imperfections of any human state, has to proceed with a tender and exacting tact, reflecting always the "disposition to preserve" and awareness that our individual "stock of reason" is small. Once again, Burke sets political action in the terms of natural relations:

> He should approach the faults of the state as to the wounds of a father, with pious awe and trembling solicitude. By this wise prejudice we are taught to look with horror on those children of their country who are prompt rashly to hack that aged parent in pieces, and put him into the kettle of magicians, in hopes that by their poisonous weeds, and wild incantations, they may regenerate the parental constitution, and renovate their father's life.⁴⁵

Members of the Revolution Society in England and the National Assembly in France are thus construed as "unnatural," prophets of magic, not reason. Burke also deploys such natural, familial or organic metaphors, to undermine his opponents' own rhetoric, appealing as it does to glorious, providential moments of revolution.⁴⁶ Burke's imagery suggests that it is the advocates of such change who are the truly "untimely." Out

---

⁴³Ibid.
⁴⁴Ibid., 153.
⁴⁵Ibid., 194.
⁴⁶Price, *Discourse*, 39-41.

of time and out of nature, they configure present conditions as grotesque extremes, themselves, perhaps, seeking to hasten them into political crisis. Thus, they celebrate violent remedy where the cautious medicine of a judicious reform will do.

Since the political environment is far more complex than "constitution mongers" dream of, far less translucent to reason, our capacity to effect change for the good is significant but severely limited. The metaphor of murderous magic and wild incantation pushes the occasion for radical change into the realm of the unthinkable, the monstrous. The effect of Burke's rhetoric is to map very tightly the limits of morally acceptable political action. His argument—and this becomes an enduring theme of later conservatism—tends to suggest that, given the destructive passions of human beings, any political environment is better than none if it brings such passions into social order. The benefit of the doubt thus belongs to the politically given, the onus of proof falling heavy on the case for change; and, where change is achieved, as in the "Glorious Revolution," its negotiation should reinsert it within the continuities of the past. Thus, though "the crown was carried somewhat out of the line in which it had before moved," the principle of hereditary succession was firmly reasserted and did not give place, as Price thought, to any monarchy by popular choice.[47] Price's error, therefore, in "A Discourse of the Love of Our Country,' was not merely in a matter of historical fact but lay much more seriously in a denial of the principle according to which human beings find and secure themselves in the continuities of time, receiving the governance and order of their social life as "a sort of family settlement."[48]

In the case of Britain, Burke believes, we find a constitution that achieves a proper analogy to nature, one in which clashes, anomalies, and local inconveniences are ultimately reconciled within the total system. Burke's view of the constitution thus approaches Pope's famous account of natural harmony. In both cases, reason's partial sight grounds a trust that transcends what reason can explicate:

All Nature is but art, unknown to thee;
All chance, direction, which thou canst not see;

---

[47]Burke, *Reflections*, 106.
[48]Burke, *Reflections*. 120.

> All discord, harmony not understood;
> All partial evil, universal good:
> And, spite of pride, in erring reason's spite,
> One truth is clear, Whatever is, is right.[49]

From the perspective of any particular generation, let alone any particular individual, there is only a small power to effect lasting good. The ordering that binds and sustains us as social creatures, preserving us from a natural existence that Burke, like Hobbes, finds thoroughly grim and unappealing, is not made according to the designs of "theorists" or "metaphysicians" in politics. Rather,

> it is a deliberate election of ages and of generations . . . made by the peculiar circumstances, occasions, tempers, dispositions, and moral, civil, and social habitudes of the people, which disclose themselves only in a long space of time.[50]

The view of history involved here makes virtues of caution and skepticism. The social order is vulnerable to human folly, conservation must always have priority over change, and promises of rational remaking must meet with a fierce suspicion. As the human capacity to mar exceeds the ability to make, action must always proceed "as if in the presence of canonized forefathers."[51] Caution and skepticism, however, are grounded in a historical optimism:

> Man is a most unwise, and a most wise, being. The individual is foolish. The multitude for a moment is foolish, when they act without deliberation; but the species is wise, and when time is given to it, as a species, it almost always acts right.[52]

---

[49] Alexander Pope, "Essay on Man," epistle 1, ll. 289-94. Burke's acceptance of a cosmic optimism more characteristic of the early Enlightenment tells against readings that connect his thought too closely with Romanticism. See C. P. Courtney, "Edmund Burke and the Enlightenment," in *England in the Eighteenth Century*, ed. Felipe Fernández-Armesto (London: Folio Society, 1998) 481-97.

[50] Edmund Burke, "Speech on the Representation of the Commons in Parliament," in *Selected Writings and Speeches*, ed. Peter J. Stanlis (New York: Anchor Books, 1963) 330-31.

[51] Burke, *Reflections*, 121.

[52] Burke, "Speech on the Representation of the Commons in Parliament," 331.

A sense of vulnerability, however, of possible calamity, distinguishes this view from modern doctrines of progress as does the disjunction between present planning or intention and eventual good. Furthermore, there is here a vital theological background which allows a reading of history that, without that context, might tread close to nihilism. On the one hand, Burke stresses the limitations of our temporally situated reason and, on the other, he insists that institutional and social history is formative in a quite thoroughgoing manner. We have our liberties, understand our rights, frame our hopes, know ourselves, only in and through this history. According to Burke, the National Assembly fell into the appalling illusion that one can 'get above' history, dismiss the past like a dishonest servant, and treat society as a blank space in which reason may build from scratch. History, however, will have its revenge through the "misrule and excess" that comes from loosening the complex ties that restrain our passions and weave us into order.[53] In other philosophical contexts, similar accounts of the situatedness of our reason, of our boundedness, fund skeptically relativist or even nihilistic positions. In Burke, however, we find an overarching optimism made possible and secured by a theology, a doctrine of providence according to which we are "disposed and marshalled . . . by a divine tactick."[54] This reading of history and reason, together with his theological convictions, distinguishes Burke's conservatism from both secular doctrines of progress and a secular conservatism that suffers some philosophical embarrassment from its implicit relativism.[55] As we shall see, it also marks a contrast with Coleridge who, unlike Burke, developed a sophisticated theology and one that significantly enlarges the scope of reason and, therefore, our capacity to read the "system" of history and being.

Imperfection and responsibility are the principle themes of Burke's doctrine of the individual and, not surprisingly, they reflect his account of the political environment and its history. Conservatism begins, as I've

---

[53] Burke, *Reflections*, 121.

[54] Edmund Burke, *An Appeal from the New to the Old Whigs*, ed. James M. Robson (New York: Bobbs-Merrill, 1962) 96.

[55] For a frank discussion of what amounts to the guilty conscience of a secular conservatism, see Roger Scruton, *The Meaning of Conservatism*, 2nd ed. (London: Macmillan, 1984) 190-91.

suggested, in suspicion, doubting the capacity of human beings to achieve a radical remaking of their social world, a remaking in which the human order becomes transparent to reason. This skepticism rests not only on finding the "private stock of reason" in any individual or generation "small" when compared to the wisdom of experience embodied in institutions, laws, manners, traditions, and "prejudices."[56] It also derives from a recognition of the unruly passions, of an internal disorder that constitutes an ineradicable, structural imperfection.[57] Society, Burke argues, meets the desperate need for the control of desires that, outside social bounds, would leave humanity in a condition of wretchedness.[58] Human beings thirst after power, and they do so immoderately. "The great object of political arrangement," therefore, is to limit the power that any one individual or group can obtain over others and to lessen the general desire for it.[59] This end cannot be completely or suddenly realized. Society is, after all, built of crooked timber even though, as Burke thought, the long haul of history, acting under the direction of providence, achieves some straightening. Following Burke, conservatism became a "philosophy of imperfection."[60]

Admittedly, conservatives have idealized the past. Most commonly, this is the medieval past, as it is for Burke who is effusive in his admira-

---

[56] Burke, *Reflections*, 182-84.

[57] In early Conservative writings, including those of Coleridge, this conviction is dependent upon accepting a Christian, and broadly Augustinian, account of the Fall. The latter remains influential but many later Conservatives, insisting on a comparable doctrine of imperfection, reject the Christian framework. See, for instance, T. E. Hulme, "Romanticism and Classicism," and "A Tory Philosophy," in *Selected Writings*, ed. Patrick McGuinness (Manchester: Carcenet Press, 1998).

[58] Burke, *Reflections*, 150-51.

[59] Edmund Burke, *An Appeal from the New to the Old Whigs*, 95. The *Appeal* was written in 1791, a year after the *Reflections*.

[60] Noel O'Sullivan, *Conservatism* (New York: St. Martin's Press, 1976) 9-18. O'Sullivan proposes the doctrine of imperfection or, more properly, ineradicable imperfection, as the key differentia of Conservatism. This, however, does not sufficiently distinguish Conservatism from other "right-wing" movements. The attitude of the Christian Right in the U.S., for instance, to the operation of the law in relation to "private" morality is in acute tension with traditional Conservatism. The attempt to find a single doctrine as defining of conservatism is probably a lost cause.

tion for feudal sentiments and institutions.[61] However, the consistent drive of Burke's position is to recognize that, in this world, whatever improvements or declensions have occurred, the peaceable kingdom lies neither ahead nor behind us. A human being cannot escape imperfection.

No more, however, may this faulty creature escape responsibility. This is the other pole of Burke's political anthropology. Conservative thinkers are noted for correlating rights and duties, pointing to the "correspondent duty which is married to every right."[62] In relation to society, therefore, human beings are as much bearers of responsibilities as possessors of rights. An obligation to belong to a society and to fulfill the conditions of belonging is, in this view, given along with the acknowledgement of rights.[63] This account of responsibility involves an understanding of the individual since embraced by many critics of liberal individualism:

> As to the right of men to act anywhere according to their pleasure, without any moral tie, no such right exists. Men are never in a state of *total* independence of each other. It is not the condition of our nature; nor is it conceivable how any man can pursue a course of action without its having some effect upon others; or, of course, without producing some degree of responsibility for his conduct.[64]

Against individualistic accounts, self-caricatured in Hodgson's "Commonwealth of Reason" where society is reduced to a conglomeration of voting atoms, Burke insists on the priority of the social. "Men without their choice derive benefits from [society]; without their choice they are subjected to duties in consequence of these benefits; and without their choice they enter into a virtual obligation as binding as any that is actual."[65]

---

[61] Burke, *Reflections*, 170-71.

[62] Russell Kirk, *The Conservative Mind: from Burke to Santayana* (Chicago: Henry Regnery Company, 1953) 42.

[63] Charles Taylor, "Atomism," in *Philosophy and the Human Sciences: Philosophical Papers 2* (Cambridge UK: Cambridge University Press, 1985) 187-210.

[64] Edmund Burke, "Letters on a Regicide Peace," in *The Works of the Right Honorable Edmund Burke*, vol. 2 (London: Henry G. Bohn, 1854) 216.

[65] Burke, *Appeal*, 95. Or as one contemporary Conservative has put it:

As we've noted, the political environment is formative of persons. This environment, however, includes other, relatively autonomous contexts of formation such as the family, religious communities, schools, localities of geography and common action. Within each context, human life is constituted as "answerable" life, life that has meaning in its response to what is given, to what is said and done *beforehand*, prior to the individual's answering words and actions. And, as the formative contexts are plural, responsibility is therefore multiple and complex. It also includes inevitable conflicts, the seriousness of which is violated whenever one context is elevated in such a way as to discount others. Despite some political ideologies, the individual is never only a citizen, only the bearer of national or racial identity, or only a member of a social class.

Burke's critique of the National Assembly's ecclesiastical policy is just one example of the conservative interest in protecting "autonomous institutions."[66] Such institutions, conservatives have argued, are vital to liberty, providing sources of resistance to rule that involves the domination of one formative context, that of nationality or class, for instance, over others. Protection of these autonomous institutions, therefore, is necessary since governments have been all too willing to sacrifice individual liberty for the pursuit of national vocation or class destiny. Even in his "radical years," Coleridge argued against Godwin, for the importance of the family as a formative context. As we shall see, in his later writings, attention to the diversity of contexts within which human beings live out and understand their lives funds his important arguments against reductionism. Regard for the plurality of formative contexts begs our recognition that human identity is complex and that it is betrayed, as Burke acknowledged, by political ideologies that boast of "simplicity" but regard society "in but one point of view."[67]

More immediate than Paine's *Rights of Man*, Mary Wollstonecraft published her *A Vindication of the Rights of Men in a Letter to the Right Honorable Edmund Burke* little more than a month after the appearance

---

"Individual man is the man who recognizes that he is no mere individual." Scruton, *Meaning of Conservatism*, 73.

[66]Burke, *Reflections*, 246-75. On "autonomous institutions," see Scruton, *Meaning of Conservatism*, 141-60; Robert Nisbet, *Conservatism: Dream and Reality* (Milton Keynes UK: Open University Press, 1986) 21-22, 47-54, 68-74.

[67]Burke, *Reflections*, 153.

of the *Reflections*.⁶⁸ This, the first of Wollstonecraft's "vindications," is a rapidly composed, angry piece in which, with some irony given her principle thesis, the author's fury sometimes overwhelms her coherence.⁶⁹ Not wishing to follow Burke through "horseway and footpath," Wollstonecraft rarely tackles the details of Burke's case directly. She does, however, recognize very clearly that Burke's is a critique of politics according to reason alone and that it implies a theory of mind. Here is the "foundation" she exposes for attack. Your book, she accuses Burke, reveals "a mortal antipathy to reason." For Wollstonecraft, Burke's judgment on the French Revolution and his defense of the British Constitution invokes an account of motivation, of the dynamics of the will as it is informed by reason, imagination, and emotion. Rather than critique in close fashion his assessment of the National Assembly, therefore, she opposes Burke's implicit philosophical psychology with her own account of mind and of the motivational conditions according to which moral and political action has integrity.

The politicians of reason, Burke claims, cast off all that is necessary "to cover the defects of our naked shivering nature."⁷⁰ The image is significant and turns about the relationship between nature and art. As was discussed above, Burke thinks that when human beings make rightly, they make according to nature.⁷¹ They embody the order of nature through the art that is politics. Reliance on reason alone, however, returns humanity to a condition of nature that is, for humanity, unnatural. The art of self-making, the art that is nature for humanity demands more than reason; it demands a harmony of faculties: understanding, imagination, and emotion. Tying the worth of obedience, or of strategies that preserve or even improve institutions, to the standard of a fully reflective awareness, an ability to justify action by a strict chain of reasoning, is not only unnecessary, it is, Burke argues, actually destructive. Much that is worthy

---

⁶⁸The *Reflections* was published on 1 November 1790 and the first edition of *A Vindication of the Rights of Men* in early December. A second, corrected edition of *Vindications* was available on 14 December. It is the latter that is discussed here.

⁶⁹The second "vindication" is *A Vindication of the Rights of Woman with Strictures on Political and Moral Subjects*, published in 1792.

⁷⁰Burke, *Reflections*, 171.

⁷¹See above, 16-17.

to be preserved eludes such an accounting. Furthermore, over and above the limitations of our temporally situated understanding, reason alone is an insufficient motivator. The British, Burke claims, wisely cherish their prejudices.[72] These are the loyalties that exceed our understanding; they foster the respect institutions need; they keep statesmen within the bounds of due caution and steady the critical decision. As bonds of agreement, prejudices issue in habits that secure the social order where fragile reason cannot, or, with its brittle abstractions, can do so only partially. Prejudice and habit involve motivation that is emotional, maintained by awe, fondness, admiration, humility. Even to the extent we grasp the wisdom behind a prejudice, we should still trust to the prejudice as much as to the reason: "[P]rejudice, with its reason, has a motive to give action to that reason, and an affection which will give it permanence."[73]

Crucial, here, is the role of the imagination. It is the imagination that hedges with nobility relationships of power and obedience, configuring them as moral relationships, imparting dignity, exciting reverence and love: "making power gentle and obedience liberal."[74] Again, Burke unites art and nature, arguing that the power of imagination brings into political life, the natural affections belonging to family and friendship. Decisions of state, made upon careful reflection, should be executed "as if in the presence of canonized forefathers," finding their measure through the force of a restraining awe. In his earlier work, *On the Sublime and Beautiful*, Burke had identified the imagination as a creative power mediating between sense, emotion, and action:

> [T]he mind of man possesses a sort of creative power of its own; either in representing at pleasure the images of things in the order and manner in which they were received by the senses, or in combining those images in a new manner, and according to a different order. This power is called imagination. . . .[75]

In the argument of the *Reflections*, the imagination appears as a moral power that responds in the form of "just prejudices," to the way of things,

---

[72]Burke, *Reflections*, 183.
[73]Ibid.
[74]Ibid., 171.
[75]Edmund Burke, "On the Sublime and the Beautiful," in *The Works of the Right Honorable Edmund Burke*, vol. 1 (London: Henry G. Bohn, 1854) 28.

the order of God's intent. Imagination and emotion, therefore, are sources of motivation relatively independent from reason. Thus, the forms with which imagination clothes political power may be "ratified by the understanding" but they are not wholly ordered by, or translucent to, human reason. A human being is not the less free, therefore, because he or she fulfills the obligations of society, not in the full glare of reason, but through an emotional attachment secured by imagination.

The *Vindication of the Rights of Men* begins with a personally focused attack on Burke, the rhetorical effect of which is to associate him firmly with the imagination while the author identifies with reason. The aesthetic categories that are the subject of Burke's earlier work are redefined, separating them from the imagination and bringing them over to the side of reason. Wollstonecraft's critique is not "a flight of fancy" but a pursuit of the truly sublime and beautiful: "For truth, in morals, has ever appeared to me the essence of the sublime; and, in taste, simplicity the only criterion of the beautiful."[76]

Burke is characterized as one swept up by imagination into vanity, subjugating reason to the service of a "shining" display of wit. The *Reflections*, therefore, is the product of a "teeming fancy," a pagoda which "plain country people," acting, one assumes, not from Burkean prejudice but in simple reason, name a "folly." With Burke "reflection inflames . . . imagination, instead of enlightening . . . understanding," and emotion run amok dispels "the sober suggestions of reason."[77] Wollstonecraft thus identifies her opponent as a parable of internal disorder, blighted by an ungoverned imagination. This opening thrust is more than a piece of infuriated abuse, it is the starting point for her attempt to trace this psychological and moral discord in the social order Burke defends.

Fastening on Wollstonecraft's critique of the imagination risks one-sidedness. She was, after all, also a writer of fiction and, even in this first treatise, her portrait of Dr. Price, for instance, is a deliberately imaginative tactic. Nevertheless, in the *Vindication*, Wollstonecraft approaches the

---

[76]Wollstonecraft, *Vindication*, 35. Her use of "fancy" is, of course, pre-Coleridgean and synonymous with "imagination." Later in this work, Wollstonecraft identifies "simplicity" with "truth" and thus completes the move by which she captures both concepts for the rule of reason: "romance destroys all simplicity; which, in works of taste, is but a synonymous word for truth," 61.

[77]Ibid., 36-37.

imagination by way of identifying it with Burkean extravagance and establishing it thereby in polarity with reason. A negative assessment of the imagination, therefore, persists throughout the work. Imagination is the source of that pomp that reconciles a populace to inequitable laws; it sanctifies unjust antiquity and the cruelties of unequal wealth. The imagination also corrupts manners and, in reducing women to objects of sensual delight, poisons relations between the sexes. Obscuring the simple truths of reason, the imagination distorts our feelings for humanity, providing us with escapist dreams and stunting the range of our pity: "a *gentleman* of lively imagination must borrow some drapery from fancy before he can love or pity a *man*."[78] Between imagination and reason are the feelings, the health of which depends upon whether they accompany and serve to enliven the latter or whether they are inflamed in unholy alliance with the imagination. Burke's appeal to blessed "prejudices" and "untaught feelings" is, therefore, merely a charter for a lazy acquiescence in the impulses of passion, a betrayal of the human vocation to cultivate reason. Mapping psychological and political order by way of each other, Wollstonecraft represents the "untaught feelings" as unauthorized by the "regal" power of reason. "Sensibility" or "common sense" is a usurper that claims an "indefeasible" right, a right, as it were, of prescription. However, unlike the rational rights of men, but certainly echoing Burke's indefinable yet discernable rights, "rights of this kind are not easily proved."[79]

Reason not emotion distinguishes humanity. Therefore, Wollstonecraft argues, however heartening or reviving the feelings, it is not emotion but reason that provides the truly human relations that form society. "Reason," here, is the exercise and product of "reflection," not the strange wisdom that trumps human folly over time, but the individual capacity for ratiocination.[80] For Burke, continuity resides in institutions and patterns of behavior dependent as much on feeling and traditions of imagination as on our powers of reflection. Wollstonecraft, however, insists that these continuities do not realize the human vocation or do so only to the extent that they are grounded in and translucent to reason. Thus we may be grateful, or at least relieved, that unthinking habits of sober behavior per-

---

[78]Ibid., 45; for the other examples, see 38, 42, 76, 54, 56, 39, 45, 39, 92, 95.
[79]Ibid., 62-63.
[80]Ibid., 73.

sist among the populace but such behavior is but "reason at second hand" and, therefore, the product of a truncated humanity.[81] What is at stake here is reason's "liberty" which requires that our reflective powers brook no partner in judging social good, that understanding alone provides the criterion of human happiness. We are free only insofar as we are consciously guided by reflection. Emotion and imagination, therefore, must be put in their place, which is clearly subordinate to reason. It is thus a necessary stage in both individual and political development that reason should "clip the wing" of fancy.[82] Here, Wollstonecraft implies an aesthetic theory that links imaginative energy to an underdeveloped understanding. Maturity requires not just the control but a clear restriction of imagination. "Truth is seldom arrayed by the Graces" and however useful the materials fancy gathers in our youth, on mature age, fancy must give them up to the judgment. An enthusiasm for Sterne at sixty, Wollstonecraft suggests, is a sign of retardation. [83]It is, we are led to assume, as dubious and untimely as an appeal to feudal color in the late-eighteenth century.

It is hardly unusual, within the tradition of Western ethics, to urge that the imagination and the passions should be governed by reason. What is significant, however, is that, unlike Burke, and in some tension with the practice of her own writing, Wollstonecraft will allow no independent value to imagination or feeling. Their humanity and their worth is dependent entirely on their being auxiliary to reason. Burke, by contrast, more skeptical of human understanding, is able to accord imagination and emotion a relative independence since individual human reason is itself only a pale and fallible reflection of the larger reason, the beneficent cunning, that informs and directs the history of enduring human institutions and practices. That larger, providential reason may be served as

---

[81]Ibid., 63-64.

[82]Ibid., 61. Just as Coleridge establishes the distinction between "imagination" and "fancy," he also introduces the equally important distinction between "reason" and "understanding," a piece of "desynonymization" that allows him to resist Burke's skepticism whilst also developing a critique of "enlightenment" rationality. The reason/understanding distinction is Kantian but Coleridge's interpretation of it is distinctively different from that of Kant. See below, chaps. 1, 2, and 5.

[83]Ibid., 91.

well, sometimes better, by actions arising from love, or lured by a reverence cultivated by imagination, as by deeds that proceed from our limited understanding. "The true lawgiver ought to have a heart full of sensibility. He ought to love and respect his kind, and to fear himself."[84] Thus, where Wollstonecraft has the rule of reason, subjugating feeling and imagination, Burke appeals to interrelating powers, potentially a harmony of powers in which deliberating reason, essential but always tending to hubristic excess, is humbled and restrained by imagination and emotion.

Even if one is only concerned with the British tradition, defining conservatism is problematic. A list of ideological features risks failing to differentiate conservatism from other "right-wing" ideologies or obscuring the variety of both contemporary and historical conservatism.[85] The convictions of Edmund Burke discussed above, however, are indisputably influential within this political tradition, though not always equally so, and they continue to find their way into contemporary expositions of what has been termed conservative "dogmatics."[86] As regards the history of conservatism, then, this book is an exercise in plotting one stage in the trajectory of some important conservative ideas, that is, from Burke's *Reflections* to a major articulation of what has been called "Romantic Conservatism."[87] Drawing an ideological trajectory involves noting the persistence and alteration of themes as they move within a changing field of discourse, practices, and institutions.[88] Thus, shifts in the social and

---

[84]Burke, *Reflections*, 281.

[85]There is an excellent discussion of the problems in *The Nature of the Right: European and American Politics and Political Thought since 1789*, ed. Roger Eatwell and Noel O'Sullivan (London: Pinter Publishers, 1989). International differences are surveyed in Pekka Suvanto, *Conservatism from the French Revolution to the 1990s* (New York: St. Martin's Press, 1997) 173-78. Suvanto's historical survey of conservatism includes Britain, France, Germany, Scandinavia, and the U.S.

[86]Scruton, *Meaning of Conservatism*, 11-13; Nisbet, *Conservatism*, 21.

[87]Frank O'Gorman, *British Conservatism: Conservative Thought from Burke to Thatcher* (London: Longman Group Limited, 1986) 18-24.

[88]I have adapted the concept of an ideological "trajectory" from its rather different use in the field of New Testament studies. James M. Robinson and Helmut Koester, *Trajectories through Early Christianity* (Philadelphia: Fortress

economic role of commerce; the influence of utilitarianism upon religious and ethical thought; a rapid secularization of political discourse; his own reading of German idealism: all these bear down on Coleridge's development of Burkean ideas and contribute to the distinctive character of his political philosophy. Above all, the impact of his own account of the mind and imagination, an account that is philosophical as well as thoroughly informed by a religious tradition, produces a conservatism to which one recent and rather dismissive description—"emotionalist conservatism in the tradition of Burke"—does, as we will see, scant justice.[89]

The Later Political Writings

Despite Coleridge's long-standing reputation as a disorganized shirker, his prose writings constitute a very sizable corpus. Over the following chapters, the discussion will range fairly extensively over his works but the political writings from the last seventeen years of Coleridge's life, treated in fair detail, will provide the main anchors for the argument.

The earliest of these texts, *The Statesman's Manual*, appeared in December 1816 and its companion, *A Lay Sermon*, in the following April.[90] Both are cast in sermonic form and directed to a specific audience. *The Statesman's Manual* is thus addressed to the "Learned and Reflecting of all Ranks and Professions, especially among the Higher Class." To this audience, Coleridge seeks to propose the Hebrew Scriptures "as a Code of true political Economy, and a specimen of bona fide philosophical history."[91] In exhorting his readers to this use of the Old Testament, Coleridge also provides an account of the hermeneutic

---

Press, 1971) 8-19.

[89]Eva Simmons, ed. *Augustan Literature: from 1660–1789* (London: Bloomsbury Publishing, 1994) 104.

[90]All references to *The Statesman's Manual* and *A Lay Sermon* are from Samuel Taylor Coleridge, *Lay Sermons*, ed. R. J. White, vol. 6 of *The Collected Works of Samuel Taylor Coleridge* (Princeton NJ: Princeton University Press, 1972).

[91]Letter to John Gibson Lockhart in *A Statesman's Manual*, which is included in Samuel Taylor Coleridge, *Lay Sermons*, ed. R. J. White, vol. 6 of *The Collected Works of Samuel Taylor Coleridge* (Princeton NJ: Princeton University Press, 1972) 244.

involved. The importance of a political reading is thus placed within a larger purpose, namely, "to recommend that state of mind" which recognizes the knowledge proper and essential to faith, turning from the extremes of either reducing that knowledge to commonly held generalities or appealing to its mysteriousness as an absolution from further thought.[92] Appended to the sermon are a series of "comments and essays," the most substantial of which concern the relationship of reason and religion; the distinction between reason and understanding; and the meaning of the term "Idea." It is in these latter pieces that Coleridge assays the task he describes as "a defense of ancient Metaphysics (principally, the Pythagorean, Heraclitic, and Platonic) contrasted with the modern."[93]

The second in what was projected as a trilogy of addresses is entitled *A Lay Sermon Addressed to the Higher and Middle Classes on the Existing Distresses and Discontents*. Coleridge describes the genesis of the work in a September 1816 letter to R. H. Brabant:

> I had been solicited by the House of Gale and Fenner, whom I had conceived at least to have felt kindly towards me, no small merit in an age of atrocious Calumny, to give them a small Tract on the present Distresses in the form of a Lay-Sermon. . . . I labored from morning to night, and found myself writing a Volume, not a Tract of a single sheet.[94]

The "present Distresses" were those of the "commercial losses and stagnation" that followed the end of the Napoleonic Wars.[95] Coleridge understood that the war had provided, a "universal stimulant" for the economy: agriculture enjoyed an extended boom; exports rose as England's European competitors suffered; and military needs accelerated technological innovation and manufacture. Peace then brought a sudden contraction of the economy in which rising domestic prices, particularly

---

[92]Coleridge, *Lay Sermons*, 46.

[93]Coleridge, *Lay Sermons*, 46.

[94]Samuel Taylor Coleridge, *Collected Letters of Samuel Taylor Coleridge*, ed. Earl Leslie Griggs, 6 vols. (Oxford: Clarendon Press, 1956–1971) 4:672.

[95]Article in *The Courier*, 25 July 1816; repr. in Samuel Taylor Coleridge, *Essays on His Times*, ed. David V. Erdman, vol. 3, pt. 2 of *The Collected Works of Samuel Taylor Coleridge* (Princeton NJ: Princeton University Press, 1978) 430.

of grain, coincided with a reduced demand for labor, itself aggravated by the influx of former servicemen.[96]

Coleridge's response to these distresses and to the discontent they provoked is twofold. First, he offers a critique of the "demagogues" who were inflaming popular passions. Though they are not named explicitly, it is not difficult to identify particular targets as William Cobbett, Sir Francis Burdett, John and Leigh Hunt, and Major John Cartwright. Coleridge attempts to expose the inadequacies of their economic interpretation and he mounts a blistering, rather intemperate, attack upon their rhetoric. The second thrust identifies the underlying cause of present turmoil as an "overbalance of the commercial spirit."[97] This critique is not of the commercial drive as such, Coleridge is now far from the damning assessment of 1795, but of a one-sided cultural development that has disturbed the dynamics of those diverse interests necessary to a healthy society. Consideration of the forces for redressing the balance brings Coleridge back to the need for principles, also the theme of *The Statesman's Manual*, and to a critical examination of the role of religion within the social order.

A third lay sermon, addressed "to the Lower and Laboring Classes," with the text "the Poor have the Gospel preached unto them," was proposed but never written. According to the advertisement printed on the back wrapper of *The Statesman's Manual*, all three sermons were to be "printed so as to make one uniform volume."[98] Even considering only the first two sermons this would have made a somewhat peculiar production. While there are clear thematic continuities between the sermons, the intended audience is different and, as a consequence, there is a marked contrast in terms of persuasive style. As Coleridge acknowledged in his letter to Lockhart, *A Lay Sermon* was

> [the] only Work (I except my Newspaper Contributions) which I had meant to be *popular*, and which, with the exception of three or four

---

[96]For a general account, see Eric J. Hobsbawm, *Industry and Empire* (London: Penguin Books, 1969) chaps. 2, 3, and 5, and diagram 37: "British Price Movements 1700–1959."
[97]Coleridge, *Lay Sermons*, 169-70.
[98]Coleridge, *Statesman's Manual*, xxxn.4.

pages, really is so—the work, which of all others was most calculated to be useful to the public and advantageous to the Author.

By contrast, *The Statesman's Manual* was of "merely general and theologicometaphysical interest addressed to the Learned."[99]

Addressing social classes in this differentiated way presupposes a rhetorical principle Coleridge recognized early in his career. In the 1795 lectures *Conciones ad Populum*, he asserts that

> in the disclosal of Opinion, it is our duty to consider the character of those, to whom we address ourselves, their situations, and possible degree of knowledge.[100]

Beyond the pragmatic counsel of rhetorical tradition, however, the practice also reflects a refusal, typical of conservative ideology, to reduce society to a mere aggregate of separate individuals. The social order realizes diverse and necessary forms of human good because, Coleridge insists, it is composed of contexts of interest and loyalty that transcend the individual and that stand in dynamic relation one to another.

The "rifacciamento" edition of *The Friend*, the largest of the works considered here, was published in November 1818. Coleridge had long intended to revise and provide supplementary numbers for this "weekly journal" that had run to twenty-seven issues between June 1809 and March 1810. The first reissue of *The Friend*, bound in a single volume, had been published in June 1812. This consisted of the first twelve issues as Coleridge had revised and slightly expanded them before the original series had ended. The 1818 edition was a much more ambitious project, a general revision that would turn the journal into "a compleat and circular work."[101] When completed, the additions to the original Friend had become so numerous that, as Coleridge explained in the advertisement:

> The present volumes are rather a *rifacciamento* than a new edition. The additions forming so large a proportion of the whole work, and the arrangement being altogether new, I might indeed hesitate in bestowing the title of a republication on a work, which can scarcely be said to

---

[99]Ibid., 244-45.

[100]Coleridge, *On Politics and Religion*, 51; see also, Coleridge, *Statesman's Manual*, xxxi.

[101]Coleridge, *Collected Letters* 4:551, letter to Joseph Cottle, 10 March 1815.

have been ever published, in the ordinary trade acceptation of the word.[102]

As is typical of Coleridge, though, his ambitions for the work exceeded his time and energy. Despite the additions and the new structure for the work, the revision of *The Friend* is very uneven. There are still a good many abrupt transitions and confusing interpolations, and passages poorly developed in the journal, such as the account of the three systems of political justice, remain without further treatment.

Through its changes in form, *The Friend* maintained a continuity of objective. Coleridge told Humphrey Davy in 1808, "I write to found true PRINCIPLES, to oppose false PRINCIPLES, in Criticism, Legislation, Philosophy, Morals, and International Law."[103] The subtitle of the 1818 edition repeats the objective: "A Series of Essays, in Three Volumes, to Aid in the Formation of Fixed Principles in Politics, Morals, and Religion, with Literary Amusements Interspersed." No more intended "for the *Multitude*" than the completed *Lay Sermons*, *The Friend* was addressed to those who "by Rank, or Fortune, or official Situation, or Talents and Habits of Reflection, are to *influence* the Multitude."[104]

What is strikingly different in the 1818 edition, however, is that, as well as adding much new material, Coleridge has given *The Friend* a new architecture.[105] Essays in the original journal were regularly interrupted by letters, poetry, and anecdotal material. This creates an impression of disorder that must have been further aggravated for Coleridge's subscribers by the way issues could begin or end in the middle of an essay.[106] By

---

[102]Samuel Taylor Coleridge, *The Friend*, ed. Barbara E. Rooke, vol. 4, pt. 1 of 2 of *The Collected Works of Samuel Taylor Coleridge* (Princeton NJ: Princeton University Press, 1969) 3. The *Oxford English Dictionary* gives the spelling as *rifacimento*, defining it as "a new modelling or recasting of a literary work." *Webster's* spells "*rifacimento* or *refacimento*," defining it as "a recasting or adaptation esp. of a literary work or musical composition."

[103]Coleridge, *Collected Letters* 3:143, letter to Humphrey Davy, 14 December 1808.

[104]Ibid.

[105]For a guide to the additions and transpositions of material, see Coleridge, *The Friend*, pt. 2, appendix D; also, E. L. Griggs, "The Friend: 1809 and 1818 Editions," *Modern Philology* (May 1938): 369-73.

[106]In more than one case, in the middle of a sentence, as in issue 5 which

contrast, for the rifacimento, Coleridge organized the material into an ascending structure of three major sections. The first, introductory section, consists of sixteen essays that discuss *The Friend* as a rhetorical enterprise, assessing its demands upon the readership, considering the ethics of literary and political communication, and justifying the pedagogical goal of empowering 'principled' thought. In the second major section, Coleridge gives his account of the principles of political philosophy; criticizes Rousseauesque arguments for universal suffrage; and discusses the character of true patriotism. The retention of material that had more immediate interest at the time of first publication, such as discussion of the British initiative to seize the Danish fleet, is justified as "giving illustration and interest" to the principles established.[107] In the final section, the reader ascends to consideration of the method of thought itself; the process by which principles are arrived at; and the relationship of that method to religion. This third part of the 1818 *Friend* is entirely new. The "Essays on the Principles of Method" that form the bulk of it are a reconstruction and reworking of the introduction for the *Encyclopedia Metropolitana*, a piece previously published in a form woefully "bedeviled," "interpolated and "topsy-turvied."[108] This section was the object of Coleridge's greatest satisfaction, surviving even his gloomiest assessment as to the enduring worth of his writings.[109] Each of *The Friend*'s three major divisions ends with a "Landing Place" or "essays interposed for amusement, retrospect and preparation."[110] Into these were gathered such "interruptions" from the earlier *Friend* as Coleridge chose to retain.

On the Constitution of Church and State in Accordance with the Idea of Each (December 1829) was the last of Coleridge's prose works to appear in his lifetime. The starting point for this systematic presentation of his constitutional theory was the bill for Catholic emancipation that

---

both begins and ends in that manner, Coleridge, *The Friend*, pt. 2, 63-64, 78-79.

[107]Coleridge, *The Friend*, pt. 1, 311-12.

[108]Coleridge, *Collected Letters* 4:825, letter to John Payne Collier, 2 February 1818.

[109]Ibid., 925: "At least, were it in my power, my works should be confined to the second volume of my 'Literary Life,' the essays of the third volume of the 'Friend' . . . with about fifty or sixty pages from the two former volumes, and some half-dozen of my poems."

[110]Coleridge, *The Friend*, pt. 1, 127.

became law in April 1829.[111] An old topic for Coleridge, he had discussed the political implications of Catholic Emancipation and of the event that drove its urgency—the Act of Union with Ireland—in articles, written in 1800, for the *Morning Post* and, in 1811, for *The Courier*.[112] In 1825, just after the House of Lords rejected Sir Francis Burdett's bill for Catholic emancipation, Coleridge attempted to complete an extended work on the constitutional problems. This proved abortive and Coleridge did not return to the task until 1829. *On the Constitution of the Church and State* was published in December of that year, some eight months after George IV, nervous for his coronation oath, gave a reluctant assent to the Catholic relief bill.[113]

This timing is important for the character and justification of a work which bears, to the events that provoked it, a relationship like that of the Napoleonic crises to the reflections in the rifacimento *Friend*. In late 1829, Coleridge could no longer hope, as in 1825, to effect the course and form of legislation.[114] This did not, however, undermine, in his view, the primary value of the treatise. Like *The Friend*, *On the Constitution of the Church and State* is an exercise in "referring things to principles." Historically produced institutions are not understood until their *rationality* is recognized, the account of reason, however, differing from both Burke and the radicals discussed above. Political change remains blind, Coleridge argues, and the historical agents that effect it do not fully

---

[111]For an account of Coleridge's engagement with constitutional theory; with the campaign for Catholic Emancipation; and of the writing of church and state, see John Colmer, *Coleridge: Critic of Society* (Oxford: Oxford University Press, 1959) 153-66; John Morrow, *Coleridge's Political Thought: Property, Morality, and the Limits of Traditional Discourse* (London: Macmillan, 1990) 126-30.

[112]*The Morning Post*, 15 and 27 January 1800, Coleridge, *Essays on His Times*, pt. 1, 105-108, 133-34; "The Courier," 13, 21, and 26 September 1811; Coleridge, *Essays on His Times*, pt. 2, 279-82, 305-13, 373-417. The Act of Union with Ireland was passed in 1800.

[113]The treatise was revised in January 1830. It is this second edition that is followed here.

[114]Coleridge had hoped, in 1825, that John Hookham Frere, the "absent friend" referred to at the beginning of "Church and State," would present his work to the Prime Minister, Lord Liverpool. See Colmer, *Coleridge: Critic of Society*, 153.

understand themselves, until such change is measured against the "Ideas" that institutions embody. *On the Constitution of the Church and State* thus develops the concept of an "Idea" introduced earlier in the appendixes to *The Statesman's Manual*. The "Idea" that animates, drives institutional development, is given in "the knowledge of [a thing's] *ultimate aim*," its telos. In the present case, the changes effected in according full political rights to Roman Catholics, and any potential threat they offer to British constitutional order, are to be assessed and judged according to the ultimate aim incarnate in a national church and in that form of political order of which it is a part. Furthermore, the famous concept of the "clerisy," developed in this context, is a response, in institutional terms, to the problems of political pedagogy and persuasion raised so passionately in the lay sermons and in *The Friend*. The clerisy, therefore, is taxed with diffusing "through the whole community, and to every native entitled to its laws and rights" the appropriate "quantity and quality of knowledge . . . indispensable both for the understanding of those rights, and for the performance of the duties correspondent."[115]

When Coleridge asked, "Have you ever heard me preach, Charles?" his friend Lamb replied, "N-n-never heard you d-d-do anything else, C-c-coleridge."[116] There is a preacher's, or at least an educator's, purpose behind all of Coleridge's later political writings. Their author seeks to foster a return to "principled thought" among those capable of "referring things to principles," of possessing *ideas*. Coleridge thus desires to "found true principles" and "to oppose false principles." Given his conviction that the health of a social order is dependent on the ideas active within it, this enterprise in political education bears upon the living powers of social formation. What is involved, therefore, is a rhetorical project with social stability and rational social change as its ultimate aim. In order to understand this project, I have paid particular attention to Coleridge's pedagogical practice, especially to the rhetorical structure of his writings. This helps show how his philosophical psychology in general, and his theory of the imagination in particular, inform his arguments, his proposals, and his persuasive approach to the reader.

---

[115]Samuel Taylor Coleridge, *On the Constitution of the Church and State*, ed. John Colmer, vol. 10 of *The Collected Works of Samuel Taylor Coleridge* (Princeton NJ: Princeton University Press, 1976) 44.

[116]This anecdote is reported in Coleridge, *Statesman's Manual*, xxxv.

One of the principle difficulties in writing on any *aspect* of Coleridge's thought, and this applies no less to his political discussions, is that one runs the risk of dividing what, in the works themselves, is vitally and, for Coleridge, necessarily united.[117] According to the division of intellectual labor among Coleridge's contemporaries, the political theorist was expected to engage a range of topics considerably broader than would be thought necessary today. Thus, William Godwin includes in the *Enquiry Concerning Political Justice* treatments of individual ethics, epistemology, philosophical psychology, language, and education.[118] Coleridge's range of concern is no less than Godwin's and in some respects, in his inclusion of historiography and hermeneutics for instance, is greater. However, more is at stake here than a recognition of contemporary expectations. The rhetorical force of Coleridge's writings depends in large measure, as shall be shown below, upon a connective, unifying movement that brings together—coadunates, to use a Coleridgean term— the processes of scientific, literary, political, ethical, and religious thinking. Furthermore, the political and social positions Coleridge takes up, the causes he espouses, few of which are original to him in themselves,[119] achieve a distinctively Coleridgean sense only within a system of connections embracing human beings, society, history, culture, nature, and the divine. Recent studies of Coleridge's political thought, in seeking

---

[117]I. A. Richards's comment on the expositions of those who would consider Coleridge's literary criticism apart from consideration of his philosophy and theology applies equally to his political ideas: "The thought so fenced off ceases to be Coleridge's and becomes something much less interesting." I. A. Richards, *Coleridge on Imagination*, 3rd ed. (London: Routledge and Kegan Paul, 1962) 5. It is significant that Miller, *Ideology and Enlightenment*, who engages very little with metaphysics, philosophical psychology, or the theory of symbolism, concludes that, as a political thinker, Coleridge is of only limited significance, primarily as a mediator of eighteenth-century political ideas into the nineteenth.

[118]William Godwin, *Enquiry concerning Political Justice*, ed. Isaac Kramnick (New York: Penguin Books, 1976).

[119]As a social critic, Coleridge was "heir to an eighteenth-century 'nostalgic' critique of commercial society." He shares fundamental perspectives, for instance, on the importance of landed wealth and the dangers of unrestricted exercise of the commercial spirit, with folk as diverse as Robert Southey; William Cobbett; and Henry Brougham. John Miller, *Ideology and Enlightenment*, 267; see also 169-97, 210-302.

to articulate the range, development, and historical context of Coleridge's political arguments, have offered expositions in which discussion of the connections between his politics and his theology, historiography, hermeneutics, doctrine of the symbol, and philosophical psychology is inevitably limited.[120] The present study treats only the later political writings, omits journalism and other short pieces, and does not seek to provide a discussion of all the arguments found therein. I do, however, seek to pay greater attention to the internal connections of Coleridge's thought, to the systematicity of one who, though he never completed his system, regarded such systematicity as an essential characteristic of rationality. To this end, the concept, discussed below, of "identification" as the goal of rhetoric, is, as Coleridge would have put it, a vital "organ of thought."

Among the various aspects of Coleridge's systematicity to which this study refers, I have laid particular emphasis upon the connections

---

[120]Colmer, *Coleridge: Critic of Society*; Miller, *Ideology and Enlightenment*; Morrow, *Coleridge's Political Thought*. Earlier, now somewhat outdated treatments, include Crane Brinton, *The Political Ideas of the English Romanticists* (New York: Russell & Russell, 1926); John Muirhead, *Coleridge the Philosopher* (London: Allen & Unwin, 1930); Alfred Cobban, *Edmund Burke and the Revolt against the Eighteenth Century: A Study of the Political and Social Thinking of Burke, Wordsworth, Coleridge, and Southey* (New York: Barnes and Noble, Inc., 1929). Other general and thematic studies of Coleridge's political and social writings include, David Calleo, *Coleridge and the Idea of the Modern State* (New Haven CT: Yale University Press, 1966); Deidre Coleman, *Coleridge and the Friend: 1809–1810* (Oxford: Clarendon Press, 1988); William Kennedy, *Humanist versus Economist: the Economic Thought of Samuel Taylor Coleridge* (Berkeley: California University Press, 1958); Ben Knights, *The Idea of the Clerisy in the Nineteenth Century* (London: Cambridge University Press, 1978); Nigel Leask, *The Politics of Imagination in Coleridge's Critical Thought* (London: Macmillan, 1988); Anya Taylor, *Coleridge's Defense of the Human* (Columbus: Ohio State University Press, 1986). Among the studies of Coleridge's work as a whole, the following should be noted as including valuable discussion of his political thought: Owen Barfield, *What Coleridge Thought* (Middletown CT: Wesleyan University Press, 1971); Geoffrey Davidson, *Coleridge's Career* (New York: St. Martin's Press, 1990); Norman Fruman, *Coleridge, The Damaged Archangel* (New York: George Braziller, 1971); Basil Willey, *Samuel Taylor Coleridge* (New York: W. W. Norton & Co, 1972).

between his politics and his theology. While it is impossible to discuss his political and social thought without some contextualizing reference to his theology, the most influential studies of Coleridge's theology pay scant attention to his politics.[121] There is, therefore, a place for the attempt to bring the theology and the politics to the fore, as it were, simultaneously. Coleridge's political thought, I propose, should be read as a "theological politics," a politics to which theological commitments are integral and essential throughout. In the final chapter, in particular, I offer a contrast between Coleridge's work and that of William Paley, citing the latter as an example of a contemporary political and ethical theory in which the connections with theology have become more tenuous. Alan Torrance has glossed the term "theological politics," in contrast to "political theology," as involving "a theologically driven approach to the state rather than a politically driven approach to God."[122]

Put as starkly as that, of course, the contrast is misleading: there is no theology that does not bear the marks of its determination by political context and interests and, in that sense, is not "politically driven." Certainly, Coleridge is no exception to this and I comment below on points at which his political anxieties inform his theology and the practical conclusions he draws from it. That said, however, I have used the term "theological politics" here in order to underline the operative role in Coleridge's politics of theological convictions, particularly in the case of *Church and State*, of incarnational and Trinitarian ones.

---

[121] J. Robert Barth, S.J. *Coleridge and Christian Doctrine* (Cambridge MA: Harvard University Press, 1969); James D. Boulger, *Coleridge as Religious Thinker* (New Haven CT: Yale University Press, 1961); James S. Cutsinger, *The Form of Transformed Vision: Coleridge and the Knowledge of God* (Macon GA: Mercer University Press, 1987).

[122] Alan Torrance, "Introductory Essay," in *Eberhard Jungel, Christ, Justice, and Peace*, trans. Alan J. Torrance and D. Bruce Hamill (Edinburgh: T. & T. Clark, 1992) xx.

2

Philosophical Psychology and Conservative Politics

From my early reading of Fairy Tales, & Genii &c &c—my mind had been habituated to the Vast—& I never regarded my senses *in any way as the criteria of my belief. I regulated all my creeds by my conceptions not by my sight—even at that age. Should children be permitted to read Romances, & Relations of Giants & Magicians and Genii?—I know all that has been said against it; but I have formed my faith in the affirmative.—I know no other way of giving the mind a love of "the Great,' and 'the Whole."—Those who have been led to the same truths step by step thro' the constant testimony of their senses, seem to me to want a sense which I possess—They contemplate nothing but* parts—*and all parts are necessarily little—and the Universe to them is but a mass of little things.*
—Coleridge, letter to Thomas Poole, 16 October 1797

Prologue: Does Fortune Favor Fools?

On 20 May 1804, two days after arriving in Malta, Coleridge visited Sir Alexander Ball, the island's governor and his future employer.[1] Ball asked him what he thought of the proverb, "Fortune Favors Fools." The answer was, almost certainly, more than he bargained for: a serpentine Coleridgean monologue weaving through metaphysics, science, psychology, linguistic analysis, and plain observation. Partly in honor of the governor, Coleridge composed an essay on the proverb for *The Friend*. In the rifacimento *Friend*, this essay opens the final section of the work—the "Third Landing Place."[2] The proverb offers an ironic challenge, this

---

[1] Richard Holmes, *Darker Reflections*, 17; Coleridge, *The Friend*, pt. 1, 532-33; pt. 2, 252-53.
[2] Coleridge, *The Friend*, pt. 1, 527-31.

piece of popular wisdom, "found in all the languages of Europe," appearing wholly unfavorable to the moral vision of *The Friend*. Coleridge has spent the previous forty-three essays urging the importance of "fixed principles in politics, morals, and religion."[3] Now, in the section designed to provide an overview of the previous intellectual progress, he considers the suggestion that all such discipline of thought is in vain. Does not fortune's smile privilege the ignorant?

Coleridge is returning to a question raised at the very beginning of *The Friend*. What is the value of his pedagogical enterprise and what hope is there of its success? Presupposing the reader's progress through the previous meditations, however, Coleridge now takes up the question from a position of some rhetorical strength. The proverb's claim is not directly assaulted. Rather, Coleridge asks after its meaning or, better, *meanings*, and seeks to render it intelligible as a product of various contexts of experience.[4]

The investigation begins by dissolving the apparent unity and straightforwardness of the proverb so as to distinguish the different functions it performs according to the experiential setting. In religious discourse, it may express compassion and pay tribute to a merciful Providence that takes "an especial care" for those least able to care for themselves. On the other hand, a psychological interest draws attention to "the safety and success which an ignorance of danger and difficulty sometimes actually assists in procuring." Alternatively, the psychologist might find the proverb to acknowledge the results of beginner's luck, those spontaneous exercises of instinctive skill unhindered by the hesitancies of reflection. An envious disposition, though, may use the proverb spitefully, taking the courage that "multiplies the chances of success" for simple folly. Finally, the words may point ruefully to the comforts gained by those who, though inferior in intellect, are more attuned to worldly concerns.

This analysis leaves Coleridge with two problems. For a start, he must clarify the meaning of "fortune," a task already indicated in the

---

[3]From the title page of the 1818 *Friend*, Coleridge, *The Friend*, pt. 1, 1.

[4]This is a procedure John Stuart Mill was later to declare distinctively Coleridgean: "By Bentham, beyond all others, men have been led to ask themselves, in regard to any ancient or received opinion, Is it true? and by Coleridge, What is the meaning of it?" "Coleridge," in John Stuart Mill and Jeremy Bentham, *Utilitarianism and Other Essays*, ed. Alan Ryan (New York: Penguin, 1987) 177.

essay's motto where the idea is described as "a galaxy or milky way . . . of certain obscure virtues without a name." Obeying a primary educational imperative of *The Friend*, Coleridge's clarification will substitute a clear concept for an obscure one. In the process, he will reclaim the idea of fortune in a manner harmonious with his metaphysics. "Fortune," he argues, refers to advantageous or disastrous events that are beyond our predictive capacities. These events elude our foresight, though, not because they are arbitrary or chaotic but because the laws that produce them are so complex as, at present, to beggar our calculation. Coleridge thereby acknowledges the experience of luck but also renders it intelligible from the perspective of his philosophical convictions concerning ideas and laws. Luck is made to add its own testimony to the moral imperative for thinking according to principles, an activity of mind that makes inroads upon the sphere of fortune.

The second problem is to account for the impression that good fortune or luck is peculiarly attracted to the ignorant. Here a simple psychological observation makes the link. Human attention is invariably arrested by the unexpected and, in this case, by instances of undeserved blessing:

> That clever men should attain their objects seems natural, and we neglect the circumstances that perhaps produced that success of themselves without the intervention of skill and foresight; but we dwell on the fact and remember it, as something strange, when the same happens to a weak or ignorant man.

"Does Fortune favor Fools?" ends with a flourish of rhetorical triumph:

> thus accumulating the one sort of facts and never collecting the other, we do, as poets in their diction, and quacks of all denominations do in their reasoning, put a part for the whole, and at once soothe our envy and gratify our love of the marvelous, by the sweeping proverb, "FORTUNE FAVORS FOOLS."[5]

The awkward proverb is expounded, acknowledged, and put in its place.

All this is a rather charming if minor example of a path of mind and rhetoric that will be familiar to the reader by the end of this study. The movement is one of diffusion and cohesion. Apparent unities and

---

[5]*The Friend*, pt. 1, 530 and 531.

seemingly stable oppositions are dissolved in order to establish new relationships. In this little essay, Coleridge dismantles the conventional understanding of fortune and undermines its immediate straightforwardness. The meaning is then reconfigured by connecting the experience of luck with the complexity of causation and a certain predisposition of social psychology.

As we'll see, these centrifugal and centripetal movements find their theoretical expression in Coleridge's theory of the Imagination: a power that "dissolves, diffuses, dissipates, in order to re-create . . . to idealize and to unify."[6] This rhetorical procedure and the philosophical psychology that underlies it serve a persistent feature of Coleridge's conservative politics: his critique of reductionism. Coleridge seeks to include, place, and relate, diverse concepts, experiences, and institutions within larger, unifying contexts of intelligibility. To the premature dispositions of French economists, Utilitarians, political demagogues, and the philosophers of mechanism, of all who "put a part for the whole," Coleridge applies the pressure of the dissolving and recombinative imagination. Their elements are released from reductive captivity for inclusion within more complex totalities.

Identification and the Goals of Rhetoric

According to classical definition, rhetoric is "speech in a manner designed to persuade" or "the faculty of discovering in any given case the available means of persuasion."[7] The rhetorical analysis of a text, therefore, is concerned with language, genre, argument, structure, imagery, all considered as means of persuasion. Again following the classical lead, the task of rhetoric—persuasion—may be analyzed further into the work of teaching, moving, and delighting. As what M. H. Abrams has called a "pragmatic" approach to literature, the analysis of rhetoric follows the

---

[6]Samuel Taylor Coleridge, *Biographia Literaria*, ed. James Engell and W. Jackson Bate, vol. 7, pt. 1 of 2, of *The Collected Works of Samuel Taylor Coleridge* (Princeton NJ: Princeton University Press, 1983) 304.

[7]Cicero, *De Oratore* 1.31.138; Aristotle, *Rhetoric* 1355^{b}30. See also Augustine, *De Doctrina Christiana* 4.25.55.

ways in which a literary text attempts to teach, move, or delight its readership.[8]

While persuasion is the most familiar element in the definitions of rhetoric, Kenneth Burke has introduced "identification" as an important supplementary term.[9] Not only persuasion, but also identification is a "generating principle" of rhetoric.[10] If rhetoric is "the use of language as a symbolic means of inducing cooperation in beings that by nature respond to symbols,"[11] then, Burke argues, it proceeds by way of identifications. At its simplest, the speaker seeks to identify his or her interests with those of the audience. To do so, what is already shared between audience and speaker is used as the basis for arriving at a new identification. Thus Aristotle discusses the shared understanding of happiness to which the orator may confidently appeal.[12] Augustine, too, recognizes the importance of identification to the art of persuasion. Someone is persuaded, Augustine comments, if

> he likes what you promise, fears what you say is imminent, hates what you censure, embraces what you commend, regrets whatever you build up as regrettable, rejoices at what you say is cause for rejoicing, sympathizes with those whose wretchedness your words bring before your very eyes, shuns those whom you admonish him to shun.[13]

Rhetoric, therefore, seeks to disclose, deploy, and achieve commonality.

Identification, of course, is not limited to narrow personal interests, nor to contexts of simple equality. Augustine's preacher, for instance, must secure his audience's identification with a sacred history and a divine ordering that transcends and includes them both. Coleridge, too, seeks to achieve his reader's recognition of the context of creation and salvation: a shared, highly differentiated context in which human beings are called to a variety of social and political responsibilities. His doctrine

---

[8]M. H. Abrams, *The Mirror and the Lamp* (Oxford: Oxford University Press, 1953) 14-21.

[9]Kenneth Burke, *A Rhetoric of Motives* (New York: Prentice-Hall, 1950) 15-46, 55-59, 174-80.

[10]Ibid., 168.

[11]Ibid., 43.

[12]Aristotle, *Rhetoric* 1360^b-62^a10.

[13]Augustine, *De Doctrina Christiana* 1.24.25.

of "Ideas," as we shall see, enables him to connect and argue for the mutual necessity of diverse social institutions. This doctrine also draws into a single embracing field, psychology, historiography, natural philosophy, and ethics. Thus Coleridge articulates the various capacities of the human mind as a "multeity in unity"[14] and maps the unity of past and present. The seminal power of "Ideas" also grounds recognition of nature as a home to the distinctive activities of human beings as rational, moral agents, an agency for which encompassing nature provides non-human analogies and symbols. In fine, Coleridge develops a system of identifications in which diverse particulars find their unity within larger contexts, the ultimate context or context of contexts, so to speak, being that of the Divine Trinity.

The world's intricacy and the moral freedom of human beings demand an intellectual progress from one context of intelligibility to another, a progress that finds its terminus only in that Logos which belongs to the divine life. In defense of this conviction and of the human vocation it involves, Coleridge takes up sometimes bitter issue with various forms of reductionism. *A Lay Sermon* includes, for instance, a critique of political economy considered as an exhaustive discourse for economic relations. Contemporary political economy, Coleridge warns, is unable to register crucial distinctions between kinds of economic relation. Commerce and trade, to which political economy is most relevant, has to be considered within the larger context of a national life dependent on agriculture as well as trade. In turn, the national life constituted by those spheres requires, for its proper understanding, the embracing context of an ethical and, ultimately, theological distinction between "persons" and "things." Of course, the reductionism that Coleridge consistently opposes also involves identification. Coleridge's arguments confront reductionism, therefore, as a strategy of identification that is socially and politically perilous. The danger lies in collapsing

---

[14][Editor's note. The now largely archaic "multeity" apparently may have been coined—it was surely "popularized"—by Coleridge. It of course means "multiplicity" or "manyfoldness." For Coleridge, the Beautiful is "that in which the many . . . becomes one." "The most general definition of beauty, therefore, is . . . Multeity in Unity." *On the Principles of Genial Criticism*, 1814.]

multiple contexts of explanation into a single context which is then treated as an adequate account of a complex field of phenomena.[15]

The practice of rhetoric, then, seeks to secure identification, to persuade of likeness or commonality. As such, it presupposes the existence of division. The field of rhetoric is a divided one, which is why rhetoric is needed. "Identification is compensatory to division. If men were not apart from one another, there would be no need for the rhetorician to proclaim their unity."[16] Rhetoric thus attempts, in some measure, to replace division with identification. Where division cannot be overcome, however, as in the case of those differences that underlie the conflict of social groups, rhetoric seeks to transform division into necessary or functional distinctions, thereby subsuming it under an overarching unity. This suggests, however, the shadow side of rhetoric, to which its apologists are frequently sensitive. In achieving identifications, rhetoric may deceive as to true interests, it may suppress or hide difference, "healing the people lightly."

This age, Coleridge laments, is one of "atrocious Calumny," the personal and literary symptom of a fragmenting culture. His admonitory list ranges widely. A science captivated by mechanism dulls our perception of Nature's "living powers" and histories that trivialize human motivation fund a dismissal of the past. While an obsessively party-minded press markets bad spirit, the easy argument and inflammatory rhetoric of demagogues excites fears and hones suspicions. Antagonistic social classes are forged by commercial practice indifferent to human consequence. In this fragmentation and opposition, knowledge of humanity itself is occluded. Religious and ethical thought, submitted to a reductionist philosophy, lose sight of the moral reason and the synthesizing power of the imagination: in other words, of the imago Dei. These are not isolated problems but symptoms of a common cultural plight that Coleridge names "the epoch of the Understanding and the Senses," or, simply, the "epoch of division and separation." A pedagogy in multiple identifications, the referral to the system of ideas, the rhetoric of connection is Coleridge's attempt to resist and transcend what he sees as his epoch's divisive pressure upon the human spirit. All that being

---

[15]At times, however, Coleridge falls into his own version of reductionism, see below, e.g., 142-43, 164-66, 172-73.

[16]Burke, *A Rhetoric of Motives*, 22.

said, however, there are, as we will see, problems in Coleridge's own system of identification: critical possibilities are evaded, difference disguised, and change resisted.

While identification, as a generating principle of rhetoric, seeks to address a divided social landscape, division itself, is also one of the tools of the rhetorician and necessary to the achievement of identification. The one who persuades may well have to divide existing unities of belief or practice, to distinguish in the interest of new identifications. Coleridge's rhetoric involves a movement of identification and differentiation in which the latter serves the drive toward unity. His theory of "desynonymization," for instance, presents language as a history of division in which clearer conceptions are enabled to emerge.[17] Such conceptual clarification makes possible the articulation of the complex system of relations that constitute reality. When a new term has been framed there is "a new organ of thought" available for the discernment of the creation's complex unity-in-difference.[18] Division is essential, too, to the polemical side of Coleridge's rhetoric. The false and reductive unities of the "mechanic philosophy," with its utilitarian reading of history and its understanding of society as an aggregate of individual atoms, have to be dissolved to make way for a far more complex, differentiated unity.[19]

Coleridge's rhetoric, then, places his readers within an unfolding system of identifications. This system is never offered complete but continues to develop in the course of his writing. Coleridge claimed:

> My system is the only attempt that I know of ever made to reduce all knowledges into harmony; it opposes no other system, but shows what was true in each, and how that which was true in the particular in each of them became error because it was only half the truth. I have endeavoured to unite the insulated fragments of truth and frame a perfect mirror.[20]

---

[17]On "desynonymization," the necessity of new terms, and conceptual clarification, see Coleridge, *Statesman's Manual*, 100-103; Coleridge, *The Friend*, pt. 1, 105-106, 177n.*, 356, 419-20; Coleridge, *Church and State*, 108n.*, 125, 167-68, 171. Also, Coleridge, *Philosophical Lectures*, 173-74, 184-85, 199-201.

[18]Coleridge, *Church and State*, 167.

[19]Coleridge, *Statesman's Manual*, 21-22; Coleridge, *Philosophical Lectures*, 195.

[20]Samuel Taylor Coleridge, *Table Talk*, ed. Carl Woodring, vol. 14, pt. 1 of *The Collected Works of Samuel Taylor Coleridge* (Princeton NJ: Princeton

Despite the ambition, however, Coleridge is notorious for his failure to complete the projected "system." Recent biographers still emphasize the self-tormented personal history that, in the view of many of Coleridge's more famous contemporaries, made up a life of unkept promise.[21] Without wishing to deny the relevance of this, it is all too easy to let Coleridge's biographical fate obscure formative elements in his thought and prejudice the explication of its internal order. My arguments here, therefore, draw attention to how Coleridge's philosophical rather than personal psychology, especially his theory of the imagination, renders us a systematicity that is "ceaseless, exploratory, incomplete," rather than something "speculative and total."[22]

Certainly, the political writings are marred by Coleridge's chaotic habits of work and by the desperately inflated intentions of an addict. Even the straightforward outline of intentions in *A Lay Sermon* remains unfulfilled, and in *The Friend* Coleridge's promised account of his preferred "prudential" approach to political decision ends up almost as abbreviated as the *Biographia Literaria*'s famous discourse on the imagination.[23] Nevertheless, these same texts display Coleridge's exploratory, open systematicity, offered as a model for thought, founded in a distinctive theory of mind. The generating principle of this systema-

---

University Press, 1990) 248, 11 September 1831.

[21] Thomas De Quincey's biographical essays on Coleridge include classic, and very influential, expressions of Coleridge the shirker, the opium eater of "indolent irregularity." De Quincey was responsible for Coleridge's first appearance in the *Encyclopedia Britannica* (8th ed., 1854). One of the more absurd amongst his damning jabs is this assessment of Coleridge's writing: "[T]he whole labors of Coleridge present the appearance of an unfinished city: the outline of the streets exhibits only how splendid they might have been; the basement of a pillar shows how gorgeous might have been its capital. A small, compact, complete beauty of poesy or thought, pains us with the reflection that it stands surrounded by mere fragments of a similar promise." More happily, the recent biographies by Rosemary Ashton and especially Richard Holmes show both the logic behind these judgments and their drastic one-sidedness.

[22] Jerome McGann, *The Romantic Ideology: a Critical Investigation* (Chicago: University of Chicago Press, 1983) 48. McGann is contrasting Coleridge with Hegel.

[23] Coleridge, *Biographia Literaria*, pt. 1, 304-306.

ticity, as we shall see, also imparts a flexibility to Coleridge's conservative politics, providing a logic for critique as well as defense, for change as well as preservation. Instead of completeness there is a restless connective movement in which Coleridge passes from nature to history, from reason to prophecy, from scripture to politics, from religion to science, from the individual to the social, from past to present and future. It is this connective movement that suggests, with a multitude of gaps remaining, not only the promised harmony of Being but the seminal power of the mind: a power capable of discerning the path by which this harmony may find finite representation. Fittingly, in a politics for which moral freedom is crucial, Coleridge states the pedagogical intent of his connective rhetoric as "to light [the reader's] own torch for him,"[24] in other words, to launch a movement of reflection that reveals the demands of the reader's place and responsibility within an unfolding system of life.

Finally, in relation to rhetoric, the concept of identification surfaces a distinctive feature of Coleridge's literary context. As Burke notes, the classical rhetoricians "consider audiences purely as something *given*." During the modern period, however, a new rhetorical situation is created by the dramatic expansion of a diverse reading audience. This invites, indeed requires, "the systematic attempt to *carve out* an audience."[25] Urging the example of his own *Lay Sermons*, Coleridge wrote, "I would that the greater part of our publication could be thus *directed*, each to its own appropriate class of Readers."[26] He had begun the second sermon in precisely this way:

> Fellow Countrymen! You I mean, who fill the higher and middle stations of society! The comforts, perchance the splendors that surround you, designate your rank, but cannot constitute your moral and personal fitness for it. Be it enough for others to know, that you are its *legal*—but by what mark shall you stand accredited to your own consciences, as its *worthy*—possessors?[27]

---

[24]Coleridge, *The Friend*, pt. 1, 16.

[25]Burke, *A Rhetoric of Motives*, 64. Also, Jon Klancher, "Reading the Social Text: Power, Signs, and the Audience in Early Nineteenth-Century Prose," *Studies in Romanticism* 23/2 (Summer 1984): 183-204.

[26]Coleridge, *Statesman's Manual*, 36.

[27]Coleridge, *A Lay Sermon*, 121.

This opening address is a simple act of rhetorical identification, bringing together author and reader as "fellow countrymen." Immediately, however, Coleridge proceeds to divide, specifying his readership as society's "higher and middle" ranks. Given this identification, the sermon asks its readers to identify themselves still more particularly: by accepting the social role Coleridge outlines for them. This social role, he argues, constitutes their identity and the bond of their community in a manner more vital and ennobling than the economic position to which he has appealed in the words "higher and middle classes." Arguments, entreaties, and literary allurements to identify with a social role appear throughout Coleridge's political writings. Thus, *The Friend* describes the rational, principled patriot and provides a model in Sir Alexander Ball, the object of its concluding epideictic. For Coleridge, membership in society carries with it, by moral necessity, some form of shared vocation. Acknowledging that vocation, and identifying with those who also share in it, belongs to that responsibility which is the form of freedom. This is at the center of Coleridge's educational intent: "You are pacing on a smooth terrace, which you owe to the happy institutions of your country,—a terrace on the mountain's breast. To what purpose, by what *moral* right, if you continue to gaze only on the sod beneath your feet?"[28]

"But how are we to guard against the herd of promiscuous Readers?"[29] A careful identification of the audience, the "direction" given to the political writings, is also Coleridge's response to that new and threatening social claim of the "Reading Public," a designation he considers as oxymoronic as the "Learned Pig."[30] Coleridge associates the expansion of readership with "the two public *ordinaries* of Literature, the circulating libraries and the periodical press."[31] These are the institutional

---

[28] Coleridge, *A Lay Sermon*, 124.

[29] Coleridge's translation of the opening line of the motto for essay VII of *The Friend*. Coleridge, *The Friend*, pt. 1, 51.

[30] See the tale of the "READING FLY," Coleridge, *Statesman's Manual*, 36-37n.*.

[31] Both these institutions were significant in increasing the numbers of middle-class readers in the early nineteenth century, although contemporary fears and the enthusiasm of subsequent historians exaggerated the extent of that increase: this is especially the case with assessments of the lower-middle- and working-class readership. Public criticism of the circulating library, especially for the provision

media of that "misgrowth of our luxuriant activity," the "Reading Public," a development Coleridge argues is a social threat precisely because it funds the oppressive influence of the "trivially learned."[32]

> The Root of the Evil is *a Public*—and take my word for it, this will wax more and more prolific of inconvenience, that at length it will scarcely be possible for the State to suffer any truth to be published, because it will be certain to convey dangerous falsehood to 99 out of a hundred.[33]

Under the influence of this "public," the writer whose works demand careful discrimination of thought and feeling is either marginalized or grossly, even dangerously, misunderstood.

Coleridge directs his writings in order to contribute to the creation of a properly differentiated literary landscape. Specifying the audience and creating a rhetoric appropriate to it, one that includes and, also, excludes, is an act of authorial resistance to the growing mass of literary levelers that, for Coleridge, are the "reading public." Here, though, he intends more than the "carving out" of one particular readership, or even, according to the original plan of the lay sermons, a series of readerships. The primary audience sought by Coleridge, in *The Statesman's Manual*, *The Friend*, and *On the Constitution of the Church and State*, is the educated man of public influence. He applies his pedagogical leverage to this point, upon those capable of grasping reflectively the "principles" that Coleridge regards as the motors of history. Educational effort, therefore, is addressed to those whose moral and intellectual integrity is essential to the well-being of the nation as a whole. To instruct this audience is to vivify the spiritual media by which "civilization" is pre-

---

of fiction, was intense at the time *The Statesman's Manual* was written. The other major contributor to changes in readership—the large-scale publication of current works in cheap editions—did not begin until 1824. See Robert Altick, *The English Common Reader: A Social History of the Mass Reading Public, 1800–1900* (Chicago: University of Chicago Press, 1957) and Arthur Simons Collins, *The Profession of Letters: A Study of the Relation of Author to Patron, Publisher, and Public, 1780–1832* (London: E. P. Dutton & Co, 1929).

[32]Coleridge, *Statesman's Manual*, 36-38. "Eruditulorum Natio," Coleridge, *Statesman's Manual*, 36n.*.

[33]Coleridge, *Collected Letters* 4:713, letter to T. G. Street, 22 March 1817.

served and extended as "culture."³⁴ However, given his view of the parlous condition of learning, the "halls of old philosophy . . . so long deserted," this audience has not only to be attracted, it has to be created. Or, perhaps better, considering Coleridge's description of the secondary imagination and his reverence for the intellectual life of pre-Restoration England, it has to be *re-created*.³⁵

Imagination and the Renewal of the Mind

I have suggested that, in Coleridge's rhetoric, "identification" involves a centripetal and centrifugal movement, one in which the process of diffusion serves that of realizing a new ordering, a new system of relations. This description recalls Coleridge's most famous statement about the imagination:

> [A power that] dissolves, diffuses, dissipates, in order to re-create; or where this process is rendered impossible, yet still at all events . . . struggles to idealize and to unify.³⁶

"Imagination" names the human capacity for identification, for the process of contextualization that Coleridge finds to be vital to the artistic, scientific, political, moral, and religious life of human beings. Without such contextualization, when the imaginative power has shrunken, grown dull, or is ill-developed, we know the world in fragments, and those fragments without the intimation of former connection. So, we "contemplate nothing but parts—and all parts are necessarily little—and the Universe

---

³⁴Coleridge, *The Friend*, pt. 1, 494, 500-502; Coleridge, *Church and State*, 42-43, 49.

³⁵Coleridge, *Biographia Literaria*, pt. 1, 304: the secondary imagination "dissolves, diffuses, dissipates, in order to re-create." Also, Coleridge, *Church and State*, 64-65: "*Before* 1660, . . . SIR PHILIP SYDNEY, the star of serenest brilliance in the glorious constellation of Elizabeth's court, communed with SPENSER, on the IDEA of the beautiful: and the younger ALGERNON—Soldier, Patriot, and Statesman—with HARRINGTON, MILTON, and NEVIL on the IDEA of the STATE: and in what sense it may be more truly affirmed, that the people . . . are in order to the state, than that the state exists for the sake of the people."

³⁶Coleridge, *Biographia Literaria*, pt. 1, 304.

... is but a mass of little things."³⁷ To see only "little things" is to lose not only the universal but the particular as well. No longer do we discern it in that imaginatively mediated light through which parts "come into their own" as *symbols*, as translucent to the whole.

The recognition and production of symbols is distinctive of the identificatory power of the imagination. As a "reconciling and mediatory power," the imagination "gives birth to a system of symbols, harmonious in themselves, and consubstantial with the truths, of which they are the *conductors*."³⁸ The relation of a symbol and the truth to which it refers is one of consubstantiality. The term "consubstantial" is theologically loaded. It translates the "homoousios" of the Nicene Creed, expressing the unity and divine equality of the Father and the Son within the Triune reality of God. The credal affirmation recognizes creation's ultimate ground in an act of identification, claiming for the divine "the deepest and highest unity possible . . . together with the most meaningful and closest relationship of difference."³⁹

Coleridge made the Christological link himself in a notebook entry of 1821, "Hast thou seen me, Philip? Thou hast seen the Father—This <last> is the consummate *Symbol* <a Tautegory>."⁴⁰ Consubstantiality is not, of course, simple identity but a differentiated unity: a "multeity in unity."⁴¹ Hence the term "tautegory," that is, "expressing the same subject but with a difference."⁴² In the same notebook entry, a few lines further on, Coleridge remarks that with increasing knowledge of the ontological relations between things, of their consubstantiality, more symbols are

---

³⁷Coleridge, *Collected Letters* 1:210, letter to Thomas Poole, 16 October 1797. Coleridge is discussing the education of children and urging the importance of fairy tales for the development of the imagination.

³⁸Coleridge, *Statesman's Manual*, 29.

³⁹Ibid.

⁴⁰Samuel Taylor Coleridge, *The Notebooks of Samuel Taylor Coleridge*, ed. Kathleen Coburn and Merion Christensen, vol. 4 of 4 thus far (New York: Pantheon Books, 1957–1990) 4832.

⁴¹Samuel Taylor Coleridge, *Biographia Literaria, with His Aesthetical Essays*, 2 vols., ed. John Shawcross (London: Oxford University Press, 1907) 2:232.

⁴²Coleridge, *Statesman's Manual*, 30, and n. 3.

disclosed. The system of identification, as it were, is more fully grasped, its density realized.

> It will often happen, that in the extension of human Knowledge what had been an *Allegory*, will become a Symbol. Thus: the identification, in genere, of the vegetable Life with the animal life, as the same <power> in a lower dignity, would raise the Homeric allegory or compound Metaphor of the Leaves into a Symbol.[43]

Symbols, then, are distinguished from allegories at the level of ontology. The relation of symbol and referent is an ontological one: a symbol "partakes of the Reality which it renders intelligible."[44] Symbols manifest reality as that system of relations in which "each has a life of its own yet all are one life" and that finds its center in the "consummate *Symbol*," the consubstantiality announced in "he who has seen me has seen the Father." Imagination, as the power that discerns and produces symbols, is the activity of the human mind capable of seeing into the consubstantiality of things, and representing what it sees.

Describing the imagination's role in this way permits a more adequate grasp of how it functions both *within* all fields of knowledge—scientific, historical, philosophical, ethical, theological, aesthetic—and as the unifying power among them.[45] In this context, I. A. Richards's description of the Coleridgean imagination serves as an instructive failure. Richards observes correctly that the imagination is responsible for more than poetry, but he then goes on to say that it gives us

> every aspect of the routine world in which it is invested with other values than those necessary for our bare continuance as living beings: all objects for which we can feel love, awe, admiration; *every quality beyond the account of physics, chemistry, and the physiology of sense perception, nutrition, reproduction, and locomotion.*[46]

---

[43]Coleridge is referring to Jupiter's speech to the gods (*The Iliad* 8.1.17-26).
[44]Coleridge, *Statesman's Manual*, 30.
[45]Cf. J. Robert Barth, "Theological Implications of Coleridge's Theory of Imagination," in *Coleridge's Theory of Imagination Today*, ed. C. Gallant (New York: AMS Press, 1989) 11.
[46]I. A. Richards, *Coleridge on Imagination*, 58, my emphasis. Here, Richards is interpreting Coleridge's "secondary imagination." The adequacy of his account of the relationship between "primary" and "secondary" imagination will be

This formulation is problematic. For a start, "invested" suggests the projection rather than the discernment of values, which is an idea foreign to Coleridge's Christian-Platonic realism. More importantly, though, the implied distinction between the imaginatively mediated world of love or wonder and the world as represented by scientific inquiry, misses the range of the imagination and its identificatory role. In so doing, Richards also misrepresents Coleridge's claims about scientific knowing. By means of the theory of the imagination, Coleridge unifies the activities of the poet and the scientist: both proceed, or should proceed, from the imaginative capacity.

According to Coleridge, then, the imagination is the generating power of scientific, as well as poetic, insight. The imagination is thus vital to his description of how scientific accounts are produced. The chemist, Coleridge claims, is "striving after unity of principle through all the diversity of forms."[47] This achievement of a unifying idea, the principle of connection that discloses a single power behind diverse forms in nature, is comparable to poetic insight:

> Thus, as "the lunatic, the lover, and the poet," suggest each other to Shakespeare's Theseus, as soon as his thoughts present to him the ONE FORM, of which they are but varieties; so water and flame, the diamond, the charcoal, and the mantling champagne, with its ebullient sparkles, are convoked and fraternized by the theory of the scientist.[48]

The scientist, like the poet, takes hold of and unifies diverse reality through "a profound and observant meditation." Here, Coleridge's language recalls an earlier description of the imagination as a "completing

---

discussed below.

[47]Coleridge, *The Friend*, pt. 1, 470. Cf. Samuel Taylor Coleridge, *Hints Toward the Formation of a More Comprehensive Theory of Life*, ed. Seth B. Watson (London: John Churchill, 1848) on a "real definition": "[I]t must consist ... in the *law* of the thing, or in such an *idea* of it, as, being admitted, all the properties and functions are admitted by implication. It must likewise be so far *causal*, that a full insight having been obtained of the law, we derive from it a progressive insight into the necessity and *generation* of the phenomena of which it is the law." Coleridge, *Theory of Life*, 25.

[48]Coleridge, *The Friend*, pt. 1, 471.

power" that unites "clearness with depth."⁴⁹ A quotation from Milton identifies then the "creative power" of such meditation as

> ... some connatural force,
> Powerful at greatest distance to unite
> With secret amity things of like kind.⁵⁰

The scientific imagination—for that is what this is—is responsible for any account of things worthy of the name "science."

There is a distinction to be made in reference to the natural sciences, but it is not the one Richards makes. The contrast is not that between a scientific account and an imaginative, evaluative one that engages emotions. Rather, we have a more complex distinction that passes through the sciences themselves and corresponds to the famous division of the imagination from the "fancy." A comparison between contemporary botany and chemistry, argues Coleridge, displays the difference between science and that which only pretends to be such. Botany has not yet arrived at that unifying idea which is the gift of the imagination. Lacking that, it can offer little more than an arbitrary catalogue: "a dictionary in which . . . an Ainsworth arranges the contents by the initials; a Walker by the endings; a Scapula by the radicals; and a Cominus by the similarity of the uses and purposes."⁵¹ There is no vital principle of connection between the elements and so the power of life that animates and unifies this variety, remains obscure. Instead, this retarded science operates with "fixities and definites," botanical counters upon a classificatory chess board. Botany, in Coleridge's view, remains, as it were, a "fanciful" rather than an imaginative enterprise.⁵² Put differently, chemistry, unlike botany, has achieved insight into symbolic relations, into the consubstantiality that enables a particular to represent the higher unity it shares with other particulars, or one reality to stand for another, being an instance of "the same power in a lower dignity."⁵³ As was noted

---

⁴⁹Coleridge, *Statesman's Manual*, 69.
⁵⁰Coleridge, *The Friend*, pt. 1, 471, from Milton's *Paradise Lost* 10.246-48.
⁵¹Coleridge, *The Friend*, pt. 1, 469.
⁵²Cf., Coleridge, *Biographia Literaria*, pt. 1, 305.
⁵³"True natural philosophy is comprised in the study and language of *symbols*. The power delegated to nature is all in every part: and by a symbol I mean, not a metaphor or allegory or any other figure of speech or form of fancy,

above, "it will often happen, that in the extension of human Knowledge what had been an *Allegory*, will become a Symbol."[54]

In the case of truly scientific insight, like that of Coleridge's admired chemists, the imagination indeed infuses an account of reality with "love, awe, and admiration." It does so, however, not *subsequent* to that discovery, as Richards suggests, but *in* it: as the imagination discloses the consubstantiality of things, that unity in which the multeity of things inheres and from which it receives its life. Thus "the serious complacency which is afforded by the sense of truth, utility, permanence, and progression, blends with and enobles the exhilarating surprise and the pleasurable sting of curiosity, which accompany the propounding and solving of an Enigma."[55]

The imagination, then, operating in the various fields of human knowledge, is that cognitive activity able to grasp the ontological relations that constitute the possibility of symbols.[56] To follow this further, it is necessary to consider the place of imagination among the other intellectual powers. An early attempt to formulate the distinction of fancy and imagination, found in a notebook of 1811, will provide a starting point. Though the entry concerns the poetic imagination, its philosophical psychology is of wider application. The passage describes two accounts of perception: one is reductionist and has unhappy theological and ethical consequences; in the other, the elements of the reductionist account are subordinated to the imagination as a higher cognitive activity.

Coleridge begins by describing the "Fancy":

> The image-forming or rather re-forming power, the imagination in its passive sense, which I would rather call Fancy = Phantasy . . . may not inaptly be compared to the Gorgon Head, which *looked* death into every thing—and this not by accident, but from the nature of the faculty itself,

---

but an actual and essential part of that, the whole of which it represents." Coleridge, *Statesman's Manual*, 79.

[54]Coleridge, *Notebooks* 4:4832.

[55]Coleridge, *The Friend*, pt. 1, 471.

[56]The "poetic" imagination is no exception to this, its creativity is predicated upon such relations and upon their recognition: "No man was ever yet a great poet without being at the same time a profound philosopher" (Coleridge, *Biographia Literaria*, pt. 2, 25-26).

the province of which is to give consciousness to the Subject by presenting to it its conceptions *objectively*.⁵⁷

The fancy is essential to the mind's experience of itself as a subject within the subject-object relation. As the "image forming or rather re-forming power," it provides the mind with stable entities, objects distinct from one another and from the subject. The language of sight dominates this passage: the fancy delivers "images" and it "makes appear."⁵⁸ Like Medusa, it *looks* "death into everything" so that the subject has experience of objects, distinct and at a distance, as it were, from its own subjectivity. The negative associations of the Gorgon, though, should be taken as a warning of the limitations of the fancy not as denying its importance.⁵⁹ Coleridge goes on to add that without the fancy "there would be no *fixation*, consequently, no distinct perception or conception": consciousness would be a delirium.

At this point, Coleridge begins to introduce language with theological overtones. His discussion shifts from the "Subject" to which the fancy presents "its conceptions objectively" to the "Soul" that is capable of knowing "symbolically." At the end of the entry, this symbolic knowing of the soul is linked explicitly with the imagination that "fixing unfixes and while it melts and bedims the Image, still leaves in the Soul its living meaning." The fancy, therefore, corresponds to a preliminary stage in human cognition, that of the "subject," whereas the imagination further constitutes the knower as "soul." Thus, through the imagination, subjectivity is taken up into soul with its associations of depth, eternity, and the divine. In a gesture that subverts what he was later to call the "despotism of the eye," Coleridge retains the language of sight here but transforms it into the "seeing through" that characterizes sacramental participation.⁶⁰ The soul perceives the "living Being . . . thro' the Body which is its Symbol and outward and visible Sign."

---

⁵⁷Coleridge, *Notebooks* 3:4066.

⁵⁸"Phantasy" from φάειν, φαίνω, "to make appear."

⁵⁹Contrast the overly negative account of the fancy in Basil Willey, "Coleridge on Imagination and Fancy," Warton Lecture on English Poetry, in *Proceedings of the British Academy* (May 1946): 32.

⁶⁰Coleridge, *Biographia Literaria*, pt. 1, 107.

The deliverances of the fancy are a stage, a necessary stage, on the way to the cognitive activity of the imagination. Unfortunately, however, a temptation lurks in the operation of the fancy that may prevent the act of completion in which symbolic vision is achieved. To take up the passage again, the fancy

> gives consciousness to the Subject by presenting to it its conceptions *objectively* but the Soul differences itself from any other Soul for the purposes of symbolical knowledge by *form* or body only—but all form as body, i.e., as shape, and not as forma efformans, is dead—Life may be *inferred*, even as intelligence is from black marks on white paper—but the black marks themselves *are truly "the dead* letter." Here then is the error—not in the faculty itself, without which there would be no *fixation*, consequently, no distinct perception or conception, but in the gross idolatry of those who abuse it, and make that the goal and end which should be only a means of arriving at it. Is it any excuse to him who treats a living being as inanimate Body, that we cannot arrive at the knowledge of the living Being but thro' the Body which is its Symbol and outward and visible Sign?
>
> From the above deduce the worth and dignity of poetic imagination, of the fusing power, that fixing unfixes and while it melts and bedims the Image, still leaves in the Soul its living meaning—.[61]

When the necessary fixities of the fancy are taken for the "goal and end" of perception, the sacramental character of such presentations, as they exist for the imagination, is missed. In its place is a "gross idolatry" with grave ethical consequences: the treatment of "a living being as inanimate Body." The consequences are not only ethical, however, they are theological as implied here by the transition from misrecognising "living being" to failing to know "living Being," or, as elsewhere, the "one life" manifesting itself in the diversity of many things. Fancy, then, presents reality in its "outside," it enables a "looking at" stabilized appearances, a mistaken attachment to which leads to the Lockean stubbornness that demands, lingering at the limits of our bodily sight, that all things should conform to the possibility "of being *seen*, if only our visual organs were sufficiently powerful."[62] Imagination, by contrast, taking the givens of the fancy, empowers a "seeing through" the "outward

---

[61]Coleridge, *Notebooks* 3:4066.
[62]Ibid.

and visible Sign" that "while it melts and bedims the Image, still leaves in the Soul its living meaning." Imagination is the condition for cognitive participation in a sacramental universe. By virtue of that, it is central, for Coleridge, to a nonreductionist account of human knowing.

On the inside back cover of his copy of volume 8 of Tennemann's *Geschichte der Philosophie*, Coleridge sketched out "the simplest yet practically sufficient order of the Mental Powers." This note places both the fancy and the imagination within the mental ordering:

Lowest	Highest
Sense	Reason
Fancy	Imagination
Understanding	Understanding
---	---
Understanding	Understanding
Imagination	Fancy
Reason	Sense[63]

The ascending structure of the powers is familiar from the above discussion of fancy and imagination. The higher activities presuppose and subsume the lower within their own activity, the lower find their intelligibility within the higher.[64] Coleridge has organized his diagram, however, in two parallel columns which suggests there are also *polar* relations between the powers—reason with sense, fancy with imagination—as well as a polarity within the understanding itself.[65]

---

[63]Samuel Taylor Coleridge, *Coleridge on the Seventeenth Century*, ed. Roberta Florence Brinkley (Cambridge UK: Cambridge University Press, 1955) 693-94.

[64]Not surprisingly, Coleridge found this ascending structure of relations throughout external nature also: "In every living form, the conditions of its *existence* are to be sought for in that which is *below* it; the grounds of its *intelligibility* in that which is *above* it." Coleridge, *Church and State*, 183. The importance of this formulation will be discussed in chap. 6 below.

[65]This discussion of Coleridge's diagram is indebted to Owen Barfield, *What Coleridge Thought*, 69-114.

In Coleridge's writings, "Reason" is the object of a series of complex attempts at definition, some of which I will consider later. However, in order to understand the polar relations of this diagram, one attempt in particular is important. In the first "landing place" of the 1818 *Friend*, Coleridge defines the reason "as an organ bearing the same relation to spiritual objects, the Universal, the Eternal, and the Necessary, as the eye bears to material and contingent phenomena."[66] As the "organ of the supersensuous," reason bears a direct, unmediated relation to its objects. Hence, the polarity with "sense" that, in the spirit of Coleridge's favorite proverb, "extremes meet," also has an unmediated, preconscious relationship to its objects.[67] This polarity explains the significance of the note written beside the diagram in Tennemann: "Fancy and Imagination are Oscillations, *this* connecting R. and U.; *that* connecting Sense and Understanding." Fancy and imagination are activities of mediation through which the objects of sense and reason enter consciousness, becoming subject to language, expression, and reflection.

The understanding is the "Clapham Junction" of the mind: all things must go through it. Reason—and sense, we may add—cannot manifest themselves "but in and through the understanding."[68] What, then, is the understanding? Coleridge's diagram shows the understanding to be itself polar, at one pole related to reason through the imagination, at the other to sense via the fancy.[69] In relation to sense, the understanding is "the

---

[66] Coleridge, *The Friend*, pt. 1, 155-56.

[67] That this is so is slightly clearer from the formulation given in Samuel Taylor Coleridge, *Aids to Reflection*, ed. John Beer, vol. 9 of *The Collected Works of Samuel Taylor Coleridge* (Princeton NJ: Princeton University Press, 1993) 223-24: "Reason indeed is much nearer to Sense than to Understanding: for Reason . . . is a direct aspect of Truth, an inward Beholding, having a similar relation to the Intelligible or Spiritual, as SENSE has to the Material or Phenomenal."

[68] Coleridge, *The Friend*, pt. 1, 156.

[69] "For the understanding is in all respects a medial and mediate faculty, and has therefore two extremities or poles, the sensual, in which form it is St. Paul's 'phronema sarkos' and the intellectual pole, or the hemisphere (as it were) turned towards the reason." For this reason, the two tables of mental powers are each divided in half, "understanding" appearing both above and below the dividing line. This polarization of the understanding also expresses the possibility of an

conception of the Sensuous, or the faculty by which we generalize and arrange the phenomena of perception."[70] The understanding receives the data of the senses, as already stabilized and made available by the fancy, and structures them so as to render the subject's world of "outward Experience." "Understanding" in this sense, as Coleridge was fond of pointing out, is possessed by animals as well as human beings.[71] Human understanding, however, exists within that ascending scheme of mental powers that culminates with the reason. As a consequence, even the understanding considered as "the Faculty of judging according to Sense"[72] is under the lunar influence of reason, the "organ of the universal." Consequently, a human understanding is enabled to carry its abstracting activity way beyond that of any animal: human beings reflect upon the logical operations of their understanding and, above all, they possess language.

It is, however, insofar as the understanding is informed by reason, through the "reconciling and mediatory power" of the imagination, that it ceases to be mere understanding and takes to itself the "power of acquainting itself with invisible realities or spiritual objects."[73] Such acquaintance is, of course, through those ordered deliverances of sense and fancy as configured by the understanding at its "sensual" pole. It is through the experienced world of subject and object but that world as now "seen through" by the imagination that operates in the light of reason. "Impregnated" by the imagination "the understanding itself becomes intuitive, and a living power," in other words, it becomes capable of recognizing and producing symbols, "organizing . . . the flux of the Senses by the permanence and self-circling energies of the Reason."[74]

Reason, as Coleridge understands it, cannot be manifest in human consciousness without the understanding. However, just as it is possible to have fancy without the imagination, it is possible, and Coleridge believes this to be the cultural fate of his time, to employ the understand-

---

overbalance of the mental faculties toward the sensual, resulting in the alienation of reason.
[70]Coleridge, *The Friend*, pt. 1, 156.
[71]Coleridge, *Statesman's Manual*, 68; Coleridge, *Aids to Reflection*, 216-22.
[72]Coleridge, *Aids to Reflection*, 215.
[73]Coleridge, *The Friend*, pt. 1, 156.
[74]Coleridge, *Statesman's Manual*, 69, 29.

ing without submission to reason as the "organ of the supersensuous." Human understanding cannot entirely rid itself of the influence of reason. Were it to do so, it would cease to be *human* understanding, a point that shows Coleridge's indebtedness to a classical account of the imago Dei. Nevertheless, the understanding can imprison itself in the forms of its own ordering activity.[75] The analytic, abstracting activity of the understanding, the activity that gives us the world of distinct entities set over against a distinct subjectivity, if taken as goal and not means, prevents knowledge of the world as a living divinely given unity. It finds and leaves the world as "a heap of little things."[76] Unless taken up into the unifying, synthesizing activity of the imagination, experience as configured by the understanding delivers up fragments: subject and object, self and other, human beings and nature, past and present. This, in addition to being an aesthetic, philosophical, moral, and theological problem, is also, because it is all of these, a political problem.

Among Coleridge's attempts to outline his theory of the imagination, the most discussed is his summary offered in lieu of the promised theoretical development at the end of *Biographia Literaria*, chapter 13:

> The IMAGINATION then I consider either as primary, or secondary. The primary IMAGINATION I hold to be the living power and prime Agent of all human Perception, and as a representation in the finite mind of the eternal act of creation in the infinite I AM. The secondary I consider as an echo of the former, coexisting with the conscious will, yet still as identical with the primary in the *kind* of its agency, and differing only in *degree*, and in the *mode* of its operation. It dissolves, diffuses, dissipates, in order to re-create; or where this process is rendered impossible, yet still at all events it struggles to idealize and to unify. It is essentially *vital*, even as all objects (*as* objects) are essentially fixed and dead.[77]

As this is a highly compressed statement, I have delayed treating it until the preceding reflections could provide a framework.

---

[75]Ibid., 93: "Individuals . . . who mistake outlines for substance, and distinct images for clear conceptions; with whom therefore not to be a *thing* is the same as *not to be at all*." See also, ibid., 60n.2.

[76]Coleridge, *Collected Letters* 1:210.

[77]Coleridge, *Biographia Literaria*, pt. 1, 304.

Philosophical Psychology and Conservative Politics 63

The majority opinion concerning this passage places the emphasis upon the "secondary" rather than the "primary" imagination. The center of gravity is taken to lie with the former. Thus, concerning the lines on the secondary imagination, Basil Willey writes:

> Here speaks the seer, the poet, and the romantic; not content with the automatic "poetry" which we all create, and which we call the world of everyday appearances, he would transcend this for a vision more intense, more true, than is afforded by the light of common day. The daily routine world may be the product of a faculty essentially creative . . . yet in itself it is cold and inanimate, filled only with "the many shapes of joyless daylight."[78]

This interpretation relegates the primary imagination to the league of the ordinary. It is the activity of the mind as productive of the daily phenomenal world. This view is repeated by I. A. Richards in an account already mentioned:

> The Primary Imagination is normal perception that produces the usual world of the senses,
> "That inanimate cold world allowed
> To the poor loveless ever-anxious crowd"
> the world of motor buses, beef steaks, and acquaintances.[79]

The products of primary and secondary imaginations are related as death to life, the latter exercising its vivifying power upon the "cold and inanimate" products of the former.

The major problem with this interpretation is that, especially in the versions just quoted, it does not reflect either a very close or a very natural reading of what Coleridge says. In an essay on the theological background to the *Biographia* passage, Jonathan Wordsworth carefully reverses the common interpretative emphasis.[80] He proposes that "primary" and "secondary" should be taken according to their most frequent usage as indicating greater and lesser importance. To support

---

[78] Basil Willey, "Coleridge on Imagination and Fancy," 4.

[79] I. A. Richards, *Coleridge on Imagination*, 58. See also J. Robert Barth, "Theological Implications," 5; and Coleridge, *Biographia Literaria*, pt. 1, lxxxix.

[80] Jonathan Wordsworth, "The Infinite I AM: Coleridge and the Ascent of Being," in *Coleridge's Imagination*, ed. Richard Gravil, Lucy Newlyn, and Nicholas Roe (Cambridge UK: Cambridge University, Press, 1985).

this, he points to the emphatic capitalization and the "grandiloquence, swelling rhythm [and] vaunting of scriptural authority" of the statement concerning the primary imagination, a rhetorical insistence that is even more marked when compared to the "business-like, even a little flat" tone of the sentence that follows. "Whatever its purpose," Wordsworth concludes, "the prose exultantly proclaims an incarnation of the eternal in the finite, a personal reenactment of God's original, an endlessly continuous moment of self-naming."[81] Not a "cold and inanimate" world, then, but the product of a "living Power" that repeats, under the conditions of the finite mind, the procession of the world from God's creative "I AM."

Wordsworth's observations may be taken further. The primary imagination is said to be "living Power and prime Agent" of all *human* perception. Human perception is distinguished from that of animals precisely by virtue of reason. As far as understanding goes, Coleridge argues, human beings differ from animals only in degree; it is as rational that they differ in *kind*.[82] In terms of the diagram discussed above, it is in the activity of the imagination, informing the understanding with reason, that the transition is made from animal to distinctively human perception.[83] As we saw, even the understanding in its employment as the "faculty judging according to the senses"—the understanding which is not unique to humanity—is under the hidden influence of reason. This influence renders that vast *degree* of difference between the human and the animal of which language is the principle indicator. Thus it is the case that the primary imagination is the "living power" of *all* human perception. It is, however, perception precisely as irradiated by reason, through the primary imagination, that constitutes the human status as imago Dei.[84]

Chapter 13 of the *Biographia* begins with a quotation from *Paradise Lost* that anticipates the climactic definition of the primary imagination. From Milton, Coleridge has chosen part of Raphael's speech to Adam

---

[81]Ibid., 24.

[82]Coleridge, *Statesman's Manual*, 67-69, 183n.*; Coleridge, *The Friend*, pt. 1, 160, 177n.*.

[83]"The completing power . . . is the IMAGINATION, impregnated with which the understanding itself becomes intuitive, and *a living power*." Coleridge, *Statesman's Manual*, 69; my emphasis.

[84]Coleridge, *Statesman's Manual*, 18-19.

describing the place of humanity in the upward movement of creation's forms, from material to intellectual. The quotation ends

> ... flow'rs and their fruit,
> Man's nourishment, by gradual scale sublimed,
> To *vital* spirits aspire, to *animal*,
> To *intellectual*, give both life and sense,
> Fancy and understanding; whence the soul
> REASON receives, and reason is her *being*,
> Discursive, or intuitive. . . . [85]

Coleridge's chapter on the "esemplastic power" thus opens with an account of the human being in created perfection. As far as the primary imagination is concerned, the implication of this is that the latter names a fullness of human perception in which all the mental powers work in concert and in their proper subordination: human perception as made in the image of God.[86] In such perception, mind and world are present in their divine depth, or, as Coleridge put it in *The Friend*, in "that intuition of things which arises when we possess ourselves, as one with the whole."[87]

That happy concert of powers in which the imagination is the "prime Agent" contains an inherent temptation, a seductive pull toward instability that is grounded in the reason itself. In *The Statesman's Manual*, Coleridge proposes a reinterpretation of the Fall in terms of the imbalance of the mental powers. This concerns, in particular the relationship between reason, and, by implication, the imagination, and the understanding and the fancy.[88] Reason, as the "*tendency* to the comprehension of all as one," contains the lure to pull away from the particularities of the understanding.

> The rational instinct, therefore, taken abstractedly and unbalanced, did *in itself*, ("ye shall be as gods!" Gen. iii.5.) and in its consequences, (the

---

[85]From Milton, *Paradise Lost* 5.482-88 (var.).
[86]Coleridge, *Biographia Literaria*, pt. 2, 15-16.
[87]Coleridge, *The Friend*, pt. 1, 520.
[88]Coleridge, *Statesman's Manual*, 60-62. *The Statesman's Manual* was written during the second half of 1816, and appeared in the December; chap. 13 of the *Biographia Literaria* was composed the previous September, although the work was not published until July 1917.

lusts of the flesh, the eye, and the understanding, as in verse the sixth,) form the original temptation, through which man fell: and in all ages has continued to originate the same, even from Adam, in whom we all fell.[89]

The "natural Man" is left, therefore, "always in a state either of resistance or of captivity to the understanding and the fancy, which cannot represent totality without limit: and he either loses the ONE in the striving after the INFINITE (i.e., Atheism with or without polytheism) or the INFINITE in the striving after the ONE, (i.e., anthropomorphic monotheism)."

It is religion, Coleridge argues, that reconciles the disrupted activity of the mental powers, the activity in which the primary imagination gifts the "repetition in the finite mind of the eternal act of creation in the infinite I AM." Religion has this function because it neglects neither the totalizing drive of the reason nor the particularizing forms of the understanding. Rather, religion is "the consideration of the Particular and Individual . . . but of the Individual, as it exists and has its being in the Universal." In religion, therefore, takes place the reconciliation and proper subordination of reason and imagination, understanding and fancy. This "union of the Universal and the Individual" is not, however, limited to religion, it is also the essence of artistic activity, albeit that the latter is subordinate to religion as its "parent and fosterer."[90] "Hence in all the ages and countries of civilization Religion has been the parent and fosterer of the Fine Arts, as of Poetry, Music, Painting, etc." The arts, therefore, and in the light of the previous discussion, truly philosophical sciences must be added here also, aim at the manifestation, the "translucence," of the universal through the particular, the necessary through the contingent, the eternal through the temporal. They seek to disclose reality in its consubstantialities, as symbolic.

Coleridge's peculiar and much repeated complaint about his age denounces it as "the Epoch of the Understanding and the Senses."[91] A "Brief History of the Last 130 Years" names the triumph of the "Mechanical Philosophy" and traces its consequences as the exclusion of imagination from art and "fancy paramount in physics." The ideal suffers

---

[89]Coleridge, *Statesman's Manual*, 61.
[90]For an interpretation of this distinction, see below 104-105.
[91]Coleridge, *The Friend*, pt. 1, 203.

eclipse "by the mere shadow of the sensible." In such an age, the "natural Man" falls into "captivity to the understanding." This is the central problem, the form of spiritual dislocation in a sorry age. The condition strikes at religion and philosophy, at poetry and at science. It does so precisely because it disables the symbolic vision, taking the deliverances of the understanding and the fancy as "goal and end which should only be a means of arriving at it."[92]

This cultural diagnosis is a needful context for reading the *Biographia*'s account of the "secondary imagination," with its opposition of a "vital power" to the "deadness" of objects differentiated within the subject-object relation. I have argued above that the "secondary imagination" refers to the agent of those activities, including poetry, in which the captivity of the understanding is overcome and the "original vision" of the primary imagination rediscovered: the vision in which "we possess ourselves, as one with the whole." It is consistent with this that Coleridge describes the poet "in *ideal* perfection" as bringing "the whole soul of man into activity, with the subordination of its faculties to each other, according to their relative worth and dignity."[93] In sum, therefore, "primary imagination" refers to the role of imagination within the created harmony of the mental powers through which the world appears in its divinely given fullness. As the mediator of reason, even under the "captivity of the understanding," its suppressed presence elevates the abstracting powers of the understanding into their *human* form. The primary imagination thus remains as the prime agent of *all* human perception, even that dominated by the understanding and the fancy. This account of the primary imagination again shows the influence of the classical Christian doctrine of the *imago Dei* that, though marred by sin, remains traceable even in the life of "natural man."[94] The role of the

---

[92]Coleridge, *Notebooks* 3:4066.

[93]Coleridge, *Biographia Literaria*, pt. 2, 15-16.

[94]Cf. J. Robert Barth, "In assessing the moral state of fallen man, Coleridge's constant preoccupation is to strike a balance between the easy optimism of the Shaftesbury sort, which fails to take account of man's real weakness of will, and a Calvinistic insistence on man's total depravity." J. Robert Barth, *Coleridge and Christian Doctrine* (Cambridge MA: Harvard University Press, 1969) 120. Thus, "as there is much beast and some devil in man, so is there some angel and God in him." Coleridge, *Table Talk*, pt. 1, 235.

"secondary imagination," therefore, is predicated upon the disruption of the created mental order, the form, though not the fact, of which is culturally variable. "Coexisting with conscious will," the secondary imagination differs from the primary in the "*mode* of its operation" working, as it does by diffusion and re-creation, upon the "fixities and definites" of a world in which the understanding has "bedimmed all the lustre and . . . dried up the sparkle and the dew drops."[95]

The "Epoch of the Understanding and the Senses" is also named, in accordance with the understanding's cognitive role, the "epoch of division and separation." It is a time in which the distinction of things is taken at face value, obscuring the unity in which all things, including the human mind, inhere and find their true intelligibility. "Man of understanding," asks Coleridge in biblical tones,

> canst thou command the stone to lie, canst thou bid the flower bloom, where thou has placed it in thy classification?—Canst thou persuade the living or the inanimate to stand separate even as thou hast separated them? . . . Do not all [things] press and swell under one attraction, and live together in promiscuous harmony, each joyous in its own kind, and in the immediate neighborhood of myriad others that in the system of thy understanding are distant as the Poles?[96]

Only where "the spirit of philosophy reigns in the learned and highest class, and that of religion in all classes" does a cultural situation exist in which, in balance to the work of understanding, "a tendency to blend and unite will be found in all objects of pursuit."[97]

As this "epoch of division and separation" is manifest in all human activity, it appears also as social and political dislocation. In this field, the self-captivity of the understanding produces false political philosophies.[98]

---

[95]Coleridge, *Biographia Literaria*, pt. 1, 80. A consequence of the interpretation proposed here is that it suggests that Coleridge departed more sharply than has often been thought from German proposals, such as those of Tetens or Schelling. For a threefold analysis of imagination and fancy, see James Engell, *The Creative Imagination: Enlightenment to Romanticism* (Cambridge MA: Harvard University Press, 1981) 119, 178, 182-84.

[96]Coleridge, *Statesman's Manual*, 77.

[97]Coleridge, *The Friend*, pt. 1, 444.

[98]Ibid., 447.

Blind to unifying principles, historical developments are read reductively as products of expedience and their origin in ideas and philosophical convictions is missed.[99] Culture is thereby alienated from the past and, in the absence of a philosophy of history, loses its foremost guide for the political future.[100] Social life, furthermore, is read in terms of utility, the understanding being the faculty of *"proximate* ends," not ultimate ones.[101] From this follows the excessive and unbalanced pursuit of commercial gain.[102] In the course of the latter, human beings are subjected to merely instrumental calculation, their identity as "persons" violated, and the considerations of society's well-being reduced to the tally of its wealth.[103]

I have argued above that behind the definition of the imagination in the *Biographia* lies Coleridge's reinterpretation of the Fall and its consequences. According to *The Statesman's Manual*, the primary human alienation consists in the disruption and imbalance of the mental powers. This disruption eclipses that original, Adamic vision in which, to use a formulation from the *Opus Maximum*, the particular is experienced "solely as the glory and representation of the plenitude of the universal."[104] The term "primary imagination," then, looks back toward created perfection, the idea of humanity in the mind of God, gifted with that knowing in which all the world is symbol. In consequence, "secondary imagination," introduces the possibility and reality of reconciliation. It is necessary, therefore, to interpret the secondary imagination against the background of Coleridge's description of religion as the "union of the Universal and the Individual" and the "parent and fosterer" of the poetic in all its forms. The secondary imagination is an agent and anticipant of redemption.[105]

---

[99]Coleridge, *Statesman's Manual*, 11, 21-22.
[100]Coleridge, *Statesman's Manual*, 10-12; Coleridge, *Church and State*, 32-33.
[101]Coleridge, *Statesman's Manual*, 74, 60n.2.
[102]Coleridge, *A Lay Sermon*, 169-70.
[103]Coleridge, *A Lay Sermon*, 209-11, 219-23.
[104]Samuel Taylor Coleridge, *Opus Maximum*, ed. Thomas McFarland and Nicholas Halmi, vol. 15 of *The Collected Works of Samuel Taylor Coleridge* (Princeton NJ: Princeton University Press, 2002) 225. For an account of the *Opus Maximum* and its significance, see below, 234-36.
[105]The focus of other Coleridgean accounts of the Fall, those in the *Opus*

Coleridge's philosophical psychology provides him with the conceptual categories for linking the classical account of the Fall with a critical analysis of contemporary culture as "an epoch of the Understanding and the Senses." The cultural situation is thus read as both an expression and a symbol of the Fall. It is with reference to this reading of his cultural situation, that Coleridge formulates the rhetoric of his later political writings. These texts attempt a liberation from "mind-forged manacles," from captivity to the understanding. They attempt to disclose the system of consubstantiality from which human life derives its worth and its intelligibility. Coleridge's theory of imagination and the closely related account of religion and reason into which that theory is eventually subsumed, determines his politics as a theological politics. According to Coleridge, political thought, no less than poetic or scientific thought, requires an education in imagination: in the exercise of a "reconciling and mediatory power," a power of identification. In the political writings of his later career, Coleridge fashions an account of his society and its proper social order according to which its particularity is irradiated and unified by that "present, other world" of the ideal: establishing its dwelling within the encompassing contexts of providential history, created nature, and the divine Trinity.[106]

Maximum, for instance, or in his marginalia on Taylor's *Unum Necessarium*, is upon the will and its corruption: the passage from free will to a will that, having chosen evil, ceases to be free. *Opus Maximum*, Huntington MS, 10-43; Samuel Taylor Coleridge, *The Literary Remains of Samuel Taylor Coleridge*, 4 vols., ed. Henry Nelson Coleridge (London: William Pickering, 1836) 3:295-328. Coleridge continued to insist, however, on the origin of the Fall within each individual, opposing the traditional doctrine of original sin as an inherited corruption.

[106]Coleridge, *Church and State*, 174-85.

3

Imagination and the Wisdom of History

Der Historiker ist ein ruckwarts gekehter Prophet.
The historian is a prophet facing backwards.
   —Friedrich von Schlegel (1772–1829), *Athenäum Fragments*, 80

Historical Method: Knowledge as Power

Politics is fraught with strange reversals. In a footnote to *A Lay Sermon*, Coleridge reflects upon the melancholy failure of Spencer Percival to abolish state lotteries.[1] Despite the prime minister's express design, despite, too, the support for abolition even from opposition members, Percival's good intentions merely preceded two lotteries rather than one during the first year of his ministry. "The door of the cabinet," Coleridge laments, "has a quality the most opposite to the Ivory Gate of Virgil. It suffers no dreams to pass through it."[2] Coleridge's remedy for despair over the taxing accidents of politics is a philosophy of history. History, he insists, must be read "in the spirit of prophecy." Only in this way will the knowledge of particulars, of history's multiple and succeeding events, find its light in knowledge of the universal. Insight will then penetrate the

---

[1] Given the amount of revenue involved, it is unlikely that Percival was committed to their abolition in the way Coleridge suggests. Coleridge, *Lay Sermons*, 124n.1. Coleridge, however, intensely disliked lotteries, their removal being one of the few immediate remedies proposed in *A Lay Sermon*. In *The Friend* he had described the public lottery as "that other opprobrium of the Nation, that *Mother vice.*" *The Friend*, pt. 2, 51. He was not entirely innocent of its attractions, though. In 1793, he entered an Irish lottery in London, hoping to pay his Cambridge debts. He lost his stake but wrote his first professional publication, the ode "To Fortune," while awaiting the results! See Richard Holmes, *Early Visions*, 51-52.

[2] Coleridge, *Lay Sermons*, 123n.*.

apparent vagaries of events to foster well-grounded hope and reasonable expectations, for "without the knowledge of Man, the knowledge of Men is a hazardous acquisition." History must be read "in the same spirit as that in which good men read the Bible." A principle objective shared by all Coleridge's late political writings is to educate his readers for this hermeneutic task. This chapter follows Coleridge as he persuades his readers of the consolation of history.

From December 1818 to the following March, Coleridge gave weekly lectures at the Crown and Anchor tavern on the history of philosophy.[3] These lectures furnish us with a working example of Coleridge's historical method and, in doing so, introduce his doctrine of ideas. The truth, the coherence, and the practical import of a historical narrative depends, Coleridge argues, upon the historian's grasp of the relation between events and ideas. According to their author, the *Philosophical Lectures* provided a much-needed corrective to the then-dominant view of philosophical history. Unlike other accounts available in England, they attempted to render a properly unified narrative, organized according to the principle that distinguishes the philosophical enterprise itself. Other works were "little more . . . than collections of sentences and extracts, formed into several groups . . . with no *principle* of arrangement, with no *method*, and therefore without unity and without progress or completion."[4] The equivalent, in other words, of those "fanciful" classifications that retarded the study of botany.[5] By contrast, Coleridge considered philosophy

> as if it were the striving of a single mind, under very different circumstances indeed, and at different periods of its own growth and development; but so that each change and every new direction should have its cause and its explanation in the errors, insufficiency, or prematurity of the preceding, while all by reference to a common object is reduced to harmony of impression and total result.[6]

---

[3]For a history of the time, place, audience, and publicity of the lectures, see Kathleen Coburn's account in Samuel Taylor Coleridge, *The Philosophical Lectures of Samuel Taylor Coleridge*, ed. Kathleen Coburn (New York: Philosophical Library, 1949) 21-37. The Crown and Anchor is on The Strand, a five minute walk east of Trafalgar Square.
[4]From the prospectus to the lectures, ibid., 67.
[5]See above, 55.
[6]Coleridge, *Philosophical Lectures*, 67.

Writing a history of philosophy is a properly 'imaginative' task, involving a struggle "to idealize and to unify." The diversity of thinkers, movements, and ideas must be grasped and ordered according to that vital principle of which these various elements are instances and symbols.

In his history of philosophy Coleridge gives Pythagoras a preeminent position as the inaugurator of truly philosophical thinking. While his contribution is anticipated in Thales and Thales's disciples, Pythagoras managed the turn from the thoughtful observation of material causes to reflection upon the mind itself. Pythagoras, therefore, is more than the first philosopher in time, he functions as Coleridge's defining instance of the philosophical mind. His is the seminal discovery that the mind and the world are isomorphous, that their relationship is governed by the principle "in the world one thing can act upon another [only] by some law of likeness." What exists, therefore, as a necessary idea in the mind is found in the world as a law of nature.[7] The external world thus embodies mathematical relations that are not derived empirically but from the reason itself. This insight frees human beings from total dependence upon the senses, upon the shifts and changes of the empirical. Pythagoras's discovery remains the abiding measure of the philosophical. Muddling him up with Archimedes, Coleridge announces that

> it is the sublimest era of human nature when Pythagoras exclaimed— "Eureka!" . . . For it assuredly was no less for the heathen world than to have found the principle of humanity itself, all that distinguishes us from the animal essentially. . . . He found a something that was above time, above accident, it was drawn from the fountain of truth that was inexhaustible, and this was in man. But it was not in his sensations . . . it was not in his understanding, for he had not deduced it from anything; but it was in the mind. It must *be*.[8]

Coleridge presents Pythagoras, therefore, as both a particular philosopher and one who embodies the entire philosophical project within himself.[9] He is a *symbol* of the philosophical though this is only recogniz-

---

[7]Coleridge, *Philosophical Lectures*, 107-109.
[8]Coleridge, *Philosophical Lectures*, 108.
[9]Coleridge, *Aids to Reflection*, 263n.*: "Why not at once Symbol and History? or rather, how should it be otherwise? Must not of necessity the FIRST MAN be a SYMBOL of Mankind? in the fullest force of the word, Symbol,

able as one contemplates the history of philosophy according to its essential idea. According to the symbol's polar dynamic, the whole is discerned through the part and the part is grasped in a discernment of the whole. As we shall see, this imaginative, symbol-producing activity has an essential role in Coleridge's historiography and biblical interpretation.

For a history of philosophy, Pythagoras is at once "portrait and ideal," to use an expression *The Statesman's Manual* applies to biblical characters. As portrait, he must have historical specificity but, as ideal, he must embody the unifying principle of philosophical history. Coleridge has, therefore, to narrate the particular details of Pythagoras's life and thought according to the "idea" of philosophy. This will reveal the individual philosopher as the common symbol in which past and present philosophy find their unity. In the difference—without which there would be no *history* of philosophy, there has to be revealed an identification—a consubstantiality—between the figure of Pythagoras and the contemporary project and situation of philosophy. It is not surprising that accomplishing this, however, turns out to require considerable construction. Coleridge achieves the identification of past and present by characterizing Pythagoras's thought in terms of what he asserts is philosophy's abiding problem—the relation of subject and object. Coherence is fashioned, therefore, by making a problem distinctive of Cartesian and post-Cartesian philosophy into the unifying theme of the whole.

Coleridge takes this procedure still further, striking off in the direction of personal apologetic. He conforms the social-educational task of ancient philosophy to that of the present by retrojecting his own philosophical and political projects into the historical narrative. Pythagoras set about the task of public education in an, of course, "most exemplary" way, a way which encapsulates Coleridge's own approach in the *Lay Sermons* and in *The Friend*, the rifacimento edition of which had been published a month before he began his lecture series.[10] Pythagoras,

---

rightly defined—viz., *A Symbol is a sign included in the idea which it represents*: *ex. gr.*, an actual *part* chosen to represent the *whole*." The measure of an adequate history of philosophy is the same as that of any history that is to be distinguished from "mere chronicle," that is, facts are discovered as either symbols of ideas or as grounded upon ideas. Cf. Samuel Taylor Coleridge, *Table Talk*, pt. 1, 256.

[10]For the account of Pythagoras's career, see Coleridge, *Philosophical*

in sturdy Coleridgean manner, is said to have addressed himself to all classes, but in a differentiated way, beginning, as does the project of the *Lay Sermons*, with "the higher classes." In the same spirit, Pythagoras placed great emphasis upon education in moral principles and employed "every possible persuasion with great eloquence," a note that recalls the objective of *The Friend* and the accompanying rhetorical claim that "my very system compels me to make every fair appeal to the feelings, the imagination and even the fancy."[11]

Coleridge's identification of Pythagoras as the symbol of the philosophical vocation informs the polemic aspect of his historical presentation. This is a history with critical intent, directed against "the histories and political economy of the present and preceding century."[12] Since it bears upon Coleridge's diagnosis of contemporary culture, the polemical character of his history of philosophy requires some further elucidation. The *Philosophical Lectures* is organized to the disadvantage of the modern philosophies Coleridge wishes to attack. The lecture series is split into two halves, the first devoted to ancient, the second to modern thought. This division is not a matter of neutral convenience but establishes a critical point. Among the ancients, Coleridge informed his hearers, "all philosophy could do or has done had been really achieved, and as well achieved, . . . by the efforts of the reason itself, as it has ever since been done."[13] Philosophy has, therefore, already inscribed its essential circle "and appeared in every possible form." Given this, the purpose of a history of modern philosophy must be "to tame the vanity

---

Lectures, 97-103.

[11]Coleridge, *The Friend*, pt. 1, 35. Coleridge even manages to slip autobiographical detail into his account of Pythagoras. But for one feature, Coleridge's summary of Pythagoras's early career is entirely dependent upon Tennemann's *Geschichte der Philosophie*: "[Pythagoras] was a man of wealth, . . . in a town then extremely thriving as a commercial town, . . . he had early opportunities of conversing with mariners and, of course, early took in the desire of seeing more than a minor island could produce to him." The mariners, of course, are not found in Tennemann. (For Coleridge's early fascination with travelers' tales, and particularly those of sea travelers, see Richard Holmes, *Early Visions*, 172-74.)

[12]Coleridge, *Statesman's Manual*, 28.

[13]Coleridge, *Philosophical Lectures*, 245.

of the moderns" by demonstrating that their work has only the status of a series of revisitations, often inferior in character.[14]

Coleridge achieves this organization of philosophical history by what amounts to a bold exercise in anachronism. A problematic distinctive of post-Cartesian philosophy—the relationship of subject and object—is said to have emerged simultaneously with philosophy itself. It is nothing less than the defining question of the philosophical enterprise, ancient and modern. A broad classification of ways of grasping the subject/object distinction provides Coleridge with both the essence and limits of the possibilities open to the philosopher. Using this classification he is able to present the history of philosophy up to the age of Justinian as having rung all the changes in the philosophical repertoire:

> There are therefore essentially but three kinds of philosophers and more are not possible: the one is those who give the whole to the subject and make the object a mere result involved in it; secondly those who give the whole to the object and make the subject, that is the reflecting and contemplating, feeling part, the mere result of that; and lastly those who, in very different ways, have attempted to reconcile these two opposites and bring them into one.[15]

Elsewhere, this scheme is given in a more familiar twofold form as the "two classes of philosophers," headed by Plato and Aristotle.[16] In the *Philosophical Lectures*, however, this divide is traced back to Pythagoras and, therefore, to the very beginnings of philosophy.

While the weight of philosophical exposition falls upon the first half of the lecture series, the rhetorical force of the way this history is structured is directed at modern philosophy, in particular at "the progress of materialism and infidelity on to the time immediately before the French Revolution."[17] Despite the expository emphasis, it is this polemical relationship to the moderns that is at issue throughout. The rhetorical effect of Coleridge's anachronistic reading of Greek and Roman

---

[14]Coleridge, *Philosophical Lectures*, 263.

[15]Coleridge, *Philosophical Lectures*, 116.

[16]Coleridge, *Philosophical Lectures*, 106. For a discussion of the reception of this scheme in nineteenth century British thought, see David Newsome, *Two Classes of Men* (London: John Murray, 1974).

[17]Coleridge, *Philosophical Lectures*, 337.

philosophy, a reading that includes some cheerful Kantianizing of the details of Pythagorean and Platonic philosophy, is to secure some borrowed modern persuasiveness for the ancients in face of their fashionable despisers.[18] It also serves to upstage the moderns, primarily the empiricists with their "wretched trash,"[19] by undermining the boast of the "Mechanical Philosophy" to revolutionary novelty.[20] Coleridge opposes this latter claim with a unified philosophical history in which the empiricists are submitted to the judgment of the past they have so woefully maligned and misunderstood. When Coleridge arrives at the philosophy of Sir Francis Bacon, this unifying interpretation pits modern philosophy's nearer origins against itself. In the teeth of Bacon's anti-Platonism and his importance as a precursor of the empiricist tradition, Coleridge harmonizes his thought with that of Plato.[21] A similar reading of Bacon is found in *The Friend*'s "Essays on the Principles of Method." There, it is of special importance as it evidences the historical unity of scientific thought: there is, and always has been, but one true philosophical method. Bacon, Coleridge proclaims, is "the British Plato"![22]

Coleridge awarded Pythagoras the status of the first philosopher because it was he who discovered the mind and its powers as the ground of philosophical knowledge. In making this discovery, Pythagoras raised human reflection into its primary and proper element. Pythagoras's predecessors, by contrast, had failed to achieve a way of thinking that drew its categories consistently from the ideal. Coleridge describes the

---

[18]See Coleridge's regret, in *A Lay Sermon*, for the parlous state of philosophical learning: "[I]n these free-thinking times, many an empty head is shook at Aristotle and Plato: and the writings of these celebrated ancients are by most men treated on a level with the dry and barbarous lucubrations of the School-men." Coleridge, *A Lay Sermon*, 193; see also 194, 170-74; and Coleridge, *Statesman's Manual*, 106-108.
[19]Coleridge, *Philosophical Lectures*, 194.
[20]Coleridge, *The Friend*, pt. 1, 446-47; and from the "chapter of contents of the moral history of the last 130 years": "The Mechanico-Corpuscular Theory raised to the title of the Mechanical Philosophy, and espoused as a revolution in philosophy, by the actors and partisans of the (so called) Revolution in the state." Coleridge, *Church and State*, 64-65.
[21]Coleridge, *Philosophical Lectures*, 331-37.
[22]Coleridge, *The Friend*, pt. 1, 488.

disciple of Thales who, possessed of the genuinely philosophical insight that the ultimate ground of phenomena (the visible) must lie in what transcends the phenomenal (the invisible), proceeded to expound that distinction in terms of the "distinguishable" and the "indistinguishable," identifying the latter with fluid.[23] Thus, this almost-philosopher conceives that which transcends the sensual as itself a particular kind of sensible thing. The struggle for freedom from the sensual, of the mind to find within itself, in its own acts, the light for the world's exegesis, Coleridge compares to a bird that,

> having been belimned [ensnared by birdlime] . . . upon a hedge or twigs, by more than usual force of genius, gets himself loose and yet still feels the lime hanging on its wings and with a sort of imperfect flutter and fright drops and again tries to rise.[24]

The difficulty conveyed in this image is an enduring pedagogical concern for Coleridge. Especially in an "epoch of the senses and the understanding," it is only with effort that reflective thought frees itself from conformity to the sensual, only with a strenuous agony does it cease to mistake imageability for conceptual clarity.[25]

With Pythagoras, however, the bird takes flight. What transcends the sensual cannot be adequately imaged, it is the ideal and ideas are the mind's own proper acts. The idea of triangularity, for instance, is not derived empirically from its sensible embodiments; it is logically prior to them as an act of the mind.[26] In reflecting upon its own acts the mind

---

[23]Coleridge, *Philosophical Lectures*, 96-97, the Egerton manuscript gives the philosopher as Anaximander.

[24]Coleridge, *Philosophical Lectures*, 97.

[25]On the fate of the "idea" in such an age, "Dr. HOLOFERNES, in a lecture on metaphysics, delivered at one of the Mechanic Institutions, explodes all *ideas* but those of sensation; and his friend DEPUTY COSTARD, has no *idea* of a better flavored haunch of venison, than he dined off at the London Tavern last week. He admits, (for the deputy has travelled) that the French have an excellent *idea* of cooking in general; but holds that their most accomplished *Maitres du Cuisine* have no more *idea* of dressing a turtle, than the Parisian Gourmands themselves have any *real* idea of the true *taste* and *colour* of the fat." Coleridge, *Church and State*, 66.

[26]Elsewhere, Coleridge identifies Pythagoras's numbers as an important antidote to the "despotism of the eye": "Under that despotism of the eye (the eman-

understands both itself *and* the world because what the mind possesses as ideas are, as laws, constitutive of empirical reality. As opposed, therefore, to any account that regards the mind as "purely contemplative," Coleridge can sum up Pythagoras's contribution to the history of philosophy:

> [It] involves an essential . . . HOMOGENEITY—a sameness . . . of the idea and the law corresponding to the idea. . . . to comprehend the philosophy of Pythagoras the mind itself must be conceived of as an act; and the numbers of Pythagoras . . . are not so properly acts of the Reason . . . as they are the Reason itself in act.[27]

Philosophy begins in the freedom of the mind's turn to its own activity, a turn upon which depends the intelligibility of the mind's objects.

The main lines of Coleridge's historiography already emerge from this discussion of Pythagoras. First, there is the concern for unity, a rational unity arrived at through contemplation of the vital principle, the "idea" embodied in historical developments. In the lectures, this desire for a unified account extends beyond the interpretation of philosophical ideas into the details of the narrative itself. Second, historical thought, rightly understood, discloses the events of history in their relation to ideas. Among the "facts of history," those that are recognized as symbols have a special role and importance: as consubstantial with the truths they reveal. Enough was said earlier concerning the role of the imagination to indicate that, understood in this way, the study of history is an imaginative enterprise. A history faithful to its subject matter is the product of that unifying and idealizing power that, infusing the understanding with reason, reveals and represents the empirical as the symbolic.

If philosophy, according to Coleridge, begins by turning to the mind's activity, so also does a proper historical method. A glance at Coleridge's own epistemological reflections will clarify this. Coleridge argues that the theory of association, especially as elaborated by Hartley and Priestly,

---

cipation from which Pythagoras by his *numeral* and Plato by his *musical* symbols, and both by geometric discipline, aimed at, as the first 'propaideutikon' of the mind)—under this strong sensible influence, we are restless because invisible things are not the objects of vision." Coleridge, *Biographia Literaria* 1:107.

[27]Coleridge, *Philosophical Lectures*, 114-15.

presents the mind as entirely passive, "a lazy Looker-on on an external World."[28] This has some exceedingly disturbing consequences with respect to both knowledge and volition. The strict denial of the *activity* of the mind in producing experience requires that consciousness be considered "as a *result*, as a *tune*, the common product of the breeze and the harp." The language of will is thus acknowledged as empty. In writing, for example,

> the whole universe cooperates to produce the minutest stroke of every letter, save only that I myself, and I alone, have nothing to do with it, but merely the causeless and *effectless* beholding of it when it is done.[29]

Furthermore, the doctrine of association cannot account for the orderliness and stability of experience. The law of association entails that "every partial representation recalls the total representation of which it was a part."[30] However, as long as no mental activity is allowed that is not itself the result of association, no reason can be given as to why experience is not a whirlpool of clashing representations:

> Consider how immense must be the sphere of a total impression from the top of St. Paul's church; and how rapid and continuous the series of such total impressions. If therefore we suppose the absence of all interference of the will, reason, and judgement, one or other of two consequences must result. Either the ideas (or relicts of such impression) will exactly imitate the order of the impression itself, which would

---

[28]Coleridge, *Collected Letters* 2:709, letter to Thomas Poole, referring to the implications of Newtonianism, 23 March 1801. His previous letter to Poole, written a week earlier, had celebrated his overthrowal of "the doctrine of Association, as taught by Hartley, and with it all the irreligious metaphysics of modern Infidels—especially, the doctrine of Necessity." Coleridge, *Collected Letters* 2:706.

[29]Coleridge, *Biographia Literaria*, pt. 1, 117.

[30]Coleridge, *Biographia Literaria*, pt. 1, 111. See David Hartley, *Observations on Man, His Frame, His Duty, and His Expectations*, 6th ed. corr. and rev. (facsimile repr.: Charlottesville VA: Ibis Publishers, 1980–1989? = London: T. Legg and Son, 1834) 41: "Any Sensations, A, B, C, etc. by being associated with one another a sufficient Number of times, get such a Power over the corresponding Ideas a, b, c, etc. that any one of the sensations A, when impressed alone, shall be able to excite in the Mind, b, c, etc. the Ideas of the rest."

be absolute *delirium*: or any one part of that impression might recall any other part and (as from the law of continuity, there must exist in every total impression some one or more parts, which are components of some other following total impression, and so on ad infinitum) *any* part of *any* impression might recall *any* part of *any* other, without a cause present to determine *what* it should be.³¹

The theory, Coleridge concludes, is applicable only to a state of complete lightheadedness.³² It fails, therefore, to make good its claim to account for the way we experience the world. The associationists provide reluctant witness to Coleridge's case that experience can only be rendered intelligible via a philosophical turn toward the mind's own activity. To the empiricist principle *nihil in intellectu quod non prius in sensu* must be added the Leibnitzian qualifier: *praeter ipsum intellectum*.³³ Upon such a turn depends a unified account of the real. And this account must embrace, in addition to the stabilizing and ordering power of the understanding and the fancy, the activity of reason and imagination. The core of such a philosophy is the mind's self-finding. Those who accept this refuse "to forget themselves, lost and scattered in sensible Objects disjoined or *as* disjoined from themselves."³⁴

If we turn from Coleridge's epistemological to his historiographical critique, we find a similar concern for an adequate account of the conditions of coherence and stability. *The Statesman's Manual* presents the case that the Old Testament should accompany contemporary political reflection as its primary source of wisdom and guidance. Having announced this, to say the least, bold thesis at the beginning, Coleridge pursues it by inquiring into the continuity of history itself. What is it that gives such unity to history that past experience can be relevant to present concerns? It is here that the aporias of associationism, considered as a complete philosophical psychology, reappear at the level of historical interpretation: the level at which people seek for a guiding order within the changes of past and present. The succession of historical events confronts the interpreter with "the fleeting *chaos of facts*." This is a bewildering flux of change to which Coleridge applies the words of

---

[31]Coleridge, *Biographia Literaria*, pt. 1, 111-12.
[32]Coleridge, *Biographia Literaria*, pt. 1, 111-12.
[33]Coleridge, *Biographia Literaria*, pt. 1, 141.
[34]Coleridge, *Notebooks* 3:3935, f69.

Heraclitus: "[I]t is impossible . . . to grasp twice any mortal substance in a permanent state . . . at the same moment it takes shape and dissolves."[35]

Contemporary historiography, Coleridge argues, fails to provide the grounds according to which we might confidently turn to the past for guidance. It is merely "the *product* of an unenlivened generalizing Understanding." "Product," here, is contrasted with "educt," the term for the symbolic narratives of Scripture. Unlike the histories that "partake of the general contagion of [the age's] mechanic philosophy," the biblical ones "are the living *educts* of the Imagination."[36] The opposition here is between the "living" and not the "dead" but the "unenlivened," that is, between the presence and the absence of the "seminal power"[37] of *ideas*. The mind possesses this power only insofar as the imagination, informing the understanding with reason, renders it "intuitive, and thus a living power."[38] Without ideas, the historian merely "snatches at truth" and, uncertain of construction, organizes the fluctuations of historical experience according to an arbitrary perspective.[39] Just as philosophy begins when Pythagoras applies to ideas—the mind's own "being-in-act"—for the light with which to render the world intelligible,[40] so must the historian turn to moral ideas—equally the generations of reason—in order to interpret the deeds, hopes, and passions of human beings. In history, just as in science and philosophy, the imagination, in the service of

---

[35]Coleridge, *Statesman's Manual*, 20.

[36]Coleridge, *Statesman's Manual*, 28-29.

[37]Coleridge, *Statesman's Manual*, 23-24.

[38]Coleridge, *Statesman's Manual*, 69.

[39]Thus, as Coleridge was reported to say much later, it is impossible to adjudicate, on this level, between competing histories: "A Whig proves his case convincingly to the reader who knows nothing beyond his author; then comes an old Tory . . . and ferrets up a hamper full of conflicting documents and notices, which prove his case per contra. A takes this class of facts; B takes that class: each proves something true, neither of course proves *the* truth or any thing like *the* Truth." Coleridge, *Table Talk*, pt. 1, 365-66, 11 April 1833.

[40]Coleridge, *Philosophical Lectures*, 109: "Applying those numbers, drawn abstractly from his own reason, to the laws of external nature and her motions, [Pythagoras] perceived the direct contrary to what the wisest of men had done before him, that instead of supposing the earth fixed and the heavenly bodies (as our senses show us) moving around us, he saw by laws derived from his own reason that the sun was fixed."

reason, opens up the mind to its own activity and, in so doing, to the vital principles of nature and humanity. The "unenlivened generalizing Understanding," on the other hand, is fated merely to arrange and rearrange, in restless uncertainty, the accumulating historical facts.

A merely empirical approach, then, is no more able to discern the unity and order in historical change than is the doctrine of association able to account for the orderliness of cognition. Furthermore, Coleridge finds eighteenth-century historians as guilty as the associationists of espousing highly reductionist accounts of human action.[41] Specifically, they eclipse the human capacity for moral 'enthusiasm,' for passionate action in the service of moral principles. From the perspective of Coleridge's philosophical psychology, this is the inevitable consequence of the "unenlivened generalizing Understanding." Save through the imagination, the understanding knows nothing of ultimate ends, only of proximate ones. In this sense, "understanding" is cognitive-instrumental reasoning: it is "the faculty of selecting and adapting means to . . . such *ends* as in their turn become means."[42]

Human actions, Coleridge insists, cannot be accounted for simply in terms of the expedient, with all other purported motives dismissed as the madness of fanaticism. In attempting such an account, David Hume was guilty of a vicious reductionism. Hume's history is dangerously abstract in that one element of human thinking and feeling, willing and acting, is selected and made out to be the whole. It is not expediency, Coleridge declares, that can account for the "*epoch-forming* Revolutions of the Christian world," however much a role it has to play in the practical arrangements of daily life. Rather, behind all developments of any note, as their inner meaning and significance, are moral ideas:

> [N]othing great was ever atchieved without enthusiasm. . . . in the genuine enthusiasm of morals, religion, and patriotism, this enlargement

---

[41]Coleridge's polemic is largely directed at Gibbon's *The History of the Decline and Fall of the Roman Empire* and David Hume's *History of England*. These are "the histories of highest note in the present age" (Coleridge, *Statesman's Manual*, 28; for a specific discussion of Hume, see ibid., 22).

[42]Coleridge, *Statesman's Manual*, 60-61n.1.

of the soul above its mere self attests the presence, and accompany the intuition of ultimate PRINCIPLES alone.[43]

Even the despised French Revolution provides evidence for this claim:

> The public roads were crowded with armed enthusiasts disputing on the inalienable sovereignty of the people, the imprescriptible laws of the pure reason, which, as rising out of the nature and rights of man as man, all nations were under the obligation of adopting.[44]

In the lay sermons and *The Friend*, the French Revolution plays the rhetorically significant role of embodying, in their extreme form, the philosophical, religious, and political developments Coleridge opposes. The mechanical philosophy reached the pinnacle of its influence in the Revolution. However, because it "recognized no duties which it could not reduce into debtor and creditor accounts on the ledgers of self-love,"[45] this philosophy is unable to explain in its own terms the very revolutionary events it acclaims.

An adequate, nonreductionist historical method, therefore, is one that does not derive from the facts of history such abstractions as will fit the confines of the mere understanding. It recognizes that "nothing great was ever atchieved without enthusiasm." The motor force of history is not expediency but moral principles expressed in struggles for political order, for fidelity to religion and national pride, for the development of culture and the protection of self, family, and property.[46] Only a historian who recognizes moral passion can do justice to the strivings of history. The

---

[43] Coleridge, *Statesman's Manual*, 23.

[44] Coleridge, *Statesman's Manual*, 16.

[45] Coleridge, *Statesman's Manual*, 76.

[46] The latter might seem reducible to "expediency" but see "How else can we explain the fact so honorable to Great Britain, that the poorest amongst us contend with as much enthusiasm as the richest for the rights of property? These rights are the spheres and necessary conditions of free agency. But free agency contains the idea of free will; and in this he intuitively knows the sublimity, and the infinite hopes, fears and capabilities of his own nature." Ibid., 24-25. Of course, it is not only Marxist historians who would point out that there certainly are other ways of explaining this "so honorable" fact. Coleridge's idealist historiography brings its own reductionism in relation to complex historical data.

historical vocation is to reveal human initiatives and institutions either as more or less adequate expressions of ideas, or as deformations, corruptions, or departures from ideas. In 1833, Coleridge summarized the historical method involved:

> You must commence with the philosophical Idea of the Thing, the true nature of which you wish to find out and manifest. You must carry your rule ready made if you mean to measure aright. If you ask me how I can know that this Idea—my own invention—is the Truth, by which the phenomena of History are to be explained, I answer, in the same way exactly that you know that your eyes are made to see with—and that is—because you *do* see with them. . . . in order to make your facts speak Truth, you must know *what* the Truth is which ought to be proved—the Ideal Truth—the Truth which was consciously or unconsciously, strongly or weakly, wisely or blindly, intended at all times.[47]

That which gives intelligibility to history, that in which appears the consubstantiality—the "unity in multeity"—of past and present, are those acts in which the mind comes to itself: ideas.

In *The Statesman's Manual*, Coleridge discusses the relevance of the past to present concerns. Deploying a rhetoric in imitation of the Old Testament prophets, he presents both the problem of historical interpretation and its resolution in two natural images. To lose oneself in accumulations of facts instead of reading history "for the sake of the general principles" is to stare at the leaves and miss the "root and sap" of the tree.[48] Similarly, to seek "the true cause and origin of public calamities in outward circumstances, persons, and incidents" is to interrogate agents that

> were themselves but surges of the same tide, passive conductors of the one invisible influence, under which the total host of billows, in the whole line of successive impulse, swell and roll shoreward; there finally, each in its turn, to strike, roar, and be dissipated.[49]

The harshness, particularly of the second image in terms of its characterization of finite "circumstances, persons, and incidents" derives from Coleridge's claim that to regard the latter as the true origin of events is

---

[47]Coleridge, *Table Talk*, pt. 1, 366-67.
[48]Coleridge, *Statesman's Manual*, 11.
[49]Ibid., 9.

"idolatrous in itself and the source of all other idolatry." The force of the image depends upon the theological nature of the historiography Coleridge proposes. To intuit within the empirical an abiding unity, to look to the ideal as "true cause and origin" presupposes

> the intuition and immediate spiritual consciousness of the idea of God, as the One and Absolute, at once the Ground and the Cause, who alone containeth in himself the ground of his own nature, and therein of *all* natures.[50]

The idea of a thing is at once its origin and end. To know an entity's nature and purpose as divinely intended is to know its idea.[51] The images of the ocean and the tree both invoke the relation of surface and depth, the perception of which reformulates the character of change, uniting the surging and dissipating waves with the continuous, causative movement of the tide's "successive impulse," and the flourishing and fading leaf with the powers of growth in root and sap. The purpose of Coleridge's historiography, focused in these images, is to establish a position from which change emerges as significant of *productive* powers, of the active presence of an ultimate origin and end, and in the light of which, may be distinguished from mere alteration or from corruption. In relation to his conservative politics, therefore, Coleridge's historiography offers a religious logic for change as well as continuity.

Understood in this way, the historical method Coleridge proposes engages with his diagnosis of contemporary culture as alienated from the past. That diagnosis also reveals the source of the culture's resistance to a proper historical method. It is "novelty," Coleridge claims, that attracts his contemporaries. In an image that anticipates the language of surface and depth in the tidal metaphor that follows, he describes this as a "restless craving for the wonders of the day, which in conjunction with the appetite for publicity is spreading like an efflorescence on the surface of our national life." Together with this passion for the new, for that which

---

[50] Ibid., 32.

[51] Cf. the later explanation of the term "idea": "that conception of a thing, which is not abstracted from any particular state, form, or mode, in which the thing may happen to exist at this or that time; nor yet generalized from any number or succession of such forms or odes; but which is given by knowledge of *its ultimate aim*." Coleridge, *Church and Society*, 12.

appears to have no precedent, is a corresponding devaluation of the past. Historical parallels, however well founded, are dismissed as pedantry, the "holy cave . . . of old philosophy" is abandoned, and "this enlightened age" adored.[52] What underlies Coleridge's attack upon the desire for novelty is the implication of historical discontinuity. The lauding of "this enlightened age" is a celebration of freedom from the past, the boast of a qualitative cultural leap that renders the consideration of history irrelevant. Coleridge's historical method is aimed at restoring his readers to the community of past and present, on the basis of which the former may guide the present and illuminate the future. If made good, claims to novelty undermine his entire project. They are claims to the unprecedented, to that which cannot be interpreted within the horizon of ideas already disclosed in the past. In typically Coleridgean fashion, however, the category of the "novel" is not simply rejected or abandoned, it is reinterpreted:

> To find no contradiction in the union of old and new, to contemplate the ANCIENT OF DAYS, his words and his works, with a feeling as fresh as if they were now springing forth at his fiat—this characterizes the minds that feel the riddle of the world and may help to unravel it![53]

Those who are alive to the creative power of ideas, discover that which is both ancient and novel.

The epistemological hinge that turns the interpreter of the present from a seeming chaos of facts to a grasp of history's underlying unity and, therefore, of the community of past and present, is the identifying power of the imagination. It is the imagination that brings into play the "ready-made measure"—the ideal state of perfection exhibited by the reason—against which the relations of historical events appear as growth or decline, anticipation or reaction, or the development of one dimension over another. The power of the imagination is "to idealize and to unify," "organizing the flux of the Senses by the permanence and self-circling energies of the Reason."[54] Here, once more, appears the reason for

---

[52]Coleridge, *Statesman's Manual*, 11, 12, 36-37, 113. See also ibid., 25; Coleridge, *A Lay Sermon*, 170-73; Coleridge, *The Friend*, pt. 1, 46-47, 109-10; Coleridge, *Church and Society*, 14n.*.

[53]Coleridge, *Statesman's Manual*, 25; Coleridge, *The Friend*, pt. 1, 110.

[54]Coleridge, *Biographia Literaria*, pt. 1, 304; Coleridge, *Statesman's Manual*,

Coleridge's repeated attacks upon the craving for novelty and upon any claim that we no longer require the guidance of the past. What is at stake is the very possibility of a history according to the unifying powers of the imagination and, therefore, the validity of the large claims Coleridge wishes to make concerning the role of that mental power across the whole field of knowledge.

The principle result of the discussion thus far is to have shown that the "turn to the mind's activity," a turn that cannot be understood apart from the theory of the imagination, is as central to Coleridge's historiography as it is to his account of philosophy, to his theory of science, and to his philosophical psychology. Without the imagination, the interpretation of history is blind. To recognize this emphasis upon ideas, upon the "acts of the mind," however, also enables an understanding of the structure of both *The Statesman's Manual* and *The Friend*.

The Statesman's Manual is a work in two parts, a sermon followed by a series of appendixes longer than the sermon itself. The impression of completeness given by the sermonic form, beginning and ending as it does with biblical texts, is disrupted by the appendixes, the internal variety of which is indicated in their overall title "appendix containing comments and essays." This material is not merely "tacked on" to the sermon. The essays are not independent, they refer to, and open up specific points in the text.[55] The integrity of the sermon—in a manner subversive of the homiletic form itself—is disturbed by explanatory interruptions, separate from the text and not themselves reflecting the sermon form. The comments and essays announce that the preacher does not expect the sermon to be understood as it stands. Its formal completeness is misleading, there is further work to be done. The appendixes continue the argument by other rhetorical means.

The appendixes, however, do not complete the work. As a whole, *The Statesman's Manual* isn't. On the flyleaf of James Gillman's copy, Coleridge described the appendixes as "nothing more than a maniple or handful of loose flowers, a string of Hints and Materials for Reflection."[56] He then gives the reason for this deliberate fragmentariness,

---

29.

[55]The exception to this is the penultimate essay (D) to which Coleridge never provided a reference within the sermon itself.

[56]Coleridge, *Statesman's Manual*, 114n.2.

> The Object . . . was to rouse and stimulate the mind—to set the reader a thinking—and at least to obtain entrance for the question, whether the truth of the Opinions in fashion is quite so certain as he had hitherto taken for granted—rather than to establish the contrary by a connected chain of proofs and arguments.[57]

"To set the reader a thinking": a similar motive governs the structure Coleridge subsequently imposed upon the rifacimento *The Friend*. The metaphor of a staircase underlies the new organization. Commenting on the interludes he calls "landing places," he explains:

> Among my earliest impressions I still distinctly remember that of my first entrance into the mansion of a neighboring baronet, awfully known to me by the name of THE GREAT HOUSE. . . . Beyond all other objects, I was most struck with the magnificent staircase, relieved at well-proportioned intervals by spacious landing places, this adorned with grand or shewy plants, the next looking out on an extensive prospect through the stately window . . . : while from the last and highest the eye commanded the whole spiral ascent with the marble pavement of the great hall from which it seemed to spring up as if it merely *used* the ground on which it rested.[58]

With stops for "amusement, retrospect, and preparation," the sections of *The Friend* form a pedagogical ascent, the concluding section of which is the "Essays on the Principles of Method." In the final form of *The Friend*, the original journal pieces become illustrative of the need and function of "fixed principles." The climax of the work, to which this varied, illustrative material leads, is the exploration of method, the means for arriving at such principles. This destination pulls all that precedes towards it: the latter springing up "as if it merely *used* the ground on which it rested." The structure, therefore, reflects Coleridge's summary of the purpose of *The Friend*: "not so much to show my Reader this or that fact, as to kindle his own torch for him, and leave it to himself to chuse the particular objects, which he might wish to examine by its light."[59]

---

[57] Coleridge, *Statesman's Manual*, 114n.2.
[58] Coleridge, *The Friend*, pt. 1, 148-49.
[59] Coleridge, *The Friend*, pt. 1, 16.

In the fourth of *The Friend*'s "Essays on the Principles of Method," Coleridge offers an indirect apologia for his rhetorical procedure. He employs the device, mentioned earlier in connection with the *Philosophical Lectures*, of identifying his own project with that of an earlier philosopher, in this case, Plato. Without an appreciation of their pedagogical intent, it is difficult, he suggests,

> to exculpate the noblest productions of the divine philosopher from the charge of being tortuous in their progress, and unsatisfactory in their ostensible results. The latter indeed appear not seldom to have been drawn for the purpose of starting a new problem, rather than that of solving the one proposed as the subject of the previous discussion.[60]

As a description of Plato's dialogues, this is open to considerable dispute. However, read as a covert apologia for Coleridge's own writing it is more intelligible, if not wholly convincing. Contemporaries accused Coleridge of writing tortuous prose that issued in unsatisfactory and anti-climactic conclusions. *The Friend* and *The Statesman's Manual* were named as particularly damning examples.[61] Certainly, there is, throughout the political writings, a persistent carelessness regarding the demands of complete exposition.[62] Any reader of *The Friend* is likely to be somewhat

---

[60] Ibid., 472.

[61] Hazlitt likened Coleridge's prose to someone talking in their sleep! In a review article, John Foster, an otherwise sympathetic reader, urged Coleridge to "a resolute restriction on that mighty profusion and excursiveness of thought, in which he is tempted to suspend the pursuit and retard the attainment of the one distinct object which should be clearly kept in view." Coleridge, *The Friend*, pt. 1, lxxiv-lxxv.

[62] In *A Lay Sermon*, Coleridge makes a somewhat untypical attempt to inform the reader concerning the topics to be covered under the heading "the Overbalance of the Commercial Spirit." In the event, only one of the proposed sections—on the implications for the agricultural world—is fully executed, the others receiving only brief mention. The apology, "for the remainder [i.e., of a proposed discussion] let the following suffice as the substitute or representative" is paradigmatic (Coleridge, *A Lay Sermon*, 169-70). Coleridge's description of a chapter in *Church and State* has a far more general application: "A treatise? why, the subjects might, I own, excite some apprehension of the sort. But it will be found like sundry Greek Treatises among the tinder rolls of Herculaneum, with titles of as large promise, somewhat largely and irregularly abbreviated in

bewildered by sudden interruptions of new material, by the abrupt transitions, and by the complex issues that are only partially discussed before they become the means of introducing a further topic.[63] Much of this is simply the product of rushed, inadequate revision and not a subtle, Platonically inspired, pedagogical strategy. However, the rhetorical rationale that Coleridge offers here—by way of Plato—remains significant at least as a guide to his educational aim, even if it does not excuse its execution.

The clue to the form of the Platonic dialogues, and by implication to that of his own work, is, Coleridge argues, their educational purpose:

> We see that to open anew a well of springing water, not to cleanse the stagnant tank, or fill, bucket by bucket, the leaden cistern; that the EDUCATION of the intellect, by awakening the principle and *method* of self-development, was [Plato's] proposed object, not any specific information that can be *conveyed into it* from without: not to assist in storing the passive mind with the various sorts of knowledge most in request, as if the human soul were a mere repository or banqueting room, but to place it in such relations of circumstance as should gradually excite the germinal power that craves no knowledge but what it can take up into itself, what it can appropriate, and reproduce in fruits of its own. To shape, to dye, to paint over, and to mechanize the mind, he resigned as their proper trade, to the sophist, against whom he waged open and unremitting war.[64]

---

the process of unrolling. In fact, neither my purpose nor my limits permit more than a few hints." Coleridge, *Church and State*, 82; the chapter title is "On the King and the Nation.".

[63] Examples would include the drastically summarized discussion of the "prudential method" in politics ("Section the First," essay iii); the suggestive but frustratingly brief account of the relation of religion and law which is dropped into the reflections upon the jury in libel cases (Coleridge, *The Friend*, pt. 1, 94-95) and then suddenly passes into a section on the distinction between tolerance and toleration (95-99); the comparison of Charlemagne and Napoleon that interrupts the essays on the liberty of the press (84-90); the extent of the explanations of "genius," "talents," "sense," and "cleverness" appended to the second section, essay i; and the only partially developed discussion of international law that becomes the occasion for the subsequent critique of Paley's "consequentialism" (289-325).

[64] Coleridge, *The Friend*, pt. 1, 472-73.

Plato's objectives are conformed here to the battle lines of Coleridge's own philosophical engagement—the critique of "passive" and "mechanical" theories of the mind—as well as to the design of his own pedagogy: "to kindle [the reader's] own torch for him." By identifying Plato's project with his own, Coleridge is doing more than stealing a little ancient authority for himself, he is laying claim to a continuous and unifying philosophical project. On the one hand, this rhetorically isolates the empiricist philosophies he opposes, on the other, it places the readers within a consubstantiality of past and present, across those flaunted disjunctions of time known as ancient and modern. The contemporary peril is not unprecedented, "the ancients, as well as the moderns, had their machinery for the extemporaneous mintage of intellects."[65]

The account of Plato's dialogues contrasts two modes of learning, each with its correspondent theory of mind. The contrast turns out to be a familiar one. There is, first, the conveying of "the various sorts of knowledge most in request" into a passive mind, the metaphor for which is the storing of a repository. Here, neither the mind nor its ideas are conceived as active. This is opposed to "the EDUCATION of the intellect" which seeks to stimulate the mind to activity, to "self-development." Knowing is an activity that shapes and determines what is given to it according to its own power, rendering it fruitful: "the germinal power that craves no knowledge but what it can take up into itself . . . and reproduce in fruits of its own." The imagination is not specifically named here, but the description of the "germinal power" that education aims to "excite" closely follows accounts of the imagination elsewhere. Thus, this power is re-creative, it transforms what is given it according to the mind's own self-intuition,[66] and it is resistant to the epistemological and educational reductionism that treats the mind as a "mechanism."

---

[65]Here, Coleridge's method allows him to draw the same moral from the history of philosophy as he does in applying his corresponding approach to the Bible. With reference to the political activities of William Cobbett and others, he writes, in the light of a passage from Isaiah, "[T]his is no new thing under the Sun! We have heard it with our own ears, and it was declared to our fathers, and in the old time before them." Colcridge, *A Lay Sermon*, 150, and see below, 118.

[66]Cf. Coleridge, *Biographia Literaria*, pt. 1, 241: "the philosophic imagination, the sacred power of self-intuition. . . . "

The use of emphatic capitals for "education" in this passage and its application to "awakening the principle and *method* of self-development" recalls Coleridge's attempt, found elsewhere, to derive his educational theory etymologically. This argument is developed in the *Logic*.[67] *Educare*, Coleridge points out, is a derivative of *educere*, "to draw forth," or "bring out," a term used originally with reference to natural growth and reproduction. Nature provides the environmental factors through which the capacities for growth and fruition, inherent in the plant, are "drawn forth" or "educed." Thus, in its primary reference, "education" refers to the human activity of so adapting the natural environment as to stimulate desired growth. It is from this context that the word is extended to apply "to the householder man in relation to the young of his own species, and made to express the collective process in which the educator is himself (instead of) the dews and showers, the sun and the breeze to the congenerous plant."[68]

From the beginning, prior to the child's engagement with formal education, the development of the intellect proceeds by means of an environment that stimulates its activity. This activity receives its earliest excitation through the profusion of stimuli that Nature provides the infant. This "promiscuous" stimulation

> solicits the mind to make for itself from the *like* effects of different objects on its own sensibility the links which it *then* seems to *find*,

---

[67]Coleridge's objectives in the *Logic* connect it with the lay sermons. It involves "knowledge of our intellectual nature" as "the substance and life of all our knowledge and the ground of intelligibility of all other objects of knowledge." As such, the *Logic* is a contribution to political education, its aims and addressees, particularly recalling those of *The Statesman's Manual*: consideration of "our intellectual nature" is "an object of duty to all who, filling or destined to fill the higher and middle stations of society, possess opportunities of leisure which have been fearfully abused if they have not been made opportunities of reflection. For these classes generally, though with especial reference to those who are forming themselves for public and professional life, the pulpit, the bar, the senate, the professor's chair, or for . . . the public press, this work was written." Coleridge, *Logic*, ed. James Robert de Jager Jackson, vol. 13 of *The Collected Works of Samuel Taylor Coleridge* (Princeton NJ: Princeton University Press, 1981) 144-45.

[68]Coleridge, *Logic*, 9-10.

unconscious that both the form, and the light by which it is beheld, are of its own irradiation and but *reflected* from external nature."[69]

Divine Providence, Coleridge goes on to argue, has ordered the child's earliest exposure to the world of objects with a view to the subsequent emergence of freedom. The very chaos of the medley that is early experience is the means for storing the mind "with all the materials for it after use" but without preempting the mind's formative activity. "Encroachment on the native freedom of the soul" is avoided. "Artificial" education must follow this example of Nature by shaping its processes to "the forms and faculties developing, or seeking to develop themselves from within." A context must be provided fit for the development of the mind's active powers and its freedom, the ultimate aim of human education being "the mind's knowledge of its own constitution and constituent faculties as far as it is obtained by *reflection*."[70]

Education, then, consists in stimulating the mind to exercise of its powers in the light of self-knowledge. It is this purpose, Coleridge claims, that justifies the form of *The Friend*, and of Plato's dialogues. The incompleteness of the political writings, the avoidance of results that

---

[69]Ibid., 11. Coleridge's *Logic* is essentially a summary and simplification of Kant's *Critique of Pure Reason*. His account of the latter inserts Kant within the reworking of the history of philosophy discussed in this chapter: "Immanuel Kant I assuredly do value most highly; not, however, as a Metaphysician but as a Logician, who has completed and systematized what Lord Bacon had boldly designed and loosely sketched out in the miscellany of Aphorisms, his Novum Organum—in Kant's Critique of the Pure Reason there is more than one fundamental error; but the main fault lies in the Title page, which to the manifold advantage of the Work might be exchanged for—An Inquisition respecting the constitution and limits of the Human Understanding." Coleridge, *Collected Letters* 5:421. On Coleridge's reading of Kant, see Rene Welleck, *Immanuel Kant in England: 1793–1838* (Princeton NJ: Princeton University press, 1931) 65-135. For treatments more sympathetic to Coleridge, see G. N. G. Orsini, *Coleridge and German Idealism: A Study in the History of Philosophy with Unpublished Materials from Coleridge's Manuscripts* (Carbondale and Edwardsville: Southern Illinois University Press, 1969); Donald M. McKinnon, "Coleridge and Kant," in *Coleridge's Variety, Bicentenary Studies*, ed. John Beer (Pittsburgh PA: University of Pittsburgh Press, 1974) 183-203.

[70]Coleridge, *Logic*, 13.

could be perverted into furnishings for a mental lumber room, is a rhetorical strategy designed to bring into play the mind's most distinctive activity: the turn towards ideas and, thereby, the formation of principles. Coleridge offers his prose as an environment for educing the "germinal power" of the mind.

The contrast found in *The Friend* between education as "educing" and the mechanical accumulation of "the various sorts of knowledge" takes, in *The Statesman's Manual*, the form of the contrast between two kinds of historical writing.[71] "The histories and political economy of the present and preceding century partake in the general contagion of its mechanic philosophy, and are the *product* of an unenlivened generalizing Understanding." On the other hand, the scriptural histories "are the living *educts* of the Imagination."[72] As educts, they are expressions of that "reconciling and mediatory power" that brings "the whole soul of man into activity, with the subordination of its faculties to each other, according to their relative worth and dignity."[73] Proceeding from this power, and unlike the historical *products* of the understanding, the Scriptures represent the human in the fullness of intellectual and moral powers. The narratives reconcile the necessity that bears down upon human beings with the freedom of the will that distinguishes them from the brute.[74] Furthermore, the Scriptures address themselves to, and seek to set in motion, the response of the "whole soul," of mind, passion, and will. By contrast, the "mechanical" histories, conformed to the terms of the understanding, present human history two-dimensionally, as "a shadow fight of Things and Quantities."[75] Appealing only to an element of human activity, they produce from a reductionist account a reductionist response: the elevation of novelty over continuity and expediency over the idea-filled "enthusiasm

---

[71]It is important here to remember the structure of Coleridge's epistemology. The "various sorts of knowledge" are not dismissed any more than is the role of the fancy; it is their relationship to the mind's activity that is at issue. Similarly, Coleridge has no desire to suggest that the historian should take lightly the "facts of history" and their discovery—again, the issue is their relation to the mind, responsive and responsible as it is, to ideas.

[72]Coleridge, *Statesman's Manual*, 29.

[73]Coleridge, *Biographia Literaria*, pt. 2, 15-16.

[74]Coleridge, *Statesman's Manual*, 31-32.

[75]Ibid., 28.

of morals, religion, and patriotism."[76] According to Coleridge, therefore, the task of the historian, taking the biblical histories as the model, is not only to expound and to unify the facts of history according to ideas but also to educe in the readers a unified activity of mind and heart.

Human knowledge, as the possession of ideas, is power: "that science, which consists wholly in ideas and principles, is power."[77] Coleridge describes the character of this power in an image of liberation:

> At the annunciation of *principles*, of *ideas*, the soul of man awakes, and starts up, as an exile in a far distant land at the unexpected sounds of his native language, when after long years of absence, and almost of oblivion, he is suddenly addressed in his own mother tongue. He weeps for joy, and embraces the speaker as his brother.[78]

The power of ideas, therefore, and in this context, the power of a proper historical knowledge, is the power to awaken the mind in response to those acts that are its own being. Through ideas, the mind finds itself and discovers in its own proper activity the continuity of past and present. Here is freedom from the bewildered alienation of those who accumulate the facts of history according to an arbitrary order, and of those who, troubled by the failure of such as Spencer Percival, "judge harshly because [they] expect irrationally."[79] The image of the exile ends with a social reconciliation. For Coleridge, the rhetoric of history and of his own historiography, because it annunciates ideas, because it awakens the mind's germinal power to the consubstantialities of past and present, contributes to the creation of social and political community.

The Scriptures: History as Prophecy

The Statesman's Manual attempts the rather daunting task of proving the Old Testament as the statesman's best source of "political skill and foresight." Coleridge's hermeneutical argument begins by breaking down

---

[76]Ibid., 23.

[77]Ibid., 24. See also, *Logic*, 42, "that alone is truly knowledge in relation to the individual acquirer which reappears as power, and the improvement of the faculties, the only sure measure and criterion of the attainments."

[78]Coleridge, *Statesman's Manual*, 24.

[79]Coleridge, *Lay Sermons*, 123n.*.

one account of scriptural authority. He then reformulates that authority so that the truth the Scriptures reveal appears as the unifying center of both historical experience and scientific understanding. The discussion thus follows the same "imaginative" movement we have observed before.

The British, Coleridge points out, are blessed. They enjoy the religious and intellectual freedoms of a Protestant nation in which "the Gospel lies open in the marketplace, and on every window seat." The addressees of *The Statesman's Manual* are members of "the higher classes" of this privileged society. For them, reflection upon Scripture is a political as well as a spiritual duty. Given such readers and such a social context, it would be invidious to argue for the unique authority of Scripture since even nominal believers must

> recur with preeminent interest to events and revolutions, the records of which are as much distinguished from all other history by their especial claims to divine authority, as the facts themselves were from all other facts by especial manifestation of divine interference.[80]

Accepting this authority, together with the "especial manifestation of divine interference" to which the Bible bears witness, Coleridge now attacks a prominent understanding of it. He does this in a short discussion and reinterpretation of the miraculous.

Coleridge castigates those who hold up the miraculous as the distinctive content of the Bible and as that upon which its authority ultimately rests. Not the sole, but certainly the most influential, representative of this apologetic tradition was William Paley (1743–1805), who is on numerous occasions the object of Coleridge's criticism.[81] Paley's *A View of the Evidences of Christianity* (1794) provides a set of interlock-

---

[80]Coleridge, *Statesman's Manual*, 9.

[81]For a few examples, see Coleridge, *The Friend*, pt. 1, 108, 313-14, 425; *Statesman's Manual*, 110; *Lay Sermons*, 186n.*- 7; *Church and Society*, 68; *Philosophical Lectures*, 461; *Table Talk*, pt. 2, 162; *Collected Letters* 2:720, 1189; *Collected Letters* 3:153, 216; *Collected Letters* 4:538; *Collected Letters* 5:138, 464-45; *Collected Letters* 6:691; Samuel Taylor Coleridge, *Anima Poetae: From the Unpublished Notebooks of Samuel Taylor Coleridge*, ed. Ernest Hartley Coleridge (Boston and New York: Houghton, Mifflin and Company, 1895) 131; *Notebooks* 3:3294, 3303, 3560; *Notebooks* 4:4838, 4903, 5200. On Paley's considerable influence in the early nineteenth century, see below, 203-204.

ing arguments to demonstrate the credibility of the apostolic witness to the miracles that attended the beginnings of Christianity. The most important of these arguments founds that credibility on the apostles' willingness to suffer for their story. If the testimony to the miraculous can be defended, Paley concludes, then "the religion must be true."[82] The truth of Christianity, then, hinges upon the miracles: apologetics finds its duty in their defense. "Miraculous evidence lay at the bottom of the argument. In the *primary* question, miraculous pretensions . . . were what they had to rely on."[83] What was the case then remains so today.

Despite the apologists' intentions, this view undermines the Bible's practical authority. Contemporary relevance stumbles over the distance the apologetic sets up between biblical events, replete with miraculous intervention, and the drearily nonmiraculous nineteenth cenury. Miracles are then used as an excuse for not heeding the Bible, for not adopting apostolic faithfulness and endurance. The evidence for biblical authority becomes a means of weakening it, at least at the motivational level: "[W]e neglect to apply truths in expectation of wonders, or under pretext of the cessation of the latter."[84] The problem, then, is set up as a distinctively Coleridgean case of fragmentation. The Bible is isolated and the biblical past severed from the present.

This alienation originates in a disorder of the mental powers. Far from encouraging a fixated attention upon physical events, the purpose of "signs and wonders" was to free the mind from the domination of the senses by presenting it with occurrences that could not be explained in terms of ordinary physical causation:

> In the infancy of the world, signs and wonders were requisite in order to startle and break down that superstition, idolatrous in itself and the source of all other idolatry, which tempts the natural man to seek the true cause and origin of public calamities in outward circumstances, persons, and incidents.[85]

---

[82]William Paley, *A View of the Evidences of Christianity, in Three Parts; and the Horae Paulinae*, ed. Richard Potts (Cambridge UK: Cambridge University Press, 1849) 125.
[83]Ibid., 43.
[84]Coleridge, *Statesman's Manual*, 10.
[85]Ibid., 9.

A miracle is a provocation to look beyond the sensual. Therefore, miracles do not occur in isolation but together with the truths for which they clear the way:

> [W]ith each miracle worked there was a truth revealed, which thenceforward was to act as its substitute: And if we think the Bible less applicable to us on account of the miracles, we degrade ourselves into mere slaves of the sense and fancy, which are indeed the appointed medium between earth and heaven, but for that very cause stand in a desirable relation to spiritual truth then only, when, as a mere and passive medium, they yield a free passage to its light.[86]

Attention to the revealed truth, provoked by the miracle, involves a reordering of the mental powers so as to bring them into their proper subordination. Thus, sense and fancy present the objects in which the understanding, made "intuitive" by the operation of the imagination, discerns the ideal.[87] And, as we've seen, it is in the ideal that human beings find motivation immediate and proper to their nature as moral agents. "The soul of man awakes" at the "annunciation of *principles*, of *ideas*." Any interpretation that makes the miracles themselves the decisive element in the biblical narrative subverts the dynamism of the mind—and of true religion. The proper vocation of mind, and the goal of religion's formative power, is to disclose and represent the union of universal and particular, the ideal and the factual.[88]

His brief consideration of miracles is significant because it clears the way for Coleridge's interpretation of the Bible as the symbolic expression of "great PRINCIPLES" and "sublime IDEAS."[89] It also provides, in the operation of miracle, a symbol for the pedagogical task itself. Coleridge has to overcome, "to startle and break down," the same idolatry that is assaulted by the miracle, namely, the attribution of

---

[86] Ibid., 9-10.
[87] Ibid., 69.
[88] Cf., ibid., 62.
[89] Ibid., 24.

national events to particular persons, particular measures, to the errors of one man, to the intrigues of another, to any possible spark of a particular occasion, rather than to the true proximate cause.[90]

Coleridge's principal interest here is in directing the reader to recognize ideas as the true powers of history. This is the purpose of his use of Scripture, his formulation of biblical authority, and the interpretation of "prophecy" and "symbol." The same interest funds also the critique of contemporary commercialism and Coleridge's discussions of historical events such as the French Revolution or social institutions such as the tax system. In all these cases, education, like miracle, intends a spiritual reformation which brings "the whole soul of man into activity, with the subordination of its faculties to each other, according to their relative worth and dignity."[91]

If, Coleridge argues, "we neglect to apply truths in expectation of wonders, or under pretext of the cessation of the latter" the appropriate response is Jesus' rebuke of the Pharisees, promising them only the "sign of Jonah," "a threatening call to repentance."[92] The introduction of Jesus at this point allows Coleridge to allude briefly to the Christological foundation—in Christ as Word—of his account of biblical authority. Also, by way of Christology, he achieves rhetorically that identity of past and present within which biblical authority is to be understood. Coleridge quotes the conclusion of the Matthean text in which Jonah is mentioned:

> Equally applicable and prophetic will the following verses be. "The men of Nineveh shall rise in judgement with this generation and condemn it, because they repented at the preaching of Jonas, and, behold, a greater than Jonas is here. The queen of the South shall rise up in the judgement with this generation and shall condemn it: for she came from the uttermost parts of the earth to hear the wisdom of Solomon, and behold a greater than Solomon is here."[93]

---

[90]Ibid., 13.

[91]Coleridge, *Biographia Literaria*, pt. 2, 15-16.

[92]Coleridge, *Statesman's Manual*, 10. The biblical reference is to Matthew 12:39.

[93]Coleridge, *Statesman's Manual*, 10-11. Matthew 12:41-42.

He then reminds the reader of the Christological doctrine of Christ's abiding presence with the church. This becomes the hinge for a reinterpretation of the Matthean passage:

> [F]or have we not divine assurance that Christ is with his church, even to the end of the world? And what could the queen of the South or the men of Nineveh have beheld, that could enter into competition with the events of our own times, in importance, in splendour, or even in strangeness and significancy.[94]

In the gospel the object of comparison with the things beheld by the men of Nineveh and the queen of the South is Jesus himself. Coleridge, however, shifts the reference to contemporary events and, by way of the doctrine of Christ's presence, identifies his own time as the context to which Christ now speaks as the Word of God. Contemporary events are thereby incorporated within the orbit of biblical ones, becoming as it were biblical in status and urgency. This interpretation dissolves the distance between past and present just as surely as a wrongheaded understanding of miracles establishes it. Past and present appear as consubstantial, the bond between them being Christ, the abiding Word, "Idea Idearum" and truth of God.[95] Coleridge has realized for the reader his historiography and his hermeneutics in a Christological miniature.

Arguing that biblical authority requires securing the evidence for miracles, establishes, in Coleridge's view, an opposition between past and present, biblical and nonbiblical history. In criticizing that apologetic, Coleridge dissolves the settled confrontation between the ancient and the contemporary. In interpreting the Matthean text, he now shifts the emphasis away from the Scriptures' "especial claims to divine authority" to that which unifies biblical and contemporary history. He maintains this emphasis as, before formulating his own view of the Bible's uniqueness, he begins to introduce his historical method, arguing against reading history "for the facts instead of . . . for the sake of the general principles." It is within this context, out of the argument for principles as the true motor force of history, that Coleridge returns to the peculiar advantages and distinctions, among all the works of human wisdom, of

---

[94]Coleridge, *Statesman's Manual*, 11.
[95]For "Idea Idearum," see below, 225-28, and *Literary Remains* 4:227.

"the Hebrew legislator, and the other inspired poets, prophets, historians, and moralists of the Jewish church." There are two factors involved in the Bible's privileged position. Biblical laws and commandments are, Coleridge claims, manifestly the expression of reason's being-in-act: universal principles and ideas. Also, however, in understanding these principles, faith and emotion come into one focus with reason. This is because they demand the "determination of the reason to have faith in itself."[96] Such faith is faith in God, the natural issue of which is joy and gratitude. So, at "the annunciation of *principles*," the one exiled in the limitations of understanding, fancy, and sense, "weeps for joy."

Coleridge concludes this argument with a summary of the relationship between the voice of reason in the Scriptures and in the sciences:

> [H]ence it follows that what is *expressed* in the inspired writings, is *implied* in all absolute science. The latter whispers what the former utter as with the voice of a trumpet. AS SURE AS GOD LIVETH, is the pledge and assurance of every positive truth, that is asserted by the reason.[97]

The structure of the distinction here parallels that of the primary and secondary imagination. In both cases a subordination is affirmed and then qualified as a subordination in terms of degree and mode but not of kind. In both cases, too, the weight placed on the first element is an explicitly theological one: here, the inspired Scriptures *express*, as oppose to imply, and "utter with the voice of a trumpet."[98] The truth expressed in the Bible and that which is the object of science is the same—the divine truth of reason—but in the former, that divine voice is present with a fullness and a clarity not possessed by the latter. This parallelism suggests that Scripture derives from and represents the activity of the primary imagination as it perceives the world in its divine depth, realizing "that intuition of things which arises when we possess ourselves, as one with the whole."[99] The development of Coleridge's argument supports this interpretation. At the climax of his hermeneutical proposal, he describes the

---

[96]*Literary Remains* 4:18.
[97]*Literary Remains* 4:20-21.
[98]Interestingly, in both passages the subordination and connection of the second element is expressed by an auditory image: the secondary imagination "echoes" the primary, the sciences "whisper" what the Scripture proclaims.
[99]Coleridge, *The Friend*, pt. 1, 520.

scriptural histories as "the living *educts* of the Imagination." This is expounded in terms that relate it to the *Biographia* definition of primary imagination. In the Bible, the divine truth and its representative symbols move in complete harmony, what is given by the senses is infused and ordered by reason. Such is the essence of the primary imagination as "the living Power and prime Agent of all human Perception," and such is also the perfection of the imago Dei. Coleridge seizes on the chariot of Ezekiel as the Scripture's self-symbol:

> *Whithersoever the Spirit was to go, the wheels went, and thither was their spirit to go: for the spirit of the living creature was in the wheels also.* The truths and the symbols that represent them move in conjunction and form the living chariot that bears up (for *us*) the throne of the Divine Humanity.[100]

The reference to the "Divine Humanity"—divinity-in-humanity, humanity-in-divinity—is both Christological and anthropological. It, too, recalls the description of the primary imagination: this relationship between God and humanity issues in the "repetition in the finite mind of the eternal act of creation in the infinite I AM."

In this parallel, then, between the definition of imagination in the *Biographia* and the doctrine of biblical authority proposed in *The Statesman's Manual*, the inspired Scriptures correspond to the primary imagination as its "living educts." What then of science, and, in particular, of historical science? The distinction between the Bible and "absolute science," that is, a science not bounded by the limits of the understanding but one that proceeds by way of ideas, suggests that Scripture is related to science as primary to secondary imagination. This is consistent with what was argued in the previous chapter. In an "epoch of division and separation"[101] an adequate historical method would read the 'facts of history' in such a way as to overcome the captivity of the understanding. The model and measure of this method is the scriptural "system of symbols": a system in which the truth is set forth with a "directness and visibility" in which "the ANCIENT OF DAYS, his words and his works" may be contemplated "with a feeling as fresh as if they were

---

[100]Coleridge, *Statesman's Manual*, 29. The reference is to Ezekiel 1:20.
[101]Coleridge, *The Friend*, pt. 1, 444.

now springing forth at his fiat."¹⁰² The implicit goal of historical science, as a labor of the secondary imagination, is the restoration of that original vision in which "we possess ourselves, as one with the whole."¹⁰³

We may now add a further instance of a distinction parallel to that of primary and secondary imagination. In his discussion of religion in appendix C of *The Statesman's Manual,* Coleridge presents both the identity and the subordination of religion and art. Religion is

> the consideration of the Particular and Individual (in which respect it takes up and identifies with itself the excellence of the *Understanding*) but of the Individual, as it exists and has its being in the Universal (in which respect it is one with the pure *Reason*).¹⁰⁴

It is precisely this "union of the Universal and the Individual" that is also the "common essence" of the arts. Religion, nevertheless, is primary as the "parent and fosterer of the Fine Arts." In works of art, the secondary imagination "dissolves, diffuses, dissipates, in order to re-create" that perception of multeity in unity that is the essence and gift of religion. This last parallel yields the following arrangement.

primary imagination	inspired Scripture	religion
secondary imagination	science, including history	arts

---

¹⁰²Coleridge, *Statesman's Manual,* 17.

¹⁰³See also, on natural science, Coleridge, *Biographia Literaria,* pt. 1, 256: "In the appearances of magnetism all trace of matter is lost, and of the phaenomena of gravitation, which not a few among the most illustrious Newtonians have declared no otherwise comprehensible than as an immediate spiritual influence, there remains nothing but its law, the execution of which on a vast scale is the mechanism of the heavenly motions. The theory of natural philosophy would then be completed, when all nature was demonstrated to be identical in essence with that which in its highest known power exists in man as intelligence and self-consciousness; when the heavens and the earth shall declare not only the power of their maker, but the glory and the presence of their God, even as he appeared to the great prophet during the vision of the mount in the skirts of his divinity."

¹⁰⁴Coleridge, *Statesman's Manual,* 62.

The interpretation here has a number of implications. First, it shows the importance of the primary/secondary imagination distinction within the argument of *The Statesman's Manual*, and more generally, to Coleridge's ordering of the relations between art and religion, science and Scripture. Second, it demonstrates further the inadequacy of any attempt to interpret his theory of the imagination within a context, a literary-critical one for instance, that abstracts it from the theological—and soteriological—framework. Finally, these parallels show Coleridge's respect for some of the classical subordinations of Christian theology—the aesthetic to the religious, the philosophical to the scriptural—at the same time as he reinterprets them to expose the underlying unity.

Returning to the distinction between the Bible and "absolute science," it is necessary, in order to gain a more precise understanding, to look first at the important category of prophecy. In order to expound the Bible's authoritative claim over present political reflection, Coleridge adopts "prophecy" as his principle interpretative category.[105] Other biblical genres, including the histories that Coleridge wishes to compare with contemporary ones, are subsumed under the prophetic. Prophecy becomes, as it were, the "form of forms" in Coleridge's reading of Scripture. The "highest formula" in Scripture, the one that governs its reading, at least for the politically aware or the would-be historian, is the prophetic declarative "AS SURE AS GOD LIVES."[106] Scripture has an "imperative and oracular form" and Coleridge compares it with the Sibylline oracles praised by Heraclitus.[107] This privileging of the prophetic is reflected also

---

[105] It is not surprising, in view of his interpretation of prophecy in terms of "eternal truths," that the category of "law" is closely linked "prophecy." Thus Coleridge refers to "the *imperative* and oracular form of the inspired Scripture" (Coleridge, *Statesman's Manual*, 18; my emphasis) and notes, in terms that elsewhere describe the inspiration of the prophet, that "*The first man, on whom the Light of an* IDEA *dawned, did in that same moment receive the spirit and the credentials of a Lawgiver*" (ibid., 42). In *The Statesman's Manual*, however, "prophecy" receives the main stress because of the link between prophecy and a "personal" God and because of the "predictive" associations of the prophetic and the sermon's concern with the bond that unites biblical and contemporary history.

[106] Coleridge, *Statesman's Manual*, 21, cf. 19.

[107] Ibid., 18 and 26.

in his citations: of some sixty-seven references to Old Testament passages, forty-five are taken from prophetic books or refer to prophetic activity. A further four are drawn from Ecclesiastes, a text Coleridge considered prophetic as well as sapiential.[108]

Early on in *The Statesman's Manual*, Coleridge indicates the meaning he will be attributing to "prophecy." "And should you," he asks his readers, "not feel a deeper interest in predictions which are permanent prophecies, because they are the same time eternal truths?"[109] As with his reinterpretation of miracles, the meaning he gives to "prophecy" contains an implicit theological critique. Now he addresses a theology for which prophecy is reduced to the status of evidence for the supernatural origins of the Bible or of the events the Bible describes. Again, Paley's *Evidences* furnishes a clear example. The truth of prophecy, Paley argues, consists in its correct description of "future transactions and changes in the world."[110] Shown to be truthful in this fashion, biblical prophecy functions as further evidence for the miraculous character of Christianity. According to Coleridge, however, prophecies are not exhausted by a particular historical fulfillment.[111] Rather, prophecy discloses, in the form of symbols, the nature of things as embodiments, fulfillments, distortions, or departures from "living ideas" that "containeth an endless power of semination."[112] Prophecy thus reveals the creative agency of God who "as

---

[108]Coleridge, *A Lay Sermon*, 145-47.

[109]Ibid., 7.

[110]For an example of this, see William Paley, *A View of the Evidences of Christianity*, 147-55.

[111]Coleridge does not ignore, let alone dismiss, the importance of "particular fulfillment," especially in the case of the Christological prophecies. Concerning the gospels, he explains: "The first three Gospels showed the history, that is, the fulfillment of the prophecies in the facts; St John declared explicitly the doctrine *oracularly* and without argument, because, being pure reason, it could only be proved by itself." Coleridge, *Table Talk*, pt. 1, 513. And for an image of prophecy that combines both "particular fulfillment" and the development of the "seminal idea" in history: "What a beautiful sermon or essay might be written on the growth of Prophecy!—from the germ, no bigger than a man's hand in Genesis till the column of cloud gathers size and height and substance, and assumes the shape of a man—girt like the smoke in the Arabian Nights' story, which comes up and at last takes a genii's shape." Ibid., 451.

[112]Coleridge, *Statesman's Manual*, 23-24.

the One and Absolute, at Once the Ground and the Cause, . . . alone containeth in himself the ground of his own nature, and therein of *all* natures."[113]

By way of example, Coleridge applies Isaiah 47:7-13 to the events of the French Revolution. According to Coleridge, what the prophet reveals, in his denunciation of Babylon as a proud and foolish queen is "the true philosophy" of the revolution. "Fulfillment" is achieved as the necessary outworking of a spiritual and ideological corruption, symbolized by the prophet and realized in France. Prophecy is the disclosure of necessities. The prophet reveals that which proceeds from the created nature of things. This being so, the language of prophecy can be applied also to the discovery of the laws of nature. Biblical prophecy is concerned with the formative powers of the moral world, deals with all that follows from the nature of human beings as moral agents, related to God and made in the image of God. The "eternal truths" of prophecy, therefore, precisely because they are eternal truths, empower prediction and political guidance. They do illuminate the future. Unlike the truths of the understanding, prophecies do not say " 'This *is*, or *ought* to be, so' [but] 'It *must* be so.' "[114] Prophecy is the truth of reason in oracular and symbolic form.

To interpret prophecy in this way allows it to have a far wider scope than when it is restricted to Christological and ecclesiological anticipations or employed as evidence for the inspiration of the Bible. The Bible is a "system of symbols," it embodies the formative powers of history, represents their ultimate unity, and names what is truly significant in the changes of time. Prophecy ceases to refer to a history within history and becomes a means for recognizing all history as prophetic.[115] Therefore, Coleridge praises Edmund Burke as simultaneously "scientific" statesman and prophet:

---

[113]Ibid., 32.

[114]Coleridge, *Table Talk*, pt. 1, 513. On the truths of the understanding, see also Coleridge, *Statesman's Manual*, 12, "Alas! like lights in the stern of a vessel they illuminated the path only that had been past over!"

[115]Natural history is to be read in this way also. Hence, nature is "prophetic up the whole vast pyramid of organic being." Coleridge, *Church and Society*, 176; see also "On Poesy or Art," in Coleridge, *Biographia Literaria with his Aesthetical Essays* 2:259-60.

Edmund Burke possessed and had sedulously sharpened that eye, which sees all things, actions, and events, in relation to the *laws* that determine their existence and circumscribe their possibility. He referred habitually to *principles*. He was a *scientific* statesman; and therefore a *seer*.[116]

In *A Lay Sermon*, Coleridge again advises his readers of their urgent need for a "principled" reading of history, for "a philosophy of history, that is, . . . history read in the spirit of prophecy." He adds:

[W]hat insight might not our statesmen acquire from the study of the Bible merely as history, if only they had been previously accustomed to study history in the same spirit, as that in which good men read the Bible![117]

Reading "in the spirit of prophecy" is not, accordingly, a means of isolating particular events but of exposing the significance, in the light of ideas, of all events, including those of especial Christological or ecclesiological significance.

By employing the category of prophecy in the way he does, Coleridge is able, via the identification of prophecy with the "truths of reason," to unite biblical and contemporary history. This also, however, opens up the strategy of interpreting those truths of reason in terms of prophecy. Prophecy places the truths of reason on the lips of the biblical God:

Herein, the Bible differs from all the books of Greek philosophy, and in a twofold manner. It doth not affirm a Divine Nature only, but a God; and not a God only, but the living God.[118]

As the announcement of "eternal truths," prophecy contributes more than biblical dressing and suggestions of guidance to an otherwise

---

[116]Coleridge, *Biographia Literaria*, pt. 1, 191. Coleridge's assessment of Burke in this respect was not always so positive: "I cannot repel the conviction from my mind [that] . . . to a certain inconsistency in his fundamental principles, we are to attribute the small number of converts made by BURKE during his lifetime. . . . The inconsistency to which I allude . . . is the want of congruity in the principles appealed to in different parts of the same Work, it is an apparent versatility of the principle with the occasion." Coleridge, *The Friend*, pt. 1, 188.

[117]Coleridge, *A Lay Sermon*, 123-24n.*.

[118]Coleridge, *Statesman's Manual*, 32-33.

bewildering future. The category of prophecy places those eternal truths beyond any association with pantheism or deism. They are the voice of the "living and personal" God of a nation in which "the Gospel lies open in the marketplace."[119]

If all history is to be read in the "spirit of prophecy," what becomes of the distinction between the truths of reason as *"expressed"* in the Scriptures and as *"implied* in all absolute science"? What is the nature of the Bible's authority when set beside the wisdom of those philosophical guides of whom Coleridge approves or beside the projected histories of those who have succeeded in making "history scientific"?[120] In the first place, the contrast is one of relative plainness, a contrast of *clarity*: in the Scriptures the "particular rules and prescripts flow directly and visibly from universal principles, as from a fountain." The Bible declares its truths in tones of explicit divine authority, speaking "as with the voice of a trumpet." Looking more closely, however, the particular character of Scripture is bound up with a certain completeness or fullness of presentation:

> Its contents present to us the stream of time continuous as Life and a symbol of Eternity, inasmuch as the Past and the Future are virtually contained in the Present.[121]

This image picks up and reverses that of the earlier Heraclitan account of the world rendered us by the understanding, in which the present never achieves being but "at the same moment it takes shape and dissolves, it comes and goes."[122] Scripture is thoroughly symbolic, its "Facts and Persons" being both "Portraits and Ideals." The biblical narratives, laws, songs, and prophecies are an abiding present, a fullness of gathered past and anticipated future. The Bible thus realizes the unified, divine-human vision of the primary imagination.

This suggestion of the Bible's completeness, that it contains all things needful for its faithful readers, appears also in the claims Coleridge makes about its adequacy as a source of political wisdom. Instancing

---

[119]Ibid., 6.
[120]Coleridge, *Table Talk*, pt. 2, 148.
[121]Coleridge, *Statesman's Manual*, 29.
[122]Coleridge, *Statesman's Manual*, 20.

"Thucydides, Tacitus, Machiavel, Bacon, or Harrington," as his examples, he asserts:

> These are red-letter names even in the almanacks of worldly wisdom: and yet I dare challenge all the critical benches of worldly wisdom to point out any one important truth, any one efficient, practical direction or warning, which did not preexist, and for the most part in a sounder, more intelligible, and more comprehensive form in the Bible.[123]

Coleridge links the worth of the Bible in regard to the temporal, political sphere with its provision of the necessities of eternal, spiritual concern. He tells his readers that just as they have found the "means as well as the pledges of our *eternal welfare*" in the "promises and information" of evangelists and apostles, yet

> not the less on this account will you have looked back with a proportionate interest on the *temporal* destinies of man and nations, sorted up for our instruction in the archives of the Old Testament: not the less will you delight to retrace the paths by which Providence has led the kingdoms of *this* world through the valley of mortal life—Paths, engraved with the footmarks of captains sent forth from the God of Armies! Nations in whose guidance or chastisement the arm of Omnipotence itself was made bare.[124]

In his use of Scripture as prophecy, these claims are reinforced. Attacking the demagogues in *A Lay Sermon*, Coleridge reads part of Isaiah 32 as a prophetic anticipation of their behavior and their rhetoric. The conformity he finds between Isaiah's portrayal of wayward Israel and the likes of William Cobbett and Major John Cartwright justifies the triumphant conclusion that

> this is no new thing under the Sun! We have heard it with our own ears, and it was declared to our fathers, and in the old time before them.[125]

In the light of a prophetic reading of the Scriptures, history contains no radical surprises. Coleridge's interpretation of prophecy achieves a

---

[123]Ibid., 17.
[124]Ibid., 8.
[125]Coleridge, *A Lay Sermon*, 150.

fundamental rhetorical purpose: it establishes the possibility of tracing history as a system of identifications, its promise placing the readers in the midst of continuities.

In the Scriptures, the imagination brings to birth a "system of symbols, harmonious in themselves." As symbolic, the biblical histories have both *specificity*, recounting a particular stretch of time with its particular institutions, practices, and expressions of belief, and *ideality*, the parts being disclosive of, and consubstantial with, the wholeness of eternal purpose. As a *system* of symbols, they confront the reader with a totality, containing all that is essential for historical interpretation, "teaching the science of the future in its perpetual elements."[126] Reflecting the traditional notion of the sufficiency of Scripture, this is the "conservative" pole of Coleridge's account of the Bible. Biblical history relates to nonbiblical in a way analogous to the relation of theme and variations in music.[127] The theme governs what is to follow, although it doesn't narrowly determine it—the range of variations possible for an interesting theme being very great. However transformed the latter becomes, though, the intelligibility of the variation still depends upon its identification with the theme. The biblical history is a comprehensive "statement of themes", in it are prefigured, in symbolic form, the moral ideas, the development of which constitutes the providential history of human beings. The

---

[126] Coleridge, *Statesman's Manual*, 8.

[127] Coleridge employs a similar analogy in *The Friend*: "[C]ertainly there is one excellence in good music, to which, without mysticism, we may find or make an analogy in the records of History. I allude to that sense of *recognition*, which accompanies our sense of novelty in the most original passages of a great composer. If we listen to a symphony of CIMAROSA [Dominico, 1749–1801], the present strain still seems not only to recall, but almost to *renew*, some past movement, another and yet the same! Each present movement bringing back, as it were, and embodying the spirit of some melody that had gone before, anticipates and seems trying to overtake something that is to come: and the musician has reached the summit of his art, when having thus modified the Present by the Past, he at the same time weds the Past *in* the Present to some prepared and correspodence Future. The auditor's thoughts and feelings move under the same influence: retrospection blends with anticipation, and Hope and Memory (a female Janus) become one power with a double aspect." Coleridge, *The Friend*, pt. 1, 129-30.

Scriptures provide the comprehensive symbolic statement of these moral ideas, promulgating them with the authority of God and explicitly relating them at all points to their divine origin.[128] The Bible, therefore, is the measure, and its ideal referents the guide, of all "scientific history."

The account of the Bible as a comprehensive "system of symbols" represents, as I have argued, the conservative pole of Coleridge's hermeneutics. The concept of the symbol itself, however, imparts to his interpretative theory a notable flexibility. Upon this, depends his representation of history both as a unity, the formative powers of which are already known, and as a reality that changes, develops, and progresses under the impact of the "seminal power" of ideas. In *The Statesman's Manual*, Coleridge argues that ideas are the true motor forces of history. History is only intelligible insofar as its 'facts' are related to ideas. In the perception of a "fact of history" as a symbol, the individual becomes "translucent" to, and representative of, the universal.[129] Not all such facts can or

---

[128]See also Coleridge, *Statesman's Manual*, 31-32: "[In the Bible] the elements of necessity and free will are reconciled in the higher power of an omnipresent Providence, that predestinates the whole in the moral freedom of the integral parts. Of this the Bible never suffers us to lose sight. The root is never detached from the ground. It is God everywhere: and all creatures conform to his decrees, the righteous by performance of the law, the disobedient by the sufferance of the penalty."

[129]Clearly, there is nothing about this understanding of the symbolic that restricts it to the scriptural histories. As was argued earlier, within Coleridge's history of philosophy, Pythagoras is accorded a symbolic function. Also, Coleridge describes Christianity itself not only as effect and means but as "symbol" of a spiritual revolution (Coleridge, *Collected Letters* 4:569). The shift from the ancient to the modern world "with respect to philosophy, poetry, politics, religion, and all that is interesting to mankind" finds its "symbol" in the building of the Christian church opposite the palace of Theodoric the Goth, "the one temple that was permitted to overlook the monarch's palace, the sole remaining object of reverence and willing submission." Coleridge, *Philosophical Lectures*, 256; and Samuel Taylor Coleridge, *Lectures 1808-1819: On Literature*, ed. Reginald A. Foakes, vol. 5, pt. 2 of *The Collected Works of Samuel Taylor Coleridge* (Princton NJ: Princeton Unversity Press, 1987) 74. And, the medieval cathedral "with all its many Chapels, its pillared stem and leaf-work Roof, as if some sacred grove of Hertha, the mysterious Deity of their pagan ancestors, had been awed into stone at the approach of the true divinity, and thus dignified by

Imagination and the Wisdom of History

will be recognized in this way: the symbolic status of the events narrated in the biblical histories, for instance, derives from their disclosing the universal and ideal in the particular and sensible with an especial force and adequacy. All symbols have their ideal referent which may be of greater or lesser scope. The monarch, for example, is the symbol of the "Unity and Majesty of the *Nation*,"[130] while the events of the history of Christ symbolize the whole history of God's redemptive work.[131] However, at the same time, all symbols reveal the ontological relations between particular and universal that constitute the intelligibility of all historical events. While not all the "facts of history" are recognized as symbols, all derive their significance from that relation of the ideal and the sensible that is disclosed in the symbol. Unless one is to be satisfied with mere 'chronicle," all "facts" must be set in relation to ideas, either as their symbols, or as arising from them, whether as embodiments or corruptions.[132]

The relation of particular and universal that is revealed in the symbol involves a tension. "An IDEA," Coleridge writes, at this point following

---

permanence into a symbol of the everlasting Gospel." Although the occurrence of the term "symbol" with reference to nonbiblical events and institutions is fairly rare, M. H. Abrams's claim that Coleridge applies the term "symbol" only "to objects in the Book of Scripture and the Book of Nature" is inaccurate. See M. H. Abrams, *The Correspondent Breeze*, New York: Norton, 1984, 221.

[130]Coleridge, *Collected Letters* 6:863.

[131]Coleridge, *Literary Remains* 3:109: "[T]he crucifixion, resurrection, and ascension of Christ himself in the flesh, were the epiphanies, the sacramental acts and *phaenomena* of the *Deus patiens*, the visible words of the invisible Word that was in the beginning, symbols in time and historic fact of the redemptive functions, passions, and procedures of the Lamb crucified from the foundation of the world."

[132]See also Coleridge, *Table Talk*, pt. 1, 256: "A Religion—that is, a true Religion—must consist of Ideas and of Facts both; not of Ideas alone without Facts,—for then it would be mere Philosophy; nor of Facts alone without Ideas of which those Facts should be the symbols, or out of which they should arise, or upon which they should be grounded—for then it would be mere History." What is here termed "mere history" is elsewhere described as chronicle as in Coleridge's adaptation of Shakespeare for the motto at the beginning of *On the Constitution of the Church and State*: "There is a mystery in the soul of state / Which hath an operation more divine / Than our mere chroniclers dare meddle with."

Schelling, "in the *highest* sense of the word, cannot be conveyed but by a *symbol*; and, except in geometry, all symbols of necessity involve an apparent contradiction."[133] "*Educts* of the Imagination," symbols incorporate "the Reason in Images of the Sense." When a sensible reality is perceived as a symbol, the powers of the mind are unified: the imagination opens up the understanding to the active presence of reason, rendering it "intuitive, and a living power," capable of discerning and representing ideas. As was noted above, the ideas of reason can be known only "in and through the understanding"[134] as the imagination makes them subject to the conditions of conscious recognition, language, and expression. Ideas, however, transcend the representational conditions of the understanding, the faculty that "conceives the sensible." Ideas "partaketh of infinity" and are, therefore, "untranslatable into any Image, unrepresentable by any particular Object."[135] Only that which is

> an educt of the Imagination actuated by the pure Reason, to which there neither is or can be an adequate correspondent in the world of the senses—this and this alone is = AN IDEA.[136]

Furthermore, ideas transcend their representatives, not only spatially, as it were, but temporally: they contain "an endless power of semination."[137] The productive power of the ideal is to continually exceed its embodiments. In referring to ideas, symbols always anticipate further symbolizations.

It is the concept of the symbol and the relationship that symbols disclose between the ideal and its embodiments that makes Coleridge a "dynamic" conservative. His philosophy of history and his biblical hermeneutics commit him to the view that the future is governed by those formative powers that have ordered, and have been revealed in, the past. The Bible "contains a Science of *Realities*: and therefore each of its Elements is at the same time a living GERM, in which the Present

---

[133]Coleridge, *Biographia Literaria*, pt. 1, 156; see also 156n.2.

[134]Coleridge, *The Friend*, pt. 1, 156.

[135]Coleridge, *Statesman's Manual*, 23 and *The Notebooks of Samuel Taylor Coleridge*, ed. Kathleen Coburn and Anthony John Harding (Princeton NJ: Princeton University Press, 2002) 6742.

[136]Coleridge, *Statesman's Manual*, 113-14.

[137]Coleridge, *Statesman's Manual*, 24.

involves the Future."[138] This philosophy of history is also, however, hostile to the suggestion that responsibility to the formative power of ideas can be achieved through the mere preservation of the forms—institutions, ideologies, social practices—of the past. Ideas exceed their embodiments: that is the energy of history.[139] Responsibility to the idea of a political constitution, therefore, cannot be identified with the preservation of a particular set of institutions. Given the continual changes of human affairs, the many forces that bear down upon them and modify the realization of moral ideas, institutional configurations have to change.[140] Thus, Coleridge appeals to the contemporary communications revolution, to "roads, canals, machinery, the press, the periodical and daily press, the might of public opinion" as a new social form through which may be achieved that balance of permanent and progressive forces, central to the idea of a constitution.[141]

The scriptural histories are *"educts* of the Imagination." As a whole, Coleridge's doctrine of Scripture is dependent upon his theory of the imagination. The continuity of past and present, of biblical and contemporary history, is recognized in the symbol, the union of universal and particular. This unity is perceived and "educed" by an intellectual dynamism that discerns and embodies the truths of reason in the forms of the understanding and the senses. The recognition and the making of symbols is, in other words, a work of the imagination. It is the theory of the imagination, too, that provides, in the distinction between primary and secondary imagination, the framework for preserving claims for the uniqueness of Scripture at the same time as presenting the dynamic of Scripture's production and the nature of its truth as the dynamic and truth of all the sciences, including the historical. The treatments of prophecy and of miracle are both directed against accounts that result in the alienation of biblical and nonbiblical history. The theory of the imagination describes the form of thought required to transcend such alienation.

---

[138]Ibid., 49.

[139]As we shall see below, however, Coleridge is much more cautious about political change than might be anticipated from this aspect of the doctrine of ideas.

[140]Coleridge, *Church and Society*, 37.

[141]Ibid., 28-29; for the term "communications revolution," see John Miller, *Ideology and Enlightenment*, 287.

Thus, the imagination is the power by which the mind, in a complex act of identification, overcomes the fixities that result from divisions made absolute. It is the activity of distinguishing without dividing and connecting without the loss of distinction.

It is now possible to summarize the rhetorical role of the doctrine of Scripture outlined above. Coleridge diagnoses his culture as suffering the consequences of philosophical and religious commitments that absolutize the analytic powers of the understanding. The consequence is a truncated rationality. Such a rationality tends toward reductionism in its accounts of nature and of human life. This is the culture of "individuals . . . who mistake outlines for substance, and distinct images for clear conceptions; with whom therefore not to be a *thing* is the same as *not to be at all*."[142]

Coleridge traces this cultural disorder into the field of historical explanation and political decision. Here, he finds both reductionist explanations of human motivation and the desperate devices of those whose blindness to ideas leaves them only with factual fragments and effects taken for causes.

> I have known men, who with significant nods and the pitying contempt of smiles, have denied all influence to the corruptions of moral and political philosophy, and with much solemnity have proceeded to solve the riddle of the French Revolution by ANECDOTES![143]

The "histories of highest note in the present age" betray a general cultural failure to achieve a unifying perspective from which rational decisions for the future can be made on the basis of past experience: "Alas! like lights in the stern of a vessel they illuminated the path only that had been past over!"[144] In claims to enlightenment and to the novelty of the present, Coleridge discerns the measure of his culture's alienation from the past.

This analysis of philosophical failure gains its urgency against a background of social change, change that Coleridge addresses most directly in *A Lay Sermon*, and *The Friend*. These texts engage specific social changes and crises from the economic slump that followed the Napoleonic Wars and extraparliamentary political demands for electoral reform to developments in communications and long-term changes in land

---

[142] Coleridge, *Statesman's Manual*, 93.
[143] Coleridge, *Statesman's Manual*, 14.
[144] Coleridge, *Statesman's Manual*, 12.

use. In the context of these developments, Coleridge's philosophy of history and his biblical hermeneutics hold out to his readers the promise that the formative powers of the past are also those of the present. He proposes a perspective from which change can be interpreted and the threat of the new to evade hermeneutic and therefore political control can be overcome. In Coleridge's own words, he seeks to provide "that steadfast frame of hope which affords the only certain shelter from the throng of self-realizing alarms".[145]

What Coleridge saw clearly was the role of the historical imagination in locating human identity across the disruptions of time. He recognized that cultural and political proclamations of radical novelty and unprecedented development may cast human beings into the temporal homelessness of a lost present. There is, however, a high price to be paid for the strong historiographical agenda that Coleridge proposes. Robert Preyer, in an essay on Coleridge's historical method, has commended him for opening "the way for the expression of an intense delight in the variousness and detail of the past."[146] It is true, as we have seen, that Coleridge's account of the relation of symbol and idea has a diversifying as well as a unifying pole. The doctrine that ideas are not fully expressible grounds the necessity of changing historical realizations. At the same time, because ideas are the true powers of history, we lose our historical selves whenever history is told as "just one damn thing after another."

It is doubtful, however, whether the task of identification, as Coleridge embraces it, can allow the recognition of historical difference in other than a highly circumscribed way. Preyer attempts to locate Coleridge within the development of modern critical historiography by pointing out that historians explain "an event by saying it was part of a movement going on at the time." They are "for purposes of narration . . . forced to act as though there are intrinsic connections between events and the purposes which they tend to realize."[147] This is, though, to appeal to a much weaker version of the historiographical claim that we find in Coleridge. Preyer ignores the metaphysical and political agenda with

---

[145]Coleridge, *Statesman's Manual*, 9.

[146]Robert O. Preyer, "Coleridge's Historical Thought," in *Coleridge: A Collection of Critical Essays*, ed. Kathleen Coburn (Englewood Cliffs NJ: Prentice-Hall, 1967) 156.

[147]Ibid., 155.

which Coleridge operates. For Coleridge, a history according to ideas promises identification, the comprehension of all history as a unity. It argues that the test of historical representation is *recognition*: disclosure of the consubstantiality of past and present. It promises, furthermore, that historical science will ground a political and cultural critique of claims to novelty and to the unprecedented. Difference is a problem to be resolved into continuity or else revealed as an "efflorescence" upon the surface of events. Coleridge was not a historian but his most extensive exercise in the field indicates the difficulties of his method. So, in the *Philosophical Lectures*, the cost of identification, of the unifying idea of philosophy, was the anachronistic conformation of ancient philosophy to contemporary controversial needs.

In relation to Coleridge's reading of the Hebrew prophets, and to his demand that we read history "in the spirit of prophecy," the interests of identification shape the prophetic in the direction of wisdom. To bring out an irony in Schlegel's dictum, Coleridge's prophets do not announce the new, either then or now: the historian is, indeed, a prophet "looking backwards." The sapientializing of prophecy means that prophecy can evoke a joyful recognition that "there is nothing new under the sun." It is telling that Coleridge, in a passing reference, casts on the author of Ecclesiastes, the mantle of the prophet.[148]

---

[148]Coleridge, *A Lay Sermon*, 145-47.

4

Social Conflict and the Balance of the Mind

We should note the double meaning of the German word aufheben. *We mean by it (1) to clear away, or annul . . . (2) to keep, or preserve. . . . We should recognize in [this] the speculative spirit of our language rising above the mere "either–or" of understanding.*

—Hegel, *Logic*

Imagination and the Extremes of Revolution

Coleridge begins *The Statesman's Manual* inviting his readers to identify themselves as members of a nation privileged to be described in biblical terms, as one that has inherited the promise of Israel:

> It is enough for us to know that the land in which we abide, has like another Goshen *been severed from the plague*, and that we have light in *our* dwellings. The Gospel lies open in the marketplace, and on every window seat, so that (*virtually*, at least) the deaf may hear the words of the Book! It is preached at every turning, so that the blind may see them. (Isai xxix.18)[1]

Britain takes form, therefore, as a "biblical" nation, and one faced with temptations also cast in scriptural mold. Contemporary political prognosticators are the misleaders of Israel redivivus, the *"wizards, that peep and mutter."* In *A Lay Sermon*, the latter theme is given a more detailed development with reference to the "demagogues" who demand political reform. There, too, the "existing distresses" are characterized as the approach of the biblical "day of trouble and of treading down and of

---

[1] Coleridge, *Statesman's Manual*, 6; the biblical references, other than the one Coleridge supplies, are to Exod. 8:22, 10:23, and Isa. 35:8.

perplexity."² All this derives from the hermeneutics discussed in the last chapter. The imagination, understood as the activity of discerning and producing symbols, makes possible this identification. The form of things present and to come are discovered in the events and relations of biblical history.

The opening of *The Statesman's Manual* places the religious condition of this biblicized Britain in contrast to those nations in which the Roman Church holds sway. Two spiritual worlds are opposed, the "enlightened and protestant land" set over against the "Church of Superstition" in which "imposture" is "organized into a comprehensive and self-consistent whole."³ The chief characteristic of the "system of delusion" is that "inversion" has become the "order of nature." In Coleridge's view, what the Roman church denies to its members is the right to exercise the mind upon the interpretation of Scripture. In the absence of intellectual activity, the senses are engaged "by vivid imagery and ritual pantomime," while the will is paralyzed by "obscure fears." Coleridge's account of Catholicism, therefore, repeats the topsy-turvy philosophical anthropology he finds in the doctrine of associationism. Activity distinctive of human beings as *human*—the activity of mind energized by reason and imagination—is disengaged, the will neutralized, and the senses made dominant. Under such conditions, interpretation loses its moorings in reason and "a jealous priesthood" finds "the applicability of the Bible to all the wants and occasions of men as a wax-like pliability to all their fancies and prepossessions."

The "allegoric vision" that introduces *A Lay Sermon* also takes up the theme of superstition. At the opening of the vision, the narrator sees himself entering the "Temple of Superstition" which stands "almost in the very entrance" of the "VALLEY OF LIFE."⁴ The details recall the descrip-

---

²Coleridge, *A Lay Sermon*, 130; Isa. 22:5.

³Coleridge, *Statesman's Manual*, 6.

⁴This allegory exists in two earlier versions, the first beginning the 1795 series of *Six Lectures on Revealed Religion and Its Corruptions* and the second constituting an article in *The Courier* for 31 August 1811. Coleridge, *On Politics and Religion*, 89-93; Samuel Taylor Coleridge, *Essays on His Times*, ed. David V. Erdman, vol. 3, pt. 2 of *The Collected Works of Samuel Taylor Coleridge* (Princeton NJ: Princeton University Press, 1978) 262-70. In the former, written in Coleridge's Unitarian days, the temple of superstition is to be understood as

tion of Catholicism in the first lay sermon. The senses are assaulted by the confusions of strange ceremony and bewildering imagery. The visionary's will is overtaken by the setting and he is "constrained" to enter the temple where he submits unresisting to ritual presentation before the idol of Superstition. Finally, before the appeal, "Read and believe: these are MYSTERIES," his intellect is disarmed. "All," the hapless narrator concludes, "was uneasy and obscure feeling." He leaves the idol "soul withered, and wondering, and dissatisfied."[5]

In the course of this allegory, Coleridge demonstrates again the applicability of the favorite saying, "extremes meet." The narrator encircles the entire valley and eventually finds himself in "a vast cavern." This turns out to be the back door into the temple of superstition which is where he started. At the mouth of the cavern stand the figures of "SENSUALITY" and "BLASPHEMY." Inside, "an old dim-eyed man" mumbles over the torso of a statue upon which is carved the name "NATURE." He applies his microscope to it and wavers between triumph and "vehement railing against a Being, who yet, he assured us, had no existence."[6] The common recourse to mystery identifies this personification of "enlightenment" atheism as the meeting extreme and, therefore, reverse side of superstition. The old man speaks "most strange mysteries," appealing to an infinity of causes and effects that stretch like blind men each clutching the skirts of the one before. There is no leader, he asserts, "for although one blind man could not move without stumbling, yet infinite blindness supplied the want of sight." Once again, reason is eclipsed in what is depicted as an act of self-imposed captivity. Atheism's object is a truncated one: the finite "torso" of nature "which had neither basis, nor feet, nor head." Like superstition, atheism involves a willful, self-blinding concentration on the finite and sensible, the transcendent and infinite prevented from coming into intellectual view. Atheism, too, is a "system of delusion" in which inversion is the order of the day.[7]

---

the Church of England. The expanded version in *The Courier*, however, explicitly associates it with Roman Catholicism: "On the base of the statue I read engraved the words: to Dominic, holy and merciful, the preventer and the avenger of soul murder." Coleridge, *Essays*, pt. 2, 263; see also 269-70.

[5]Coleridge, *A Lay Sermon*, 135.
[6]Ibid., 137.
[7]The allegory closes by rendering explicit the connection between the

Before entering the cavern of atheism, the visionary meets with the other main figure in the allegory, that of "RELIGION." Significantly placed midway between the extremes of superstition and atheism, religion makes her appearance as the "virtuous mean" whose modesty of appearance is equidistant from the fanaticism of superstitious and atheistic extremes. In her, passion and reason are appropriately conjoined. "Deep reflection, animated by ardent feelings" is displayed in her countenance. These, together with the certainty of religious hope, are unified by a power, the description of which at once suggests both the Holy Spirit and the imagination: "Deep reflection . . . ardent feelings . . . hope . . . and a something more than all these, which I understood not; but which yet seemed to blend all these into a divine unity of expression."[8]

Religion is given the power to liberate and protect those suffering under the delusions of superstition and atheism. She heals the blindness that afflicts the extremes between which Coleridge has placed her. Leading the visionary "to an eminence in the midst of the valley," she opens the view from which he may perceive the order of things in their interrelationships and in their place in the whole. As in *The Statesman's Manual*, religion is "the consideration . . . of the Individual, as it exists and has its being in the Universal." An "optic glass" supplies a glimpse of that larger sphere within which all things exist:

> [The glass] enabled us to see far beyond the limits of the Valley of Life: though our eye even thus assisted permitted us only to behold a light and a glory, but what we could not descry, save only that it *was*, and that it was most glorious.[9]

Whereas atheism is myopic, restricted to a "microscopic" view, religion's gaze gathers all things and extends beyond their boundaries to a vision of the transcendent. The "optic glass," furthermore, "assisted without contracting our natural vision." Coleridge thus images the unity and continuity of the knowledge of science and of religion. Religion does

---

extremes of superstition and atheism: "[A]s [the old man] started forward in a rage, I caught a glance of him from behind; and lo! I beheld a monster bi-form and Janus-headed, in the hinder face and shape of which I instantly recognized the dread countenance of SUPERSTITION—and in the terror I awoke."

[8]Coleridge, *A Lay Sermon*, 135-36.
[9]Ibid., 136.

indeed approach "that which is too deep for words": there is indeed mystery. This, though, is not an arbitrarily declared mystery, stifling reason and forbidding its employment, it is rather that mystery to which, in its unfettered exercise, reason itself leads.

The strange opposition and likeness that exists between superstition and rationalistic atheism is found also in *The Statesman's Manual*, not in the form of an allegory but as a structural principle of the argument. The opening description of the "Church of Superstition" finds its atheistic counterpart in Coleridge's references to the French Revolution. He presents the Revolution, which is a theme of both the sermon and its appendixes, as the dark and threatening end of political, religious, and philosophical tendencies that also exist as corrupting forces in Britain. The specific discussion of religion in appendix C has its coordinates, like the "allegoric vision," in the threefold relation of superstition, religion, and atheism. Here, however, atheism is construed differently from its personification in the allegory. In the latter, the dim-eyed man has no other counters to work with than the categories of the understanding to which he gives an absolute status in the description of an endless train of finite causes and effects. In appendix C, though, atheism is the end not of a captivity to the understanding but of an inappropriate resistance to it in the name of "abstract reason." Superstition, by contrast, then appears in terms of the dominance of the understanding: the "excellence of the *Understanding*" as "the consideration of the Particular and Individual" falls into Superstition when the universal is forgotten.[10]

The threefold organization of superstition, religion, and atheism has here, therefore, been articulated upon the epistemological distinction, so vital for Coleridge, between the reason and the understanding. As a result, true religion, according to appendix C, achieves the balance between reason's two "primary factors": "ONENESS and ALLNESS," unity and infinity.[11] Put differently, on one side of true religion stands atheism for

---

[10]Coleridge, *Statesman's Manual*, 62; see also 60-61.

[11]Coleridge, *Statesman's Manual*, 60. Also, "we can neither rest in an infinite that is not at the same time a whole, nor in a whole that is not infinite." The philosophical theology here has roots in Neoplatonism. Plotinus's attempts to say something about the "unspeakable" One that "no name names" may be read as a struggle to articulate that which is infinite but, at the same time, not simply indeterminate or indefinite. See J. M. Rist, *Plotinus: the Road to Reality*

which specificity and unity is lost in the rational striving for the infinite. The other side finds superstition as the loss of infinity in the interests of specificity, driven by the understanding. These threatening extremes are explicit in, on the one hand, Jacobinism's bloody sacrifice of each "to the shadowy idol of ALL" and, on the other, of that superstitious concentration upon the particular that,

> becoming more and more earthly and servile, as more and more estranged from the one in all, goes wandering at length with its pack of amulets, bead rolls, periapts, fetishes, and like pedlary [i.e., peddlery], on pilgrimages to Loretto, Mecca, or the temple of Jaggernaut.[12]

The social expressions of this fundamental imbalance demonstrate the grim meeting of these extremes. Both the revolutionary Terror and the murderous mobile idol of Jaggernaut[13] forsake the human person as particular yet uniquely related to the divine, as an end that must not be reduced to a mere means.[14]

As the above account will have suggested, Coleridge's treatment of the French Revolution is complex. For a start, his presentation has a

---

(Cambridge UK: Cambridge University Press, 1967) 21-37.

[12]Coleridge, *Statesman's Manual*, 63-64. [Editor's note. "Jaggernaut," the "mobile idol" of Sri Krishna (worshiped as an incarnation of Vishnu), usually appears as "Juggernaut" or, after the Hindi, as "Jagannath" or "Jagganath" (lit. "lord of the world").]

[13]Coleridge, *The Friend*, pt. 1, 98-99: "And can He be pleased with the blood of thousands poured out under the wheels of Jaggernaut?" [Editor's note. Annually at the Puri festival "Jagganath" appeared in procession on an enormous cart drawn by hundreds of pilgrims, some of whom were said to court martyrdom and a blessed eternity in Paradise by throwing themselves under the wheels of the god's chariot as it progressed. "Juggernaut" thus came to mean something very big and virtually unstoppable.]

[14]Coleridge adopts the Kantian distinction between "persons" and "things." Thus, Coleridge, *A Lay Sermon*, 218n.*: "On the distinction between . . . Things and Persons, all law human and divine is grounded. It consists in this: that the former may be *used*, as *mere* means; but the latter *dare* not be employed as the means to an end without directly or indirectly sharing in that end." Cf. Immanuel Kant, *Foundations of the Metaphysics of Morals*, trans. Lewis W. Beck (New York: Macmillan, 1969) 52-53. For a comparison of the ethical thought of Kant and Coleridge, see Orsini, *Coleridge and German Idealism*, 149-59.

twofold character. On the one hand, while the revolution as a whole appears as the extreme, atheistic counterpart of the "Church of Superstition," its origins and progress are analyzed as *internally differentiated* into the two extremes represented by superstition and atheism. In this analysis, the latter opposition is configured, as it is in appendix C, according to the distinction of reason and the understanding.

Unlike Burke, of course, Coleridge was writing well on the other side of the Terror and of the Napoleonic empire. His analytical focus, therefore, is upon "Jacobinism"; for him, a synonym of revolutionary ideology, ambitions, and practices. Jacobin politics, he argues, is the consequence of abstract reason run wild. Each is "sacrificed to the shadowy idol of ALL" in the name of a reason that will have no truck with, and brook no resistance from, the particularities of social and individual history. This is reason taken without reference to the truth that reason has to be known, expressed, and applied under the forms of the understanding. It is reason exalted in a refusal to recognize that the political sphere is fashioned out of the inequalities of human beings and nations and formed by the many contingencies of their history. As such, though a social order may more or less adequately approach them, it can never perfectly realize ideas, the principles of reason.

In *The Friend*, Coleridge's critique of politics within the limits of reason, of reason as the sole ground of political decision, is an expanded version of an argument only sketched in the first lay sermon.[15] Coleridge points out that as soon as a constitution is sought on the basis of such a politics, its framers inevitably and quickly leave the narrow path of reason.[16] Reason alone, for instance, cannot legitimate the institution of property except on the most abstract level and certainly not the "inequalities inseparable from the actual existence of Property"[17] It is not on the basis of "pure reason," either, that the franchise is denied to

---

[15]Coleridge, *The Friend*, pt. 1, 186-202. Coleridge defines the political principle at issue as "nothing is to be deemed rightful in civil society, or to be tolerated as such but what is capable of being demonstrated out of the original laws of the pure Reason. . . . Whatever is not *every where* necessary, is *no where* right." He finds the social application of this principle developed most fully in Rousseau's *The Social Contract*.

[16]Coleridge, *The Friend*, pt. 1, 195-96.

[17]Ibid., 200.

children but because of the particular degree of their power to exercise reason: "the faculty is not yet adequately developed." In decisions of this kind, human beings take into consideration matters not of necessity but of contingency and degree:

> Nothing, which subsists wholly in degrees, the changes of which do not obey any necessary law, can be subjects of pure science, or determinable by pure Reason. For these things we must rely on our *Understandings*, enlightened by past experience and immediate observation, and determining our choice by comparisons of expediency.[18]

The attempt to ground political order upon reason alone is self-deceiving and callously blind to the existing and not wholly rational conditions in which human beings live. Riding roughshod over the special, historically forged, circumstances of a particular society, it takes form as Jacobin Terror or Napoleonic despotism.[19]

According to Coleridge, then, the reason that is celebrated by the revolutionaries is reason in a hubristic and illusory flight from its proper relationship with the activity of the understanding. At the religious level, this has its natural issue in the "shadowy idol of ALL": the atheism that sacrifices unity, the "ONE," in seeking to grasp the infinite.[20] Coleridge finds the typifying expression of revolutionary atheism in the "atheists who deified the human reason in the person of a harlot during the earlier part of the French Revolution." In a marginal note to a copy of *The*

---

[18]Ibid., 196.

[19]Coleridge, *The Friend*, pt. 1, 197: "REASON is the sole sovereign, the only rightful legislator: but Reason to act on man must be impersonated. The Providence which had so marvelously raised and supported [Napoleon], had marked HIM out for the representative of Reason, and had armed him with irresistible force, in order to realize its laws. In Him therefore MIGHT becomes RIGHT, and HIS cause and that of destiny (or as the wretch now chuses to word it, exchanging blind nonsense for staring blasphemy) HIS cause and the cause of God are one and the same. Excellent postulate for a choleric and self-willed tyrant! What avails the impoverishment of a few thousand merchants and manufacturers? What even the general wretchedness of millions of perishable men, for a short generation? Should these stand in the way of the chosen conqueror . . . or prevent "a constitution of things, which erected on *intellectual* and *perfect* foundations, groweth not old?"

[20]Coleridge, *Statesman's Manual*, 60-61.

Statesman's Manual given to John Anster, Coleridge specified the incident he had in mind:

> They dressed up a Courtezan in the costume of Minerva, and under the name of the Goddess, Reason, and actually performed worship of her![21]

The participation of the "harlot" is, for Coleridge, especially appropriate and ironic. A harlot also appears as a climactic expression of the corruptions of superstition:

> Superstition . . . becoming more and more earthly and servile . . . arm and arm with sensuality on one side and self-torture on the other [is] followed by a motley group of friars, pardoners, faquirs, gamesters, flagellants, mountebanks, and harlots.[22]

Asocial and rootless, the harlot is the exchangeable person, the human being as mere means: the fate of the human under both revolution and superstition. Extremes meet. Neither revolutionary reason nor superstition as "captivity" to the understanding can provide a social order for the well-being of creatures who are made to be faithful to the particular in the spirit of the universal.

This characterization of the French Revolution in terms of abstract reason run wild is not the only, nor indeed, the most emphasized, element of Coleridge's analysis. Taking into consideration *The Friend* as well as *The Statesman's Manual*, the stress falls on the revolution as the sorry and extreme manifestation of an age that has *forgotten* reason as the "organ of the Supersensuous."[23] In its place, this epoch has
absolutized the understanding, conforming all things to the limits of the finite and sensible, exchanging ultimate for proximate ends. In the lay sermon, Coleridge identifies the thought of the French "Encyclopaedists"

---

[21]Coleridge, *Statesman's Manual*, 62n.1. There were a number of such incidents, although the "goddess" could be "Liberty" as easily as "Reason," and moral uprightness was generally an essential criteria in her selection. There was, however, a festival at Amiens in 1793 that corresponded more closely to Coleridge's description. See John McManners, *The French Revolution and the Church* (London: SPCK, 1969) 98-105.

[22]Coleridge, *Statesman's Manual*, 64-65.

[23]Coleridge, *The Friend*, pt. 1, 156.

as the culmination of a process in which the understanding was alienated and assumed a hubristic self-sufficiency:

> Under the influence of Voltaire, D'Alembert, Diderot, say generally of the so-called Encyclopaedists, and alas!—of their crowned proselytes and disciples, Frederick, Joseph, and Catherine, ... the Human Understanding, and this too in its narrowest form, was tempted to throw off all show of reverence to the spiritual and even to the moral powers and impulses of the soul; and usurping the name of reason openly joined the banners of Antichrist, at once the pander and the prostitute of sensuality, and whether in the cabinet, laboratory, the dissecting room, or the brothel, alike busy in the schemes of vice and irreligion.[24]

Coleridge traces the trajectory by which the "works of the understanding" came to be valorized as the acme of science and intellect to the burgeoning of the commercial spirit and the successes of the "experimental philosophy." Characteristically, this argument is followed by a quick balancing qualification: both of these cultural developments are "good and beneficial" in themselves. For Coleridge, they only imperil a culture when they become its primary determinants and the sole measure of value and verity. A society that absolutizes the understanding is a society that loses its grip upon *ultimate* aims and goods, for the understanding knows only of means and "proximate ends." The cultural consequence is rampant sensuality and selfishness, its quintessence is a "French nature of rapacity, levity, ferocity, and presumption."[25] The latter is stated with not a little of what, in *The Friend*, Coleridge termed his "anti-Gallic spleen."

Coleridge associates the Enlightenment, as "the epoch of the understanding," with the claim to intellectual maturity and autonomy.[26] In an interesting reversal of the theme of enlightenment and coming of age,

---

[24]Coleridge, *Statesman's Manual*, 75.

[25]Coleridge, *Statesman's Manual*, 77.

[26]Coleridge, *Statesman's Manual*, 11: "I well remember, that when the examples of former Jacobins, as Julius Caesar, Cromwell, and the like, were adduced in France and England at the commencement of the French Consulate, it was ridiculed as pedantry and a pedant's ignorance to fear a repetition of usurpation and military despotism at the close of the ENLIGHTENED EIGHTEENTH CENTURY."

Coleridge identifies the understanding as rightly and properly a "ward," and not of an authority that may be outgrown or legitimately overcome. The due governor of the understanding is "faith and reason":

> [The understanding] was placed as a ward of honour in the courts of faith and reason; but it chose to dwell alone, and became a harlot by the wayside.[27]

Once again, the figure of the harlot returns. Here she is an image of the self-sufficient understanding, linked with the woman of Isaiah who says in her pride, "None is my overseer!"[28] The harlot is thus a figure of radical alienation who has, by her own hubris, lost the larger context upon which well-being depends. "By the wayside," she is without home or divine order. The harlot, an image informed both by Hebrew prophecy and Christian apocalyptic,[29] is used by Coleridge to represent that dynamic, whether epistemological, religious, or social, in which necessary distinction becomes the basis of division: the dynamic in which one element, in a destructive "overbalance," fragments from the whole.

It has become apparent that the structure of Coleridge's analysis of the French Revolution derives from the distinction between the reason and the understanding. In the lay sermons and in *The Friend*, the revolution and its Napoleonic aftermath serve as the contemporary exposition of the Fall, the new history of the old Adam. The history of the first temptation and its consequences is strung "from Adam, in whom we all fell, to the atheists who deified the human reason in the person of a harlot during the earlier period of the French Revolution."[30] In Coleridge's account, therefore, the revolution manifests both poles of the

---

[27]Coleridge, *Statesman's Manual*, 74. And compare, of course, Kant's metaphor of enlightenment as achieving intellectual maturity, freedom from guardians: "What Is Enlightenment?" in *Kant's Political Writings*, ed. H. Reiss (Cambridge UK: Cambridge University Press, 1970).

[28]Coleridge, *Statesman's Manual*, 75. Coleridge had already applied his version of the text from Isaiah 47 to "the true philosophy of the French Revolution" in the course of the sermon itself.

[29]The Book of Revelation represents the city of Rome as Babylon, "great whore": "Babylon the great, mother of whores and of all the obscenity upon earth" (Rev. 17:5).

[30]Coleridge, *Statesman's Manual*, 61-62.

epistemological tussle with which the "natural Man" is afflicted, being always in "a state either of resistance or of captivity to the understanding and the fancy."[31]

In the earlier discussion of the *Biographia*'s definition of imagination, we argued that the distinction between primary and secondary imagination invokes the Christian doctrines of the Fall and of Adam's "original perfection." We may also find this connection between the Fall and the loss of the imagination in the first lay sermon's account of the French Revolution. It is, after all, the imagination that unites the reason and the understanding, bringing them into their proper order and subordination. Coleridge's description of revolutionary France is a description of a cultural and political situation in which the mediating and reconciling power of the imagination is eclipsed: in which the "predominant system of speculative philosophy" has no place for it.[32] The central moral distinction between person and object appears only in the light of the imagination: the power to discern the universal within the individual. This distinction is violated by both the revolution's rationalism and its sensuality. In the Scriptures, as educts of the imagination, "every agent appears and acts as a self-subsisting individual: each has a life of its own, and yet all are one life."[33] By contrast, the distinctive revolutionary

---

[31]Ibid., 60-61. See the first three essays of *The Friend* in which Jacobinism is described as the "lawless alternation" (Coleridge, *The Friend*, pt. 1, 165) between a "Hobbesian" politics—that "denies all truth and distinct meaning to the words, RIGHT and DUTY, and affirming that the human mind consists of nothing, but manifold modifications of passive sensation, considers men as the highest sort of animals" (ibid.)—and the Rousseauesque misapplication of universal principles.

[32]Cf. Coleridge, *Collected Letters* 4:757: "Taste and Character, the whole tone of Manners and Feeling, and above all the Religious (at least the Theological) and the Political tendencies of the public mind, have ever borne . . . a close correspondence, . . . [a] distinct and evident an Analogy to the predominant system of speculative Philosophy."

[33]Coleridge, *Statesman's Manual*, 31. Coleridge also describes the Shakespearean imagination in these terms: "[I]n all his various characters, we still feel ourselves communing with the same human nature, which is everywhere present as the vegetable sap in the branches, sprays, leaves, buds, blossoms, and fruits, their shapes, tastes, and odours. . . . we may define the excellence of *their* method as consisting in that just proportion, that union and interpenetration of the

product is a constitution built on the assumption that all states are machines and their members merely parts. Coleridge describes the essential character of Jacobinism as a grotesque parody of the imagination's unifying power, made up

> in part of despotism and in part of abstract reason misapplied to objects that belong entirely to experience and the understanding. . . . In all places Jacobinism betrays its mixt parentage and nature.[34]

Jacobin politics is a *"monstrum hybridum."*

In appendix C of *The Statesman's Manual*, Coleridge denounces "French wisdom" as under the domination of the understanding. At the climax of this polemic he confronts the "man of understanding" with a series of questions that echo the Creator's address to the biblical Job:

> [C]anst thou command the stone to lie, canst thou bid the flower bloom, where thou hast placed it in thy classification?—Canst thou persuade the living or the inanimate to stand separate even as thou hast separated them? And do not far rather all things spread out before thee in glad confusion and heedless intermixture, even as a lightsome chaos on which the Spirit of God is moving?—Do not all [things] press and swell under one attraction, and live together in promiscuous harmony, each joyous in its own kind, and in the immediate neighborhood of myriad others that in the system of thy understanding are distant as the Poles? If to mint and remember names delight thee, still arrange and classify and pore and pull to pieces, and peep into Death to look for Life, as monkeys put their hands behind a looking glass![35]

The understanding, therefore, analyzes, clarifies, and generalizes, but it cannot grasp or represent the living connectedness of things. It is blind to the complex of relations within which, and only within which, the particular has life. The understanding alone, therefore, is not capable of discerning the totality present in the individual, the whole anticipated and present in each of the parts, which elsewhere Coleridge terms the "ALL in EACH."[36] This discernment, too, belongs to the imagination. The sug-

---

universal and the particular, which must ever pervade all works of decided genius and true science." Coleridge, *The Friend*, pt. 1, 457.
[34]Coleridge, *Statesman's Manual*, 63-64.
[35]Coleridge, *Statesman's Manual*, 77.
[36]Ibid., 50.

gestion here of Job's quizzing by God implies the connection between the imagination, the absent power of comprehension, and the Spirit of God as the divine orderer of creation. The imagination is the Spirit's repetition in the finite mind, following in its discernments and echoing in its productions, the creative knowing of God.

When the categories of the understanding are made absolute, the consequences in politics, as in science and religion, are reductionist. Thus, within the social sphere, that which is *relatively*, not absolutely, good becomes decisive for the whole: "*Worth* was degraded into a lazy synonym of *value*; and value was exclusively attached to the interests of the senses."[37] Coleridge sees the result in terms of a drastic restriction of the notion of the common good in which "well-being" is equated with "wealth." Given that the understanding is the capacity for identifying only "proximate ends," it recognizes "no duties which it could not reduce into debtor and creditor accounts on the ledgers of self-love." "Utility" in personal and social ethics becomes the measure of the good. The process is represented by *The Friend* in the form of "a brief history of the last hundred years":

> Imagination excluded from poesy; and fancy paramount in physics; the eclipse of the ideal by the mere shadow of the sensible—subfiction for supposition. *Plebs pro Senato Populoque*—the wealth of nations for the well-being of nations, and of man![38]

This "brief history," one that Coleridge reworked for the treatise on the church and state, traces his familiar cultural woes—alienation from the past; reductionism in politics; revolution; the "plebification" of learning—to their origin in "Mechanical Philosophy hailed as a . . . revolution in philosophy."[39]

In *A Lay Sermon*, as in *The Friend*, William Paley comes in for attack as the English representative of an ethics that remains within the instrumental categories of the understanding. As Coleridge reads him, Paley dissolves the distinction between prudence and virtue by interpreting the latter as prudential action in relation to our eternal rather than our merely temporal happiness:

---

[37] Ibid., 74.
[38] Coleridge, *The Friend*, 447.
[39] Coleridge, *The Friend*, pt. 1, 447; cf. Coleridge, *Church and State*, 64-65.

> Thus, the great principle of the Gospel, that we are bound to love our neighbours as ourselves and God above all, must, if translated into a consistency with this theory of enlightened Self-love, run thus: On the ground of our fear of torment and our expectation of pleasure from an infinitely powerful Being, we are under a prudential obligation of acting towards our neighbours *as if* we loved them equally with ourselves; but ultimately and in very truth to love ourselves only.[40]

This critique is, of course, generated out of the radical distinction between reason and understanding. From this perspective, reason is eclipsed in Paley's ethics, morality being only another application of the instrumental activity of the understanding. As a consequence, our "neighbors" and virtue itself are reduced to "proximate ends."[41]

Coleridge's argument sets the reductionism of revolutionary philosophy—a reductionism he sees repeated in the very different context of Paley's ethics—in opposition to that distinctive object and product of the imagination: the symbol. Both are explicated in terms of the relationship between whole and part. In the case of the symbol, the whole is represented in the part that is "translucent" to it without loss of its individuality: a symbol "is an actual and essential part of that, the whole of which it represents." Reductionism, on the other hand, *equates* the whole with the part. Furthermore, whereas the latter is a static relation, the part simply substituted for the whole, the symbol is dynamic, provoking a movement between part and whole, between particular and universal. The imagination is an essentially antireductionist concept. By

---

[40]Coleridge, *A Lay Sermon*, 186-87n.*.

[41]Paley's *The Principles of Moral and Political Philosophy* was enormously influential during the last quarter of the eighteenth century, particularly at Cambridge where after 1786 it was required for examinations. Of Paley's major works, however, it was also the object of the most vigorous assault, especially following the publication in 1789 of Thomas Gisborne's *Principles of Moral Philosophy*. Coleridge's criticism of Paley both responds to the extent of the latter's influence and also shares common themes with that of Evangelicals like Gisborne. The Evangelicals, too, condemned Paley's doctrine of expediency and accused him of reducing morality to selfish calculation. They also made the link between the ethics and the practice of commerce. Nineteenth-century criticism of Paley is discussed in D. L. LeMahieu, *The Mind of William Paley: A Philosopher and His Age* (Lincoln NE: University of Nebraska Press, 1976) 153-83.

it, Coleridge locates the uniqueness of the human mind, that which distinguishes it from the animal, in its capacity to unify and connect. The imagination, proceeding in an activity directly opposite to reductionism, relates each to each "in promiscuous harmony." Thus it reads the elements of the experienced world as embodiments and anticipations of a totality proceeding from the One who "containeth in himself the ground of his own nature, and therein of all natures."[42] The revolutionary world, as Coleridge rhetorically constructs it, is a world from which symbolic perception has been banished, and with it the *imago Dei*, leaving "the *caput mortuum* of human nature evaporated."[43] The revolutionary, dividing in order to rule, does not emancipate but rather excommunicates himself: separates from a sacramental universe.

Earlier, I argued that Coleridge configures the French Revolution as an extreme counterpart to "the Church of Superstition." A closer look at the analysis of the revolution and its philosophical antecedents revealed that Coleridge also portrays the French revolution as itself exposed to the "lawless alternation" of the two extremes. This unstable opposition appears as the ideological and political expression of the tension between the dynamics of reason and understanding: "[T]he natural Man is always in a state either of resistance or of captivity to the understanding and the fancy."[44] The fruitful interpenetration of reason and understanding is only achieved through the mediating and reconciling power of the imagination. Coleridge thus constructs his polemical analysis in terms of opposed and "meeting" extremes. This rhetorical device, as we will see, produces a critique of "extremism" that is also an apologia for religion and, with it, for the concept of the imagination.

In *The Friend*, the fifth essay of the section on "the principles of political knowledge" is entitled "On the Errors of Party Spirit: or Extremes Meet." The second half of this essay sets an antirevolutionary extremism over against the revolutionary one. Coleridge mounts a critique of the conservative and aristocratic response to the revolution in France

---

[42]Coleridge, *Statesman's Manual*, 32.

[43]Coleridge, *Statesman's Manual*, 77. The editor of *Lay Sermons* explains *caput mortuum* as a technical term in alchemy, used for "the residuum left after distillation" (*Lay Sermons*, 77n.2). After French philosophy has had its way with the human, all that is left is the animal residue.

[44]Ibid., 60.

insofar as that response itself became a form of extremism. Originally this critique had appeared in the issue of *The Friend* for 19 October 1809. The "anti-Jacobins" Coleridge has in mind include Pitt and his war ministry between 1793 and Pitt's resignation in 1801.[45] In *The Morning Post*, Coleridge had described the members of this ministry as "base and venal creatures . . . blind and furious bigots."[46] This unflattering summary was provoked by a series of repressive measures against "sedition," beginning in 1792 with a royal proclamation condemning "divers wicked and seditious writings." Thereafter, habeas corpus was suspended in 1794; the range of treasonable offenses was extended in 1795; a system for the registration of printing presses was introduced in 1796; and a program of anticombination legislation was completed in the Combination Acts of 1799 and 1800. More generally, the essay "On the Errors of Party Spirit" addresses the Tory reaction among the aristocracy and gentry throughout the 1790s. Coleridge himself had been among the targets. In 1800, the satirical journal *The Anti-Jacobin*, a prominent organ of Tory polemic, republished Gillray's 1798 cartoon "The New Morality." This depicts Coleridge as an ass, surrounded by other "English Jacobins," reciting his "Dactylics" before a revolutionary altar mounted by the three French crones, Justice, Philanthropy, and Sensibility. A year earlier, George Canning's poem *New Morality* had been republished in *The Beauties of the Anti-Jacobin* with the addition of the scurrilous note referring to Coleridge as having "left his native country, commenced citizen of the world, left his poor children fatherless and his wife destitute. *Ex uno disce* his friends Lamb and Southey!"[47]

---

[45]The Peace of Amiens was signed by the Addington government in the following year.

[46]On 21 October 1802. Coleridge, *Essays*, pt. 1, 368.

[47]Gillray's cartoon is reproduced as a plate in Richard Holmes, *Early Visions*, between pp. 112 and 113. [Editor's note. The caption is quoted by Coleridge in chap. 3 of his *Biographia Literaria*, pt. 1, 67n.*.] Among publications to which Coleridge was more sympathetic, Burke's *Reflections on the Revolution in France* also failed to maintain, in Coleridge's view, a just balance: "The extravagantly false and flattering picture, which Burke gave of the French Nobility and Hierarchy, has always appeared to me the greatest defect of his, in so many respects, invaluable Work." Coleridge, *The Friend*, pt. 1, 215n.*.

Coleridge describes this anti-Jacobin reaction as a grim, conservative mirror of revolutionary extremism. The vigor of a malicious passion overcomes reason and sweeps its subjects into a blind repetition of the worst features of their opponents:

> [T]hese pretended Constitutionalists recurred to the language of insult and to measures of persecution. In order to oppose Jacobinism, they imitated it in its worst features, in personal slander, in illegal violence, and even in the thirst for blood. They justified the corruptions of the state in the same spirit of sophistry, by the same vague arguments of general Reason, and in the same disregard of ancient ordinances and established opinions, with which the state itself had been attacked by the Jacobins.[48]

In the intensity of an extreme reaction, important distinctions, clearly seen in more sober moods, are ignored:

> While they lamented with tragic outcries the injured Monarch and exiled Noble, they displayed the most disgusting insensibility to the privations, sufferings, and manifold oppressions of the Continental population, and a blindness or callousness still more offensive to the crimes and unutterable abominations of their oppressors. Not only was the Bastille justified, but the Spanish Inquisition itself—and this in a pamphlet passionately extolled and industriously circulated by the adherents of the then ministry.[49]

---

[48]Coleridge, *The Friend*, pt. 1, 216.

[49]Ibid., 215. The pamphlet referred to has not been traced, the ministry was that of Pitt. It should be noted that the ideological polemic with which Coleridge is concerned in this essay, while it was important in generating popular support and, as Asa Briggs puts it, in transforming "a war of prudence into a war of honour," did not furnish the reasons for Pitt's controversial decision to challenge the French in 1792. At that point, it was French policy in the Netherlands, opening up the River Scheldt to traffic after its navigation had been guaranteed to the Dutch, that was the ground for protest. Disturbance of the economic balance of power, therefore, not concern for foreign monarchies or nobilities, was the decisive provocation. See Asa Briggs, *The Age of Improvement, 1783–1867* (New York: Longman, 1979) 117-49; Eric J. Hobsbawm, *The Age of Revolution, 1789–1848* (New York: New American Library, 1962) 101-25.

Without the regulation of a sober regard for truth, political opposition turns into an extreme that meets its own enemy as a brother in corruption and folly.

From this critique of extremism, Coleridge derives a rhetorical principle: "The first duty of a wise advocate is to convince his opponents, that he understands their arguments and sympathizes with their just feelings." Indeed, Coleridge has already taken care to provide, at the outset of this essay, an example of such a procedure in his treatment of Major John Cartwright.[50] Cartwright is acknowledged for his moral integrity, for his repudiation of inflationary rhetoric, and for the rationality and austerity of his, albeit misapplied, principles.[51] The critique of anti-Jacobinism that follows this ends with a defense of those youthful enthusiasts whose idealism led them to overestimate the substance of revolutionary hopes.[52] The conservatives are admonished:

> Having first sympathized with the warm benevolence and the enthusiasm for Liberty, which had consecrated it, [the aristocratic party] should have then shewn the young Enthusiasts that Liberty was not the only blessing of Society; that though desirable, even for its own sake, it yet derived its main value as the means of calling forth and securing other advantages and excellencies, the activities of Industry, the security of Life and Property, the peaceful energies of Genius and manifold Talent, the development of the moral Virtues, and the independence and dignity of the nation in its relations to foreign powers: and that neither these nor Liberty itself could subsist in a country so various in its soils, so long inhabited and so fully peopled as Great Britain, without difference of ranks and without laws which recognized and protected the privileges of each.[53]

---

[50] Coleridge's attitude to Cartwright was to change. In *A Lay Sermon* Cartwright is included, and denounced, among the "demagogues" in a reference to "*Patriots*, who aim at enlargement of the rights and liberties of the people by inflaming the populace to acts of madness that necessitate fetters—pretended heralds of freedom and actual pioneers of military despotism." Coleridge, *A Lay Sermon*, 150, see also n. 1.

[51] Coleridge, *The Friend*, pt. 1, 205-209. Coleridge takes Cartwright as representative of a politics grounded solely upon reason.

[52] Of which, of course, Coleridge was one.

[53] Coleridge, *The Friend*, pt. 1, 220.

The essay "On the Errors of Party Spirit" thus begins and ends with an appeal for a rhetoric that, by taking the measure of truth in opposing positions, seeks the balance in which they may both receive due recognition. "Avoid extremes" becomes a rhetorical imperative.[54]

Underlying the description of Jacobin and anti-Jacobin extremes is, once again, the epistemological distinction of reason and understanding. While the distinction is nowhere explicitly mentioned, Coleridge characterizes anti-Jacobinism, as he has Jacobinism, in terms of the unstable oscillation between abstract rationalism and an alienated understanding. Thus,

> if the Jacobins ran wild with the Rights of Man, and the abstract sovereignty of the people, their antagonists flew off as extravagantly from the sober good sense of our forefathers, and idolized as mere an abstraction in the Rights of *Sovereigns*.[55]

At the same time, however, national independence as an expression of the *idea* of freedom is reduced to the inviolability of a nation as the *property* of its ruler.[56] The sovereign, too, ceases to be regarded according

---

[54] Suspicion of extremism was a feature of Coleridge's journalism in the *Morning Post*. In a leader article of 1799, he admonished the "*Friends* of Freedom": "Passion makes men blind; and these men, by the alarm which their intemperate zeal, unfixed principles, and Gallican phraseology excite, form around the Minister a more effective phalanx of defence, than all his bodyguard of Loan jobbers, Contractors, Placemen, and Pensioners, in and out of Parliament. But these are times in which those who love freedom should use all imaginable caution to love it wisely. . . . Good men should now close in their ranks. Too much of extravagant hopes, too much of rash intolerance, have disgraced all parties." Coleridge, *Essays*, pt. 1, 39-40. Coleridge, however, did not always obey his own principle. The attack on the demagogues in *A Lay Sermon* descends to the same kind of rhetorical violence and personal invective that Coleridge rejected in his opponents.

[55] Coleridge, *The Friend*, pt. 1, 216.

[56] Ibid., 217: "I could mention possessions of paramount and indispensable importance to first-rate national interests, the nominal sovereign of which had delivered up all his seaports and strongholds to the French, and maintained a French army in his dominions, and had, therefore, by the law of nations, made his territories French dependencies—which possessions were not to be touched, though the natural inhabitants were eager to place themselves under our

to its idea as a symbol of the nation's "unity and majesty" and is considered as a mere individual property holder: "[I]nstead of the interest of mighty nations, it seemed as if a mere lawsuit were being carried on between John Doe and Richard Roe!"[57]

Anti-Jacobinism, therefore, "playing the same game" as Jacobinism, albeit "with different counters," demonstrates the same "lawless alternation" between false abstraction and false, reductionist concretion.

As Coleridge sets it up, what is at stake in extremism, and in the appeal to avoid extremes, is the balance of the mind. Extremism is configured as a distortion of the relationship between reason and understanding, one that inspires the ungodly passions of hatred and vengefulness. Behind the demand for a rhetorical practice that eschews extremes is the ideal of the proper relation and subordination of reason, understanding, and passion: the "total act of the soul" of which the imagination is the regulator.

Coleridge's theory of the imagination, as the mediator and reconciler of reason and understanding, is a theological theory. This needs stressing. "Imagination" cannot be adequately understood unless it is interpreted within the context of Coleridge's theology. There is more to this, however, than saying that Coleridge treats "imagination" as a religious or theological concept. In *The Statesman's Manual*, in particular, the distinctive characteristics of the imagination as a cognitive power merge with the description of religion as the power of reconciliation between humanity and God.[58] Thus, what Coleridge terms "*essential* Religion" has its being in the "living and generative interpenetration" of reason and understanding.[59] In the context of the theory of mind, that "living interpenetration" takes place through the imagination. Also in this

---

permanent protection—and why?—They were the *property* of the king of—!" Coleridge is referring to Malta where, in 1805, he was acting public secretary to Alexander Ball, the British high commissioner.

[57]Coleridge, *The Friend*, pt. 1, 217; Coleridge, *Collected Letters* 6:863.

[58]"RELIGION, at the birth of which we receive the spirit of adoption, whereby we cry Abba, Father; the Spirit itself bearing witness with our spirit, that we are the children of God." Coleridge, *Statesman's Manual*, 90.

[59]Ibid., 90; cf. 62-64, where religion is said to be the power that reconciles reason's interest in the universal and the understanding's concern with "the Particular and Individual."

passage, which invites comparison with the *Biographia*'s account of the "primary imagination," religion is described as a symbol of the divine Spirit. By being a "total act of the soul," religion "doth finitely express the unity of the infinite Spirit." Furthermore, by virtue of its consubstantiality with that Spirit, religion enables men and women to discern in all created things, the image of "the Almighty Goodness." It is the unifying power that sees all things in God and God in all things. Consequently, under the inspiration of religion, we long for and anticipate the renewal of creation in which the latter is freed from its fragmentation.[60]

While Coleridge's formulation is somewhat unclear at this point, he seems to propose a cosmic fall in which all things express, at their own level, that egocentricity by which human beings fail of their created purpose as living symbols of God:

> [Religion] seeth that same image [of God] throughout the creation; and from the same cause sympathizeth with all creation in its groans to be redeemed. "For we know that the whole creation groaneth and travaileth in earnest expectation" (Romans viii.20-23) of a renewal of its forfeited power, the power, namely, of retiring into that image, which is its substantial form and true life, from the vanity of Self, which then only *is* when *for itself* it hath ceased to be.

Expressed, as it is here, in a soteriological context, the reconciling power, at the human level, is named "*essential* Religion." Expressed, however, in the context of his philosophical psychology or his aesthetics, that same power is imagination. "Religion" and "imagination," and the contexts in which they appear, thus mutually interpret one another.[61] This point becomes especially important when considering *A Lay Sermon*. In that piece, while the imagination receives no significant mention anywhere, it is nevertheless present throughout in the function Coleridge accords to religion.[62]

The rhetorical structure of *The Statesman's Manual* confronts its readers with extremes: with those internal to the French Revolution and

---

[60] Ibid., 90.
[61] Cf. Coleridge, *Philosophical Lectures*, 157: the spirit of Christianity is "THE ALL-COMBINING, ALL-PENETRATING, ALL-TRANSORMING SPIRIT OF UNION AND ENNOBLEMENT."
[62] See below, 167-79.

its philosophy and, set up from the beginning, with those of the "Church of Superstition" and revolutionary irreligion. Between those extremes, Coleridge places that "biblicized" Britain to which he appeals as the sermon opens. This is the land that has "like another Goshen *been severed from the plague*,"[63] the nation in which, as Coleridge subsequently gives thanks, "open infidelity" is still not socially acceptable.[64] By means of this structure, Coleridge projects his readers as living in this cultural condition: between extremes. Placed in this position, one that is precarious as well as privileged, Coleridge's readers are both exhorted to patriotic gratitude and offered a prophetic warning.[65]

This analysis of political events and social developments in terms of extremes is, of course, the product of a rhetorical decision, one on which Coleridge's critique of extremism depends. Coleridge had had a long fascination with the dynamics of extremes. The proverb "extremes meet" was an early favorite and Coleridge discerned in it an organizing principle of large scope. "To collect and explain all the instances and exemplifications" of this saying, he claimed in *The Friend*, "would constitute and exhaust all philosophy."[66] The *Philosophical Lectures* offer some illustration of this claim. Coleridge describes the unifying design for the course as "the striving of a single mind, under very different circumstances indeed, and at different periods of its own growth and development." The execution of that design, though, displays the working of the beloved proverb. The mind's historical pilgrimage, in Coleridge's account, seeks a middle way between the extremes of philosophies that derive all things either from the subjective or from the objective pole.[67]

In the lay sermons, Coleridge's interest in the dynamics of extremes extends its range and depth of relevance by virtue of his interpretation of the Fall. The temptation to which the human person succumbs, Coleridge

---

[63] Coleridge, *Statesman's Manual*, 6.
[64] Coleridge, *Statesman's Manual*, 84.
[65] Coleridge, *Statesman's Manual*, 6: "The glories of our country will form the blazonry of our own impeachment, and the very name of Englishmen, which we are almost all of us too proud of, and scarcely any of us enough thankful for, will be annexed to that of Christians only to light up our shame, and aggravate our condemnation."
[66] Coleridge, *The Friend*, pt. 1, 110.
[67] Coleridge, *Philosophical Lectures*, 116.

argues, is inherent within the dynamics of the mind, specifically in the relationship of the reason and the understanding. The "natural Man," to whose condition Coleridge opposes the reconciling power of religion, is seduced either by the rational drive toward the universal or by the need for the "Particular and Individual" that constitutes "the excellence of the *Understanding*."[68] This interpretation of the Fall in which the dynamics of the mind "overbalance" toward one or other of two extremes, determined either by "reason" or "understanding," provides, as we have seen, the terms for a cautionary account of the French Revolution. Reason and understanding have come, in addition to their epistemological roles, to signify philosophical, political, and social extremes.

By employing his epistemological categories to provide a framework for his political and cultural analysis, Coleridge produces for his political philosophy, an ordering parallel to that of the *Philosophical Lectures*. Contemporary history and social organization is configured after the dynamics of "a single mind." Much of the polemical force of Coleridge's analysis, though, depends upon the way the disrupted dynamics of reason and understanding are developed in terms of opposing extremes, extremes to the full length of which, but for the grace of God, the fallen mind is doomed to rush.[69] The result is that analytical edges are satisfyingly sharpened and Coleridge's polemic gains in rhetorical force. There is also, however, a severe cost in terms of social and historical description. The complexities and differentiations of the history of revolutionary France are all absorbed into the "lawless alternation" of either resistance or captivity to the understanding. Coleridge's analysis reduces the French revolution to the history of "Jacobinism." The logic of this identification scarcely differs from the claim "once a Jacobin, always a Jacobin" that Coleridge condemns in *The Friend*.

---

[68]Coleridge, *Statesman's Manual*, 59-65.

[69]Cf., F. W. J. Schelling, "Philosophical Investigations into the Essence of Human Freedom and Related Matters," in Fichte, Jacobi, and Schelling, *Philosophy of German Idealism*, ed. Ernst Behler, trans. Priscilla Hayden-Roy (New York: Continuum, 1987) 253-54.

Reason and the Critique of Commerce

Introducing *A Lay Sermon*, Coleridge writes: "[I]t has been my purpose, throughout the following discourse to guard myself and my Readers from extremes of all kinds." Initially, the extremes are the political diagnoses and prescriptions of "the political Empirics of the day," and then, in the main body of the work, those of an unchecked commercialism.[70] The sermon was written to "offer counsel concerning circumstances of great distress, and of still greater alarm,"[71] that is, the economic troubles and social discontent that followed the end of the Napoleonic Wars.[72] After

---

[70] Under this description and the term "demagogue"—though without explicitly naming any of them—Coleridge lumps together William Cobbett, Sir Francis Burdett, John and Leigh Hunt, Major John Cartwright, Henry "Orator" Hunt, Henry Brougham, and Samuel Whitbread, men who, in fact, though all urging political and economic reform, differed widely in terms of political proposals, diagnoses, and tactics. Coleridge, *A Lay Sermon*, 144nn.1 and 2, 145n.1, 149nn.3 and 4, 152n.5. Coleridge's critique proceeds at two levels. First, and most dramatically, an attack upon their motives and upon their personal and intellectual morality in which any individual detail is swept up into the "type" of the false prophet conjured out of the language of Jeremiah and Isaiah. Most of the force of Coleridge's treatment of the reformers derives from this unpleasant, "demonizing" rhetoric. He has also, however, identified two economic arguments common amongst radicals of the period: that distress is aggravated by high taxation and government spending and that pensions and sinecures significantly increased the economic burden upon the nation. Though firmly rejected, these arguments, particularly the former, receive a more measured and careful critique. See J. Morrow, *Coleridge's Political Thought*, 107-11; R. J. White, *Waterloo to Peterloo* (London: William Heinemann Ltd., 1957) 122-51.

[71] Coleridge, *A Lay Sermon*, 139.

[72] The Napoleonic Wars had encouraged British farmers to grow increasing quantities of corn. High prices and the absence of competition encouraged landowners to invest in more land and in reclamation projects, this expansion being financed by an overconfident granting of credit by local banks. The end of the war and the renewal of foreign competition coincided with an exceptionally good harvest in 1815 and the consequent decline in prices left many farmers unable to meet interest payments. The price of wheat fell from 71s 9d a quarter in March to 55s 9d in December 1815. The price structure, therefore, which deter-

the assault upon the "demagogues,"[73] the burden of the sermon is the argument that current distresses are due to the weakness or absence of the traditional means by which bounds were set to the influence of commercialism within the social order. While the "commercial spirit" brings undoubted blessings, its extension to certain spheres, especially that of agriculture, is necessarily destructive, owing to a fundamental incompatibility of aims.[74]

The term "commerce" is used in a number of ways in Coleridge's writings, reflecting a similarly various usage in the political debates of the eighteenth century. In the polemical context of Tory opposition, commercial wealth, perceived as a threat to the constitutional position of landed interests, was identified in particular with the providers of loans and loan-broking services for the government.[75] In an article in the *Morning Post* for 1 February 1800, Coleridge sets commerce over against wealth derived from agriculture and manufacturing. He goes on to question whether a decrease in wealth derived from banking and credit would really be disadvantageous to the nation. This article, entitled "Our Commercial Politicians," echoes the political fears of Tories:

---

mined rent payments and agricultural income at all levels, was put into crisis. A general collapse in commercial activity followed in 1816, the economic depression lasting until 1821. See E. Halevy, *The Liberal Awakening 1815–1830*, rev. ed. (New York: Peter Smith, 1949) 3-79; A. S. Link, "Coleridge and the Crisis in Great Britain, 1816–1820," *Journal of the History of Ideas* 9 (1948): 323-38.

[73]In his critique of the demagogues, Coleridge is grappling with attempts, by such as Cobbett and Cartwright, to channel economic distress into political protest and reform agitation. The disturbances upon which fastened anxious fear of revolution did not, however, achieve a coherently political character until 1819. Before then, episodes of rioting and machine breaking are to be understood as expressing economic discontent in a traditional way. See R. J. White, *Waterloo to Peterloo*, 101-13.

[74]Coleridge, *A Lay Sermon*, 169n.*: "My opinions would be greatly misinterpreted if I were supposed to think hostilely of the spirit of commerce to which I attribute the largest proportion of our actual freedom (i.e., as *Englishmen*, and not merely as *Landowners*) and at least as large a share of our virtues as of our vices."

[75]Mark Francis and John Morrow, *A History of Political Thought in the Nineteenth Century* (London: Gerald Duckworth & Co., 1994) 103-22.

> On the supposition that . . . we could be and remain the monopolists of the commerce of Europe, is it quite ascertained, that it would be a real *national* advantage? . . . Is it quite certain, that it would not give such a superiority to the moneyed interest of the country over the landed, as might be fatal to our Constitution? Has not the hereditary possession of a landed estate been proved, by experience, to generate dispositions equally favourable to loyalty and established freedom? Has not the same experience proved that the moneyed men are far more malleable materials? that ministers find more and more easy ways of obliging them, and that they are more willing to go with a Minister through evil and good? . . . Have not loans and other Ministerial job-work created injurious and perhaps vicious objects for moneyed speculations?[76]

By 1815, Coleridge had adopted a far more positive position with regard to commerce, acknowledging many of the social benefits claimed by its Whig defenders. At the same time, "commerce," comes to have broader, nonpolemical associations and in *A Lay Sermon* the "commercial spirit" is used synonymously with the "Spirit of Trade."[77] The fundamental contrast is now between land-based wealth and wealth derived from trade, manufacturing, banking and credit, all considered as expressions of the "commercial spirit."[78]

What, then, is the essential character of commercial reasoning? It is, according to Coleridge, to view persons and things solely in terms of their relation to the system of credit and exchange. The commercial mind, as it were, conforms the objects of its experience to the "medium of the market." The distinction between "persons" and "things," founded upon the uniqueness of human beings as rational, moral agents, is not, indeed cannot be, recognized within the confines of a relationship conducted strictly in the "spirit of Trade":

> In Trade, from its most innocent form to the abomination of the African commerce nominally abolished after a hard-fought battle of twenty years, no distinction is or can be acknowledged between Things and

---

[76]Coleridge, *Essays*, pt. 1, 143-45.

[77]Though critical associations are by no means entirely absent, see below, 164-66.

[78]See J. Morrow, *Coleridge's Political Thought*, 1-10; 43-125; J. Miller, *Ideology and Enlightenment*, 210-51.

Persons. If the latter are part of the concern, they come under the denomination of the former. . . . The personal worth of those, whom I benefit in the course of the Process, or whether the persons are really benefited or no, is no concern of mine. The Market and the Shop are open to all.[79]

Coleridge is not interested in criticizing the commercial relationship as such, his concern is with the consequences of a failure to recognize the abstraction involved: that, for certain limited purposes, it is necessary to consider persons only as means.[80] The danger is that, under the impact of commercial success and of the material benefits derived from it, the commercial relationship may become a culture's paradigm for the construal of human beings and their mutuality.

Coleridge believes that this is precisely what is occurring in early nineteenth century Britain. As a consequence, other social institutions, relationships, and activities are inappropriately conformed to the categories of commercial thinking. Put in this way, it is possible to appreciate that the argument about commercialism is a transposition, to the economic and social sphere, of that concerning the understanding. The logic of commerce is the logic of the understanding: within it, only "proximate ends" appear, "*ends* as in their turn become means."[81] "Person" refers to the human being as rational, as having the capacity for free agency and, therefore, as an end that may not be reduced, without violation, to a mere means.[82] Recognition of this ultimacy is itself a

---

[79]Coleridge, *A Lay Sermon*, 220.

[80]For Coleridge, of course, it would not be possible to defend the commercial relationship as such without recourse to the distinction between persons and things. The fact that *within* the relationship persons are treated as means is defensible on the grounds that the commercial system as a whole produces benefits for human beings as persons.

[81]The cognitive divide between moral and commercial discourse comes out well in Coleridge's account of how moral qualities such as honesty are reconfigured under the aegis of the commercial spirit: "[A]s a tradesman, I am bound to regard honesty and established character themselves, as *things*, as *securities*, for which the known unprincipled dealer may offer an unexceptional substitute."

[82]Coleridge, *The Friend*, pt. 1, 189-90: "[A]ll morality is grounded in the reason. Every man is born with the faculty of Reason: and whatever is without

product of reason: it cannot be derived from within the categories of the understanding. The consequence, therefore, of the general extension of the commercial spirit is the breakdown of social ties that embody the recognition of human beings as persons.[83]

Coleridge proceeds with his stated intention to describe the effects of the "overbalance of the commercial spirit" by dividing this task under four heads, "1. In the COMMERCIAL WORLD itself: 2. In the Agricultural: 3. In the Government: and, 4. In the combined Influence of all three on the more numerous and labouring Classes."[84] In the initial section on the "overbalance as displayed in the commercial world itself" Coleridge instances the extremes of economic instability associated with the "system of credit."[85] He argues that

---

it, be the shape what it may, is not a man or a PERSON, but a THING. . . . as the faculty of Reason implies free agency, morality (i.e., the dictate of Reason) gives to every rational being the right of acting as a free agent, and of finally determining his conduct by his own will, according to his own conscience: and this right is inalienable except by guilt, which is an act of self-forfeiture, and the consequences therefore to be considered as the criminal's own moral election."

[83]In *A Lay Sermon*, Coleridge has in mind, especially, those social relations associated with agriculture, i.e., the responsibility of the landlord for the moral, religious, and educational, as well as the physical well-being of his tenants, and the respect, loyalty, and deference on their side. His depiction of these relationships in the second *A Lay Sermon*, however, is not free from idealization and nostalgia, see below, 160n.118.

[84]Coleridge, *A Lay Sermon*, 169-70. The execution of this plan is only partial and does not extend beyond the section on agriculture in which, according to Coleridge, the influence of commercialism is essentially alien and socially most destructive. Despite the stated intention, there is a certain rhetorical completeness about Coleridge's account of the "overbalance of the commercial spirit," the emphasis falling upon the contrasted "worlds" of commerce and agriculture, analogous in their distinction and relation to reason and understanding. See below, 164-66.

[85]Coleridge, *A Lay Sermon*, 202. The formulation is potentially misleading. However, Coleridge is not inconsistently suggesting, as John Morrow (*Coleridge's Political Thought*, 202) reads him, that there exist counterbalancing forces within the commercial sphere itself but that the failure of modifying influences such as religion has consequences within the commercial world, particularly by not curbing reckless greed. Coleridge's thought, here, seems to be that commer-

within the last sixty years or perhaps a somewhat larger period, there have occurred at intervals of about 12 or 13 years each, certain periodical Revolutions of Credit. . . . certain gradual expansions of credit ending in sudden contractions, or, with equal propriety, ascensions to an utmost possible height . . . but in every instance the attainment of this, its ne plus ultra, has been instantly announced by a rapid series of explosions (in mercantile language, a *Crash*).[86]

Such crashes, Coleridge maintains, are preceded by periods of mounting overconfidence in financial speculation. He characterizes the audacious ascent of reckless credit, as he does the misuse of the understanding, as arrogant and hubristic. He invokes the figures of Icarus, Phaethon, and Milton's Satan:

For a short time this Icarian Credit, or rather this illegitimate offspring of CONFIDENCE, to which it stands in the same relation as Phaethon to his parent god in the old fable, seems stunned by the fall; but soon recovering, again it strives upward, and having once more regained its mid region,
"—thence many a league,
As in a cloudy chair ascending rides
Audacious!"
till at the destined zenith of its vaporous exaltation,

---

cial logic alone, given its abstraction from the distinction between persons and things, is insufficient to check, for instance, the kind of shortsighted speculation that seeks to "get rich quick," irrespective of the long-term social cost.

[86] Coleridge, *A Lay Sermon*, 202. This stands as evidence that Coleridge's grasp of economic activity was considerable, despite J. S. Mill's judgement that he wrote like an arrant driveler on such matters. See J. Colmer, *Coleridge: Critic of Society*, 140: "With little reliable statistical information to work on and with the whole science of political economy in its infancy, Coleridge was nevertheless able to detect in the history of the previous sixty years 'periodical revolutions of credit,' occurring at intervals of about twelve or thirteen years. His treatment of these booms and crashes differs from that of the economists of the day, who neither enquired into their causes nor lamented their effects on the health and happiness of the people." For a similarly sympathetic account of Coleridge's economics, see W. Kennedy, *Humanist versus Economist: The Economic Thought of Samuel Taylor Coleridge*. Mill's judgment may be found in his "Coleridge," 217.

> "*all unawares*
> *Flutt'ring its pennons vain plumb down he drops!*"[87]

In *Paradise Lost*, Coleridge's quotation is preceded by a description of the "eternal anarchy" before the gates of hell, presided over by Chaos and Chance.[88] This image informs Coleridge's final evaluation of speculative irresponsibility through which "the movements of Trade become yearly gayer and giddier, and end at length in a vortex of hopes and hazards, of blinding passions and blind practices, which should have been left where alone they ought ever to have been found, among the wicked lunacies of the Gaming Table." Abuses of the credit system plunge the participants into uncertain chance and into a chaos with disastrous economic consequences.

The miserable results of heedless speculation fall hard upon those least able to bear their burden. Coleridge's protest is emotional, even melodramatic:

> In the cruelty of suffering, when the old Laborer's Savings, the precious robberies of self-denial from every day's comfort; when the Orphan's Funds; the Widow's livelihood; the fond confiding Sister's humble Fortune; are found among the victims to the remorseless mania of dishonest Speculation, or to the desperate cowardice of Embarrassment, and the drunken stupor of a usurious Selfishness that for a few months respite dares incur a debt of guilt and infamy, for which the grave itself can plead no statute of limitation.[89]

Against the evocation of this chaos, Coleridge places an image he derives from contemporary political economy:[90]

---

[87]Coleridge, *A Lay Sermon*, 203-204. From *Paradise Lost* 2.929-31 and 932-33 (var.).
[88]*Paradise Lost* 2.895ff.
[89]Coleridge, *A Lay Sermon*, 208.
[90]The term "political economy" had two related meanings in contemporary discussion. In a narrower sense, it referred to the science associated in particular with the Scots, Sir James Stewart, Adam Smith, Adam Ferguson, and John Millar but also with the French "Physiocrats" and with Malthus. A more general use "describes a perspective that stressed the general benefits that flowed from the increasing prominence of a commercial order in politics, and a commercial ethos in social relations." John Morrow, *Coleridge's Political Thought*, 102. Cole-

We shall perhaps be told too, that the very Evils of this System, even the periodical *crash* itself, are to be regarded but as so much superfluous steam ejected by the Escape Pipes and Safety Valves of a self-regulating Machine.[91]

Reductionist accounts of social institutions in terms of mechanism are, for Coleridge, paradigmatic of the attempt to comprehend a society of persons within the limits of the understanding. Here, the sharp contrast of practices that precipitate the rule of chance and anarchy with the image of a "self-regulating Machine" uncovers political economy functioning as an ideological justification for financial practices reckless of their human consequences. In Coleridge's view it requires the rational distinction between persons and things to expose the full context and, therefore the moral character, of such practices.

Coleridge's attack upon "the reputed Masters of Political Economy" continues with a passionate denunciation of the claim that "in a free and trading country *all things find their level*."[92] His objections to this are

---

ridge's qualified recognition of the social and political benefits of commerce did not prevent him from harsh criticism concerning "political economy" in the former sense. Even here, however, caution is necessary: first, Coleridge's economic views demonstrate an appreciative reading of Stewart, and his analysis of the postwar economy and the dangers of retrenchment (Coleridge, *The Friend*, pt. 1, 228-44; *A Lay Sermon*, 155-68) draws close to that of Malthus, of whose celebrated *Essay on the Principle of Population* he is highly critical. See William F. Kennedy, "Coleridge's Economic Views on Postwar Depression: 1817," in *Coleridge: A Collection of Critical Essays*, ed. Kathleen Coburn (Englewood Cliffs NJ: Prentice-Hall, 1967) 142-51. Second, the real target of Coleridge's ire is the reductionism involved when "political economy" is elevated and isolated as *the* discourse for reflection upon social and economic matters, see below, 153-55.

[91]Coleridge, *A Lay Sermon*, 205.

[92]As he makes clear in the letter to the *Morning Post* article "Monopolists and Farmers" (Coleridge, *Essays*, pt. 1, 255; cf. *Essays*, pt. 2, 176), Coleridge's source for this is Adam Smith. Thus, "the natural price, therefore, is, as it were, the central price, to which the prices of all commodities are continually gravitating. Different accidents may sometimes keep them suspended a good deal above it, and sometimes force them down a good deal below it. But whatever may be the obstacles which hinder them from settling in this center of repose and

twofold. First, he detects a linguistic slight of hand in the metaphor: it disguises, by suggesting an eventual resting place, what is, in fact, a continual state of fluctuation:

> [I]nstead of saying all things *find*, it would be less equivocal and far more descriptive of the fact to say, that Things are always *finding* their level: which might be taken as the paraphrase or ironical definition of a storm.[93]

Coleridge thus shifts the metaphor from that of temporary shifts in water level, such as occur when a dam is released, to that of a storm.[94] This makes possible a further transition:

> ... but would be still more appropriate to the Mosaic Chaos, ere its brute tendencies had been enlightened by the WORD (i.e., the communicative Intelligence) and before the Spirit of Wisdom moved on the *level-finding* Waters.[95]

Coleridge glosses the reference to "the Spirit of Wisdom" with "that is, Reason in Act or Energy." In invoking the "Mosaic Chaos" and the creative, unifying and ordering Logos, he returns his discussion of political economy to its theological and epistemological framework. This critique and reinterpretation of the "level" metaphor exposes the ideological function of that metaphor within economic discourse. It further suggests the necessity of grasping the processes of economic

---

continuance, they are constantly tending towards it." Adam Smith, *The Wealth of Nations* (Chicago: University of Chicago Press, 1976) 1:65. For the "water and level" image see the following note.

[93]Coleridge, *A Lay Sermon*, 206.

[94]Cf. Smith, *The Wealth of Nations* 2:18: "Open the floodgates, and there will presently be less water above, and more below, the damhead, and it will soon come to a level in both places." In *The Wealth of Nations*, the metaphor appears in connection with the taxation and restriction, by the Spanish and Portuguese, of gold and silver exports. The government restraints and their effects upon the internal and external value of gold and silver, together with other commodities, are likened to the difference in water level created behind and in front of a dam. Were the artificial restraints to be given up, the value of gold and silver, "their proportion to the annual produce of land and labor, will soon come to a level, or very near to a level."

[95]Coleridge, *A Lay Sermon*, 206.

fluctuation within a larger context opened up through the ordering and modifying power of reason. With the image of chaos and Wisdom, Coleridge provides a rhetorical miniature of the burden of *A Lay Sermon*: that, within society, commerce, as an affair of "proximate ends," must be counterbalanced, integrated within an embracing moral context, by "the permanence and self-circling energies of Reason." The passage also constitutes another illustration of the use of scripture, discussed earlier, as a "system of symbols."

The second objection to the economists' claim that all things find their level is that it is an abstraction and, what is more, a socially pernicious abstraction. The metaphor of waters "finding their level" belongs to a discourse, the elements of which are *things*. In the analyses of political economy, persons are only considered as more or less calculable factors in the market:

> But Persons are not *Things*—but Man does not find his level. Neither in body or soul does the Man find his level! After a hard and calamitous season, during which the thousand Wheels of some vast manufactory had remained silent as a frozen waterfall, be it that plenty has returned and that Trade has once more become brisk and stirring: go ask the overseer, and question the parish doctor, whether the workman's health and temperance with the staid and respectful Manners best taught by the inward dignity of self-conscious support, have found *their* level again![96]

To the reified, abstract world of political economy, "a shadow fight of Things and Quantities," Coleridge opposes the concrete particularity of human beings.[97] A vivid, emotional exhortation discloses the genuinely homiletic element in the rhetoric of *A Lay Sermon*:

> Alas! I have more than once seen a group of children in Dorsetshire, during the heat of the dog days, each with its little shoulders up to its ears, and its chest pinched inward, the very habit and *fixtures*, as it were, that had been impressed on their frames by the former ill-fed, ill-clothed, and unfuelled winters. But as with the Body, so or still worse with the Mind.[98]

---

[96]Coleridge, *A Lay Sermon*, 206-207.
[97]Coleridge, *Statesman's Manual*, 28.
[98]Coleridge, *A Lay Sermon*, 207.

Here is a suffering and a moral claim that cannot appear within the categories of the economists' system, a *"product,"* as it is, "of the unenlivened, generalizing Understanding."

"Political Economy," Coleridge wrote to William Mudford in May 1818,

> is a science that begins with abstractions, in order to exclude whatever is not subject to a technical calculation: in the face of all experience, it assumes these as the *whole* of human nature.[99]

Considered only in terms of the market, the human being is not present either in its individuality or its situated connectedness within village, town, and nation. The individual, insofar as he or she is an object of political economy is replaceable: "the mutton must be eat somewhere, and what difference where? If three were fed at Manchester instead of two at Glencoe or the Trossacs, the balance of human enjoyment was in favour of the former."[100] Coleridge's recognizes the worth of this abstraction as a necessary tool for analyzing certain aspects of economic activity. That is not his quarrel. His critique engages this abstraction where identified with "the whole of human nature."[101] Such an identification has fallen prey to what Coleridge depicts as an abiding temptation of the understanding: to take the part for the whole. Coleridge's description of political economy places it, as a science, close to the merely classificatory efforts of contemporary botany. Thus, its abstractions, however useful for certain descriptive or predictive tasks, are at a remove

---

[99] Coleridge, *Collected Letters* 4:856.
[100] Coleridge, *A Lay Sermon*, 211.
[101] Hence the final paragraph of the fifth "Monopolists and Farmers" letter: "I have often heard unthinking people exclaim, in observing the differences of price in various parts of the country, What has become of Adam Smith's *level*? I, God knows, am no *Friend* to those hardhearted comparisons of human actions with the laws of inanimate nature. Water will come to a level without pain or pleasure, and provisions and money will come to a level likewise; but, O God! what scenes of anguish must take place while they are coming to a *level*! But still the sneer against Adam Smith, as to the simple fact, is absurd. The tide in the rivers Trent and Parrot flows in a *head*. Now if a spectator should exclaim to a writer on fluids, What has become of your *level* now? Would he not answer, *stay* and see!?" Coleridge, *Essays*, pt. 1, 255.

from the essential character of human beings as persons and from those historically formative powers, moral ideas. The cognitive divide, of course, is that between the mere understanding and the understanding made "intuitive, and a living power" through imagination's mediation of reason.

The discussion of political economy in *A Lay Sermon* illustrates well the "identifying" role of the Coleridgean imagination as it informs the argumentative process. Coleridge's criticism is directed against a reductionist discourse, one that constrains and thus obscures the complex, multileveled connections that make up nature, society, and history. In exposing and critiquing the reductionism, Coleridge moves to a larger context in which the problematic discourse, of which there is, as it were, an "overbalance," is put in its place—in both senses of the phrase.[102] The contribution of the political economist thus finds both its critique and its qualified recognition in the context of an appeal to that which cannot be derived from political economy: the differentiation of persons from things, human beings from beasts.[103]

---

[102]While Coleridge never raises it to the level of an explicit systematic principle, this description of his movement of thought suggests Hegel's famous "to cancel and preserve" (*aufheben*), the reference of the epigraph to this chapter. Like Hegel, Coleridge conceives of rationality as the means of transcending cultural, social, and religious fragmentation, the consequences of captivity to the understanding. Unlike Hegel, of course, Coleridge places the primary emphasis upon rationality as expressed in religion.

[103]For Coleridge, the Kantian formulation of the distinction between persons and things is also a way of articulating the doctrine of human beings as made in the image of God. It might be objected that "things" and "beasts" are not synonymous but the dualism of the categories, "persons" and "things," makes them so for ethical purposes. Thus, Coleridge argues, "we plant a tree, and we fell it; we breed the sheep, and we shear or kill it; in both cases wholly as means to *our* ends. For trees and animals are *things*. The woodcutter and the hind are likewise employed as *means*, but on agreement . . . which includes them as well as their employer in the *end*. For they are *persons*." Kant recognizes both the need and the difficulty of grounding, in these terms, duties with respect to animals. He proposes that our responsibilities are based upon the analogies between human and animal behavior: "Animal nature has analogies to human nature, and by doing our duties to animals in respect of manifestations which correspond to manifestations of human nature, we indirectly do our duty toward

Coleridge's critique of commercialism, then, concerns commerce and the furthering of commercial interests, not as such, but "taken as the paramount principle in the Nation at large."[104] In other words, the aims of social organization and of government cannot be reduced to those of commercial interest. The reason for this is that commercial interests necessarily abstract from recognition of human beings as persons. The ends or "final causes" of the state, therefore, as Coleridge formulates them in *A Lay Sermon*, are carefully antireductionist. They reflect, in language and organization, the distinction and relation of reason and understanding:

> We suppose the negative ends of a State already attained, viz. its own safety by means of its own strength, there will then remain its positive ends:— 1. To make the means of subsistence more easy to each individual. 2. To secure to each of its members THE HOPE of bettering his own condition or that of his children. 3. The development of those faculties which are essential to his Humanity, i.e. to his rational and moral BEING.[105]

The three ends are arranged in an ascending order. That which is distinctively human—rationality, speculative and practical—is distinguished as the subject of the final and climactic member.[106] In a way that

---

humanity." Immanuel Kant, *Lectures on Ethics*, trans. Louis Infield (Indianapolis: Hackett Publishing, 1963) 239.

[104]Coleridge, *A Lay Sermon*, 206.

[105]Coleridge, *A Lay Sermon*, 216-7. In *The Friend*, Coleridge gives a slightly different, fourfold formulation of the "ends of government." The additional member is placed second, "that in addition to the necessaries of life he should derive from the union and division of labor a share of the comforts and conveniences which humanize and ennoble his nature; and at the same time the power of perfecting himself in his own branch of industry by having those things which he needs provided for him by others among his fellow citizens, including the tools and raw or manufactured materials necessary for his own employment." Coleridge, *The Friend*, pt. 1, 252. The underlying structure, as described in connection with *A Lay Sermon* remains, however, the same.

[106]The distinction and continuity between the first two and the third ends of the state also reflects the distinction made in both *The Friend* and in *On the Constitution of the Church and State* between "civilization," corresponding to the first two ends and "cultivation" as the subject of the third. See Coleridge, The

immediately recalls the structure of Coleridge's philosophical psychology, the third member both presupposes the two former and, in its turn, grants them their final intelligibility as *human* acts of subsistence and progression.[107] The "ends of government," therefore, express Coleridge's theological anthropology: they are the ends of the imago Dei, possessed by creatures both continuous and radically discontinuous with the rest of the animal creation.

A significant element in Coleridge's account of the purposes of the state is his emphasis upon development and hope. The latter is further underscored by way of a footnote:

> [H]is Maker has distinguished [man] from the brute that perishes, by making Hope an instinct of his nature and an indispensable condition of his moral and intellectual progression.[108]

This stress is rooted in the doctrine of the mind as *active* both in cognition and as a moral agent. The mind, for Coleridge, is a "progressive" power, requiring a "sphere of activity" and the opportunity for the exercise and enlarged use of its capacities.[109] The dynamic of the mind is to "appropriate and reproduce in fruits of its own."[110] Coleridge's fulminations against contemporary radicals are funded by this theory of mind and its social transposition into the ends of the state:

Friend, pt. 1, 494-95, 500, 502; and Coleridge, *Church and State*, 42: "[C]ivilization is itself but a mixed good, if not far more a corrupting influence, the hectic of disease, not the bloom of health, and a nation so distinguished more fitly to be called a varnished than a polished people; where this civilization is not grounded in *cultivation*, in the harmonious development of those qualities and faculties that characterize our *humanity*."

[107]Compare also Coleridge's philosophy of nature and creation, which see above, and Coleridge, *Church and State*, 183: "In every living form, the conditions of its *existence* are to be sought for in that which is *below* it; the grounds of its *intelligibility* in that which is *above* it."

[108]Coleridge, *A Lay Sermon*, 216n.*.

[109]This, it will be remembered, is the sole rational basis of the institution of property.

[110]Coleridge, *The Friend*, pt. 1, 473.

> That the Cobbetts and the Hunts address you (= the lower Ranks) as Beasts who have no future Selves—as if by a natural necessity you must *all* for ever remain poor and slaving.[111]
>
> The Demagogues address the lower orders as if each Individual were an *inseparable* part of the order—always to remain, *nolens volens* [willy-nilly], poor and ignorant—How opposite to Christianity, which forever calls on us to detach ourselves spiritually not merely from our rank, but even from our Body and the whole World of Sense.[112]

His philosophical psychology commits Coleridge to a view of social order in which well-being is bound up with the continuing development of the whole and with improvement as a possibility for each of its members.[113] It becomes the basis for a protest against the ultimacy of class as a determinant of individuals:

> One of the ominous characteristics of this reforming age, the custom of addressing "*The Poor*," as a permanent Class, assumed to consist ordinarily of the same individuals. . . . The Ideal of a Government is that which under the existing circumstances most effectually affords Security to the Possessors, Facility to the Acquirers, and *Hope* to all. Poverty, whatever can justify the designation of "the Poor," ought to be a transitional state—a state to which no man ought to admit himself to belong, tho' he may find himself *in* it because he is passing *thro'* it, in the effort to leave it. Poor men we must always have, till the Redemption is fulfilled, but *The Poor*, as consisting of the *same* Individuals! O, this is a sore accusation against any society![114]

---

[111]Coleridge, *Notebooks* 3:4311, April 1816.

[112]Coleridge, *Notebooks* 3:3317, May 1808.

[113]Cf. Coleridge's suspicion, elsewhere, of language in which he perceives an acceptance of disadvantage as the permanent condition of a social class: the "ominous but too appropriate" expression the "Labouring Poor" (Coleridge, *A Lay Sermon*, 207), for instance, unites, as an accepted condition, the coexistence of human effort with an inability to achieve the conditions for independence or betterment.

[114]Coleridge, *Notebooks* 5:6655. Coleridge's protest registers one of the most important features of social and economic change in the early nineteenth century: the transformation of social structure in which "the vertical connections and horizontal solidarities of class came for the first time, clearly, unmistakeably, and

Given the human ideal which Coleridge projects, the possibility of improvement must be intellectual and moral as well as physical. To be sure, he never supposed, nor thought it either possible or desirable, that society would cease to be an ordering of inequalities.[115] The state, however, must seek to ensure, or, at the least, not to prevent, the conditions for the development of persons, that is, of rational, moral agents. Such conditions are those in which hope of physical betterment, in a like manner to the relation of understanding and reason, is orientated toward and the necessary ground for intellectual and moral development. Although Coleridge abandoned his early egalitarian vision, expounded in the *Lectures on Revealed Religion*, his insistence upon the possibility of improvement represents a continuation of his youthful idealism. While property would be, according to the older Coleridge, forever unequal, the

---

irrevocably, to supplant the vertical connections and horizontal rivalries of dependency and interest." Harold Perkin, *Origins of Modern English Society* (New York: Routledge & Kegan Paul, 1969) 209. The category, however, in which this change is registered—"the Poor, as a permanent Class," rather than that of a working class as opposed to other class solidarities—reflects the social descriptions of the eighteenth century, as does the naive appeal to social mobility.

[115]Cf., Coleridge, The *Friend*, pt. 1, 253: "Reflect on the direful effects of casts in Hindostan, and then transfer yourself in fancy to an English cottage,
  Where o'er the cradled Infant bending
  Hope has fixed her wishful gaze
and the fond mother dreams of her child's future fortunes—who knows but he may come home a rich merchant, like such a one? or be a bishop or a judge? The prizes indeed are few and rare; but still they are possible: and the hope is universal, and perhaps occasions more happiness than its fulfillment.... [And, commenting on the last "end of government,"] The poorest Briton possesses much and important knowledge, which he would not have had, if Newton, Luther, Calvin, and their compeers had not existed; but it is evident that the means of science and learning could not exist, if all men had the right to be made profound Mathematicians or men of extensive erudition. Still instruction is one of the ends of Government: for it is that only which makes the abandonment of the savage state an ABSOLUTE DUTY: and that Constitution is the best, under which the average sum of useful knowledge is the greatest, and the causes that awaken and encourage talent and genius, the most powerful and various."

institution of property ownership should not be so ordered as to create social groups whose members are incapable of bettering their lot.

Discussion of the ends of the state is introduced into *A Lay Sermon* because of the special relationship that Coleridge sees to exist between the state and agriculture. Landed property is "essentially different" from the property that is the object of Trade: "a gentleman ought not to regard his estate as a merchant his cargo, or a shopkeeper his stock."[116] The difference lies in the interests served by the two forms of property. Trade serves the private interest of the merchant, businessman, manufacturer, or dealer. While a healthy commercial life is of great public benefit, it is so indirectly, the direct aims of commerce being private ones. The interest served by landed property, however, is nothing less than "the maintenance, strength, and security of the State."[117]

Ownership of land, therefore, must be considered as a form of trust, entailing public responsibilities. The aims of agriculture, Coleridge concludes, coincide with those of the state. They embrace both the physical well-being of the nation's populace and also the conditions for "the development of those faculties which are essential to his Humanity." On the one hand, this makes agriculture, as a sphere of social relations, radically different from the world of commerce. On the other, the inroads of the commercial spirit into the ownership and maintenance of landed property are thus peculiarly destructive to social good. Unlike commercial relations, the relationships involved in agricultural ownership and production are moral in character. They are, or should be, relations between persons. The association of landlord and tenant, for instance, should not permit of that abstraction by which persons are taken for things. In the sphere of agricultural production are formed bonds of mutual responsibility, loyalty, deference, and respect. Such bonds constitute a moral framework within which individuals may hope for the betterment of themselves and their children.[118] Furthermore, they serve for

---

[116] Coleridge, *A Lay Sermon*, 215.

[117] Ibid., 217.

[118] Despite Coleridge's discussion of the Scottish Highlands, one would not gather from *A Lay Sermon* the extent to which the paternalist ideal had been abandoned by Britain's landowners. By 1800, for instance, the laissez-faire argument was proof against any attempt to fix wages by parliamentary legislation. In the counties, during the bread crisis of 1795, there were hardly any

social restraint and so, in Coleridge's view, are essential to the survival of a social order based upon the unequal distribution of property.[119]

Coleridge illustrates his case from a journey taken through the Highlands of Scotland. He provides two anecdotes involving the elimination of small farms in favor of sheep rearing and the consequent displacement of Highland communities. Coleridge regards this development as clear evidence of landlords preferring economic advantage to social responsibility.[120] The anecdotes, particularly the first, are significant

---

magistrates who even debated a scale of minimum wages. Harold Perkin, *Origins of Modern English Society*, 183-95. The gap between ethical ideal and social reality makes Coleridge's appeal to the community bonds of agricultural society a nostalgic one. In this regard, at least, Coleridge is bedfellow with the hated Cobbett.

[119]The social role Coleridge accords to landed property and its system of social relations presupposes, of course, "a society which retained a sufficient body of landholders and was not wholly or largely commercial." J. Morrow, *Coleridge's Political Thought*, 120. In the light of recent work in economic history, however, there is a risk of anachronism if one ascribes to Coleridge, as does A. S. Link ("Coleridge and the Crisis in Great Britain, 1816-1820," 326 and passim), "the attitude of rural Englishmen who refused to acquiesce in all the social and economic consequences of a revolution that had transformed England from an agricultural state into an industrial nation." Prior to 1832, Britain's economy remained dominated by agriculture and by traditional technologies. Whilst there was growth during this period, only cotton increased exponentially (that Coleridge appreciated the latter appears from his pamphlets and correspondence on child labor in the cotton factories). See J. C. D. Clark, *English Society 1688-1832: Ideology, Social Structure, and Political Practice during the Ancien Regime* (New York: Cambridge University Press, 1985) 64-93.

[120]The economic potential of the Highlands was vastly expanded by the introduction of the Cheviot in the 1790s: under sheep, land produced two shillings (2s) an acre compared with two pennies (2d)—that is, twelve times as much—under the traditional black cattle. The ejectments that followed upon this tempting opportunity were extreme and completed the destruction of the old clan society. See John Prebble, *The Highland Clearances* (London: Secker and Warburg, 1963) and Malcolm Gray, *The Highland Economy: 1750-1850* (Westport: Greenwood Press, 1957) 3-54. Prebble's verdict on the Highland Clearances is a very Coleridgean one: "[W]e have not become so civilized in our behaviour, or more concerned with men than profit, that this story holds no lesson for us."

for the way Coleridge has carefully fashioned them into symbols of his human and social ideal. As with the passage concerning the economists' "level," they carry a much greater rhetorical weight than that of simply illustrating the immediate argument.

At the outset, though, we should note that Coleridge's picture of the traditional social structure of the Highlands is an idealized one and hides the complexities of history. The subtenants, who made up the majority of those who farmed their own land, possessed no written leases and, long before the "coming of the Great Sheep," were the victims of arbitrary ejectment, intimidation by the "tacksmen," and acute poverty. Furthermore, military support was a condition of tenure and its continuation rather than, as Coleridge suggests, a simple expression of loyalty. However, contemporary research does confirm Coleridge's claim that his anecdotal narratives were expressive of common distress and embitterment in the closing years of the eighteenth century.

The first anecdote concerns a widow ejected from her farm. Coleridge is careful to indicate the security and social mobility possible within an agrarian setting not driven by commercial interest alone:

> She said, [her ejectment] bore with comparative lightness upon her, who had saved up for her a wherewithal to live, and was blessed with a son well to do in the world.[121]

In a delightful contrast with the dull sheep that now populate the Highlands, Coleridge describes the woman in highly active terms. She began "with a deep sigh and a suppressed and slow voice which she suddenly raised and quickened after a first drop or cadence"; as she spoke, "she made a movement with her hand in a circle, directing my eye meanwhile to various objects as marking its outline." The woman evokes that energy of mind that distinguishes the human from the beast and signals the moral divide between them. Her Coleridgean account of the Highlands is articulated in terms of a populated diversity replaced by an empty monotony:

> Within this space—how short a time back! there lived a hundred and seventy-three persons: and now there is only a shepherd, and an underling or two. Yes, Sir! One hundred and seventy-three Christian

---

[121]Coleridge, *A Lay Sermon*, 209.

> souls, man, woman, boy, girl, and babe; and in almost every home an old man by the fireside . . . Instead of us all, there is one shepherd man, and it may be a pair of small lads—and a many, many sheep![122]

With the abandonment of the farms, the impoverishment has extended into the natural world itself:

> [T]hey are gone, and with them the bristled bear, and the pink haver, and the potatoe [sic] plot that looked as gay as any flower garden with its blossoms! I sometimes fancy, that the very birds are gone, all but the crows and the gleads![123]

The woman's description is a social symbol of the reductionism that Coleridge attacks as a product of unchecked commerce in particular and of the "epoch of the understanding" in general. Instead of a diversity of human and natural life unified in a common and sustaining moral order, there is homogeneity and the exchange of a moral community for a collection of beasts.

In the second of the two anecdotes, Coleridge represents the threat such agricultural policies pose to the social order itself. Again, traditional agricultural relations engaging loyalty and eliciting courage and love, are broken down in the interests of profitability. The ejectments are portrayed as a betrayal of the responsibilities a landlord owes to a tenantry willing to endanger their lives on his behalf. A disaffected former tenant tells Coleridge how the same laird who once raised a militia from among his tenantry, now ends their leases:

> [A]nd what were the thanks . . . for those that fell in battle, fighting before or beside him? Why, that their fathers were all turned out of their farms before the year was over and sent to wander like so many gipsies, unless they would consent to shed their grey hairs, at tenpence a day, over the new canals. Had there been a price set upon his head, and his enemies had been coming upon him, he needed but have whistled, and a hundred brave lads would have made a wall of flame about him with the flash of their broadswords! Now if the _____ should come among us . . . let him whistle to his sheep and see if *they* will fight for him![124]

---

[122]Coleridge, *A Lay Sermon*, 209-10.

[123]Coleridge, *A Lay Sermon*, 210.

[124]During the fifty years that followed Culloden, the lairds raised, from

The story of ejection is the same but it is now "told with a far fiercer indignation" that intimates rebellion, "eager hopes mingled with vindictive resolves." Alarmed by the threatening tone, Coleridge remonstrates with an elderly man whom "I took to be a schoolmaster." This figure, a telling representative of former community bonds and hopes, responds, "O, Sir, it kills a man's love for his country, the hardships of life coming by change and with injustice." Coleridge then concludes his anecdotes by presenting them ironically to "a very sensible person who had studied the mysteries of political economy." He is told

> that more food was produced in consequence of this revolution, that the mutton must be eat somewhere, and what difference where? If three are fed at Manchester instead of two at Glencoe or the Trossacs, the balance of human enjoyment was in favor of the former.[125]

The economists reply exposes again the burden of the whole critique: that a practice indifferent to the suffering particular, that abstracts from the *personality* of human beings is, unqualified and unchecked, morally and socially intolerable. "I still think," Coleridge reflects, that "men ought to be weighed not counted. Their *worth* ought to be the final estimate of their value."

Thus far, we have argued that Coleridge's social analysis in the second lay sermon presupposes his philosophical psychology and, specifically, the distinction between the cognitive powers of reason and understanding. Commercial logic demands only those considerations that fall within the purview of the understanding. What is decisive for the social implications of commerce, insofar as those implications are potentially negative, is that, within this sphere, persons and their moral qualities, such as honesty or loyalty, are configured as objects of the understanding, that is, as things. Over against commercial activity, Coleridge sets the sphere of agricultural production. This opposition appears all the more starkly given that Coleridge abandoned the original plan for a fourfold discussion of "the overbalance of the commercial spirit," and covered only the commercial sphere itself and the extension

---

among the Highlanders, no less that twenty-two regiments for the Crown. See John Prebble, *The Highland Clearances*, 28-29.

[125]Coleridge, *A Lay Sermon*, 164.

of its influence in agriculture. That influence is a pernicious one because the agricultural world is responsible for the maintenance of social relations that are properly *rational* in character, that is, they are determined by recognition of persons and their moral qualities. As we've seen, this recognition derives from reason.

The epistemological framework that Coleridge employs in his social analysis does, however, constrain that analysis in regrettable ways. Despite his claim, made in a footnote, to attribute to commercial activity "at least as large a share of our virtues as of our vices,"[126] Coleridge does not consider ways in which the existence and the practices of the commercial sphere might themselves contribute, albeit indirectly, to ends that involve "those faculties which are essential to . . . Humanity, i.e., to . . . rational and moral Being."[127] This is, as it were, a blind spot that derives from the epistemologically informed structure, according to which commerce is tied closely and firmly to the understanding on the one hand and opposed to agriculture on the other by virtue of the latter's association with reason. This opposition is then reinforced by the polemical interest in criticizing the "overbalance of the commercial spirit." Furthermore, this structure licenses an assessment of the commercial sphere that does not bother to differentiate among forms of commercial activity. Well aware of the analytic purchase gained by the process of desynonymization, Coleridge here indulges in its opposite: a synonymous use of terms that might have allowed a more discriminating analysis of the commercial sphere and its relation to "rational and moral Being." Thus Coleridge does not distinguish between "commerce," "trade," and "manufacturing" as expressions of the commercial spirit.[128] He can even

---

[126]Coleridge, *A Lay Sermon*, 169n.*.

[127]Ibid., 216-17.

[128]Recent social history has shown how the "agricultural" social relations that Coleridge opposes to those of "commerce" might be found to persist as the model for relations and responsibilities within manufacturing industry. J. C. D. Clark (*English Society*, 67) cites John Aiken who commented on the textile industry in and around Manchester as "highly favourable to the paternal, filial, and fraternal happiness—and to the cultivation of good moral and civil habits—the sources of public tranquility." Also, "the ironmasters might, like the Crawshays of Cyfartha, demand—and often receive—political loyalty from 'their' men which recalls the relation between squires and the farming population rather

identify the latter as the "Spirit of Barter" and refer to its "accompanying disposition to overvalue Riches with all the Means and Tokens thereof." Here, this synonymous use of a term is freighted with a value judgment and, indeed, a disdain, that would be distortive of any social analysis.

John Morrow's study of Coleridge's changing attitudes to property has shown how Coleridge comes to "combine perspectives on the political and moral significance of property that were usually seen as alternatives."[129] Arguments in support of the special importance of landed property within the state are joined by a qualified appreciation of commercial activities. Morrow has demonstrated the extent to which Coleridge, in his mature years, came to defend the national significance of the commercial sphere. This is important as it reveals the inadequacy of views of Coleridge's conservatism that construe him as one "crying in an age of commercialism for a return to idealistic, nonmaterialistic Christian values . . . [clinging] tenaciously to the ideals of an age that had passed."[130] My proposal here is that, in *A Lay Sermon*, Coleridge's epistemology provides him with the structure by means of which he is able to combine an acknowledgement of the value of commerce with a primary, though certainly not uncritical, allegiance to the political and social role of the landowner. It should be remembered, however, that while the epistemological framework within which Coleridge's argument is cast allows for a somewhat appreciative assessment of commerce, it also circumscribes the extent of that appreciation, disclosing an abiding suspicion of the commercial spirit. A measure of this suspicion is his rhetorically contaminating association of trade with slavery, the extreme case of the reification of human beings: "In Trade, from its most innocent form to the abomination of the African commerce . . . no distinction is or can be acknowledged between Things and Persons."[131]

---

than between industrial employers and their operatives" (Hobsbawm, *Industry and Empire*, 57).

[129] Morrow, *Coleridge's Political Thought*, 100.

[130] A. S. Link, "Samuel Taylor Coleridge and the Economic and Political Crisis in Great Britain, 1816–1820," 338.

[131] Coleridge, *A Lay Sermon*, 219-20.

5

Social Criticism and the Religious Imagination

> *"If I had not a place of profit that forces me to go to Church,"* said Inflam-mable Gass, *"I'd see the parsons all hang'd,—a parcel of lying—."* *"Oh!"* said Mrs Sigtagatist. *"If it were not for churches & chapels I should not have liv'd so long. There was I up in a Morning at four o'clock, when I was a Girl. I would run like the dickens till I was all in a heat. I would stand till I was ready to sink into the earth. Ah, Mr Huffcap would kick the bottom of the Pulpit out with Passion— would tear off the sleeve of his Gown & set his wig on fire & throw it at the people. He'd cry & stamp & kick & sweat, and all for the good of their souls."* *"I'm sure he must be a wicked villain,"* said Mrs Nannicantipot, *"a passionate wretch. If I was a man I'd wait at the bottom of the pulpit stairs & knock him down & run away!"* *"You would, you Ignorant jade? I wish I could see you hit any of the ministers! You deserve to have your ears boxed, you do."* *"I'm sure this is not religion,"* answers the other.
> —William Blake, *An Island in the Moon*, chapter 4

True Religion and Proper Interests

The "true seat and source" of the contemporary economic and political crisis is an "overbalance of the commercial spirit." This is the critical claim of *A Lay Sermon*. If this is so, what cultural conditions have permitted this spirit to exceed its due bounds? Coleridge's answer is that the overbalance has occurred owing to the "absence or weakness" of traditional countervailing forces.[1] He identifies three such forces but attends in detail to only one of them: religion. As to the other two, he sees scant contemporary evidence of a "genuine intellectual Philosophy with an

---

[1] Coleridge, *A Lay Sermon*, 169.

accredited, learned and philosophic *Class*," while "the ancient feeling of rank and ancestry," he acknowledges to be in inevitable decline.² What I have termed Coleridge's "dynamic conservatism" appears in his view of ancient deference. The system of "rank and ancestry" has undergone significant historical change, change that has made way for "far more important blessings." Regret for an earlier form of that system would be idle. Its decline yields present advantages and reestablishing the institution as it was is impossible. The question concerning the *function* of the earlier form, however, remains for Coleridge a live one: What is now to furnish the necessary checks to the absolutizing of the commercial motive?

Religion receives extended treatment within *A Lay Sermon* as the primary means to achieve a proper balance among the diversity of rightful human concerns. Religion regulates the equilibrium of human interest: without it, "all the pursuits and desires of man must either exceed or fall short of their just measure."³ The reason for emphasizing religion, as opposed to philosophy, is partly to do with the shift in audience. Whereas *The Statesman's Manual* was addressed "exclusively *ad clerum*," to the "Learned and Reflecting of all Ranks and Professions, especially among the Higher Class," *A Lay Sermon* has a nonscholarly audience in mind and was, in Coleridge's own words, the "only Work (I except my Newspaper Contributions) which I had meant to be *popular*, and which, with the exception of three or four pages, really is so."

Coleridge's treatment of religion takes the form of a critique of contemporary religious thought and practice together with a proposal as to why it currently fails as a counterweight to commercial motivation. Coleridge focuses his critique upon the Unitarian movement and upon the Society of Friends, choosing these groups because, in his view, they represent the religious assumptions and attitudes most influential among the "higher and middle classes."⁴ Both Unitarians and Quakers, Coleridge

---

²Coleridge, *A Lay Sermon*, 170.
³Coleridge, *A Lay Sermon*, 174-75.
⁴Thus, on Unitarianism: "Whether it be on the increase, as a Sect, is doubtful. But it is admitted by all—nay, strange as it may seem, made a matter of boast,—that the number of its secret adherents, outwardly of other denominations, is tenfold greater than that of its avowed and incorporated Followers. And truly, in our cities and great manufacturing and commercial towns, among Law-

argues, and the form of religion they exemplify, evidence a reductionism that prevents their spiritual practice from acting as a counterbalance to their commercialism. Both conform their religion to their commerce rather than allowing the practice of faith to put their business in its due place, for their good and that of others. This, though, is not a matter of simple hypocrisy. Were that Coleridge's accusation, he would not be off to a very novel or promising start. His analysis, rather, claims to surface a way of thinking about religion that, for all the sincerity, eagerness, and self-discipline involved, nevertheless emasculates faith's critical power.

Unitarianism, Coleridge tells us, has inherited the Socinian animus to the classical theological tradition, asserting that Christianity is "comprised in a few plain doctrines, and contains nothing not intelligible, at the first hearing, to men of the narrowest capacities."[5] The appeal to simplicity, though, is equivocal, providing the cover whereby the intellectual content of belief is reduced to the memorized sections of a catechism. Furthermore, such contraction is not economically innocent: a religion that demands no intellectual effort on the part of its adherents leaves energies aplenty for acquisitive concerns. In this, Unitarianism holds an attraction grasped by many outside its membership.

> [T]he Religion of best repute among us holds all the truths of Scripture and all the doctrines of Christianity so very transcendent, or so very easy, as to make study and research either vain or needless. It professes, therefore, to hunger and thirst after Righteousness alone, and the rewards of the Righteous; and thus habitually *taking for granted* all truths of spiritual import leaves the understanding vacant and at leisure for a thorough insight into present and temporal interests: which, doubtless, is the true reason why its followers are in general such shrewd, knowing, wary, well-informed, thrifty, and thriving men of business.

Religious reductionism serves economic practice.

The Quakers have a particularly important rhetorical place in Coleridge's argument. He describes the Society of Friends as a sect that originated in an especial concern for restraining worldly-mindedness.

---

yers and such of the Tradesfolk as are the ruling members in Book clubs, I am inclined to fear that this has not been asserted without good ground." Coleridge, *A Lay Sermon*, 181.

[5]Coleridge, *A Lay Sermon*, 177.

Their religious dedication and "undoubting belief in the threats and promises of Revelation, and a consequent regularity of personal, domestic, and social demeanor" is a matter of general note.[6] So also is their business acumen and commercial enthusiasm. They may, therefore, Coleridge concludes, stand for

> the strict, but unstudied and uninquiring Religionists of every denomination. Their characteristic propensities will supply, therefore, no unfair test for the degree of resistance, which our present Christianity is capable of opposing to the cupidity of a trading people.[7]

If we are to discover it anywhere, surely among the Quakers, "we may expect to find Christianity tempering commercial activity and sprinkling its holy damps on the passion of accumulation." Sadly, Coleridge reflects, we don't. The Quakers merge with the crowd of "Christian Mammonists," heading off like laden camels "all at full speed, and each in the confident expectation of passing through the EYE OF THE NEEDLE, without stop or halt, both beast and baggage."[8] This is a delightfully mischievous image but it is hardly to Coleridge's credit that he does not bother to argue for his negative conclusion as to Quaker piety. He permits himself the luxury of a simple appeal to common knowledge: "[I]f the almost universal opinion be tolerably correct, the question is answered."[9]

The Quakers are rhetorically important, then, as a negative example. They represent a combination of religious commitment with commercial zeal in which the unifying principle is that of "prudential motive," the "prudence" of Paley's ethics.[10] Their religion is an extension of their commerce. While its object may be transcendent, the form of relation is

---

[6]Coleridge, *A Lay Sermon*, 185-86.
[7]Coleridge, *A Lay Sermon*, 191.
[8]Coleridge, *A Lay Sermon*, 190.
[9]Coleridge, *A Lay Sermon*, 190.
[10]Coleridge, *A Lay Sermon*, 186. The footnote criticizing Paley's concept of "prudential obligation" is attached to the passage on the Society of Friends. Paley provides a theological defense of economic inequality and competition in the second half of *Natural Theology*, chap. 26. See also A. M. C. Waterman, "The Ideological Alliance of Political economy and Christian Theology, 1798–1833," *Journal of Ecclesiastical History* 34/2 (April 1983): 231-44.

worldly. The Quakers, therefore, function as a negative type of the relationship between religion and trade. They furnish another instance of that "inversion" that Coleridge found in both superstition and atheism: categories appropriate only to the particular and contingent are applied to the universal and necessary.

Despite the original, "spiritualizing" intention of the Society of Friends, their "scheme of faith and worship" fails to provide an adequate counterpoise to the "Spirit of Trade." The fault, according to Coleridge, lies in an omission disastrous for the flourishing of a religion that claims the "Spirit that *searcheth* all things, yea the deep things of God himself":[11]

> In the zeal of their Founders and first Proselytes for perfect Spirituality they excluded from their system all ministers specially trained and educated for the ministry, with all Professional Theologians: and they omitted to provide for the raising up among themselves any other established class of learned men, as teachers and schoolmasters for instance, in their stead.[12]

Whereas theological reductionism is deliberately pursued by Unitarians, among Quakers it is the product of neglect. The absence of institutional provisions for theological learning means that there is no check to the confining of Christianity "in confession and practice . . . to feelings and motives." Quaker religion and the religion of the like multitude of "strict, but unstudied and uninquiring, Religionists of every denomination" is shorn of reflective interest in those truths that cannot be conformed to the categories of the understanding. This is the crucial point, not the trivial one that time in the library is time away from the counting house. The truths that 'pass understanding' are truths of reason, the "organ of the supersensuous." They are qualitatively different from the objects proper to the understanding and "cannot be contemplated, much less can they be the subject of frequent meditation, without dimming the lustre and blunting the rays of all rival attractions."[13] These truths alone, therefore, possess the capacity to liberate us from the cramping context of prudence, setting "things" in the light of "persons,"

---

[11]Coleridge, *A Lay Sermon*, 175.
[12]Coleridge, *A Lay Sermon*, 190.
[13]Coleridge, *A Lay Sermon*, 196.

and gifting us ends that are ultimate not proximate. They acclimatize the mind to the perspective of eternity. "Truths of reason" generate energies of concern that, within the individual and, by extension within society, modify and restrain commercial interests within their good and appropriate bounds.

The contrast between the place accorded to doctrine by Unitarians and Quakers and the religious and cultural role for theological reflection proposed by Coleridge, turns out to be a familiar one. Instead of that which is stored in the mind "as if the human soul were a mere repository or banqueting room,"[14] we have truths that draw the mind into its full activity. Just as associationism, as Coleridge came to interpret it, represented, with unhappy cultural effects, the mind as a merely passive receiver, so influential forms of contemporary religion offered a Christianity "poured in on the Catechumen all and all at once, as from a shower bath: and which, whatever it may be in the heart, yet for the understanding and reason is from boyhood onward a thing past and perfected!"[15] This celebrated "simplicity" mistakes Christianity, that "Faith, which in endless evolution *'teaches us of all things and is truth.'* " Christianity should stir up the dynamism of the mind *and sustain it in its activity*.

> [E]very new knowledge [is] but a new organ of sense and insight into this one all-inclusive Verity, which, still filling the vessel of the understanding, still dilates it to a capacity of yet other and yet greater Truths, and thus makes the soul feel its poverty by the very amplitude of its present, and the immensity of its reversionary, wealth.[16]

If the doctrinal content of Christian faith is not treated reductively, if it is allowed to become the object of *thought*, then it engages and exercises the human mind in the state proper and distinctive to it: the mediation of the objects of reason, by the imagination, to the understanding.

For his account of Unitarians and Quakers, Coleridge returns to the analysis of extremes, the same rhetorical strategy discussed above in connection with the Jacobins of *The Statesman's Manual*. Not surprisingly, this account is problematic in similar ways. The two religious move-

---

[14] Coleridge, *The Friend*, pt. 1, 473.
[15] Coleridge, *A Lay Sermon*, 191.
[16] Coleridge, *A Lay Sermon*, 179.

ments, like Jacobinism, are taken as symbolic of the mind's disordered dynamics, as those dynamics take social form. Again, as with Jacobinism, they express a false mediation, in this case, between religion and commerce. In other words, they represent a social condition in which imagination has failed to disperse and reconfigure the fixities of understanding and fancy. The difficulty is that Coleridge first construes these groups as extreme instances—the end of religion under the domination of the understanding—and then, without any empirical justification, accords them a representative status. The reader is supposed to recognize in the Society of Friends and in Unitarianism, the sobering inner truth of contemporary religion. The argument is rhetorically forceful because these groups are depicted as the inevitable extreme—the logic of the understanding in a pure form. The claim, however, upon which the whole argument depends—that Unitarians and Quakers are representative of a general religious condition—is left without empirical warrant. The affinity Coleridge finds between these forms of religion and economic practice is highly suggestive; indeed, it anticipates the sociological analyses of Weber and Tawney. It remains the case, however, that a complex historical landscape has, once again, been coerced by the epistemological typology.

The critical analysis of *A Lay Sermon* identifies religion as the vital counterweight to commercialism: the balancing and ordering power without which all human concerns "exceed or fall short of their just measure." The choice of religion, as opposed to the philosophy and philosophical education recommended in *The Statesman's Manual*, certainly reflects the shift in intended audience. Much more than that, though, Coleridge is now making, at least by implication, a fundamental proposal about the role of religious as opposed to philosophical knowledge. Whereas philosophy is, quite properly, an aristocratic business, its pursuit limited to the privileged few, religion engages, and extends, the intellectual activity of all. Ultimately, philosophy and religion share a common object, participate in a common quest.[17] Furthermore, though the

---

[17]During the twentieth century, Paul Tillich provided perhaps the most widely influential statement of this claim, although developing an account of God that, given Tillich's privileging of "being" over "will," Coleridge would not have accepted, see below, 220-25. Paul Tillich, *Biblical Religion and the Quest for Ultimate Reality* (Chicago: University of Chicago Press, 1955).

form of knowing differs, both bear the same relationship to the identity of human beings as made in the image of God. "Every Christian," Coleridge paraphrases St. Paul, "in proportion as he is indeed a Christian, has received the Spirit that *searcheth* all things, yea the deep things of God himself."[18] That theological anthropology in which the *imago Dei* is expressed in the activity of reason and imagination lies behind Coleridge's polemic against the Socinian and Unitarian advocacy of a "simple faith." Or perhaps we may say, if faith is simple, it is not easy. "Energies of the intellect, increase of insight, and enlarging views": these are the gifts of a faith that pursues its vocation to thought. Mobility of mind is essential to religion because it is essential to humanity. Some degree of intellectual striving is expected of all and belongs to faith as such. Thus, Coleridge is furious at the implications of the policy: "No Notes! No Comment! Distribute the Bible and the Bible only among the Poor!" and celebrates the enthusiasm of "crowded and promiscuous Audiences" for the sermons of Donne and Jeremy Taylor.[19] True religion excites to intellectual activity and of all interests "it is calculated to occupy the whole mind, and employ successively all the faculties of man." Religion is "the Poetry and Philosophy of all Mankind."[20]

The claim that religion is the universal "poetry and philosophy" invites comparison with Schelling's doctrine of art in the *System of Transcendental Idealism*. Coleridge plagiarized this work extensively in the *Biographia* and it remains influential in the third appendix of *The Statesman's Manual*.[21] The comparison illuminates the connection between religion and imagination in Coleridge's thought. In brief, *A Lay Sermon* accords to religion the role that is given to art in the final section of Schelling's *System*. In the latter, Schelling makes two claims about art and about the relation of art to philosophy, both of which are echoed in Coleridge's discussion of religion. First, Schelling argues that only a few will ever be capable of that "special direction of the mind" necessary in philosophy. This limitation, however, is transcended in that the principle

---

[18]Coleridge, *A Lay Sermon*, 175.

[19]Coleridge, *A Lay Sermon*, 197, 201.

[20]Coleridge, *A Lay Sermon*, 197.

[21]Richard Holmes reconstructs the personal and social dynamics of Coleridge's plagiarisms with fine insight and a tactful restraint from easy judgment. See *Darker Reflections*, 254-55, 280-81, 399-402.

from which philosophy begins—the ultimate identity of spirit and nature—becomes available for all, the few and the many, in the work of art. There, it is given "universal currency." The "intellectual intuition" which belongs to philosophy and that "makes no appearance at all in ordinary consciousness," in art "*can* at least figure in every consciousness."[22] Coleridge's hostility to contemporary attempts to "popularize" philosophy needs to be understood against the background of a similar division of labor, in this case between philosophy and religion.[23] Not doing so, we risk reading his undoubted elitism too crudely.[24] The epistemological discussions that are so important a part of *The Statesman's Manual* are notably absent from *A Lay Sermon*. Such reflection, vital to a philosophical education, belonged in the first lay sermon because it was aimed at those among whom Coleridge hoped to find and to stir the embers of properly philosophical thought. For Coleridge, philosophy's distinguishing task is reflection upon the mental powers that make possible, for philosopher and nonphilosopher alike, the *religious* apprehension of the world as symbolic: "in all things and each thing . . . in each, the meanest object, [religion] bears witness to a mystery of infinite solution."[25]

The second claim Schelling makes for art also receives a Coleridgean transposition in the lay sermons. Philosophy raises a human being to the highest contemplation. However, "it brings to this summit only, so to say, the fraction of a man," whereas art, Schelling continues, "brings *the whole man*, as he is, to that point, namely, to a knowledge of the highest, and this is what underlies the eternal difference and the marvel of art."[26]

---

[22]Schelling, *System of Transcendental Idealism (1800)*, trans. P. Heath (Charlottesville: University Press of Virginia, 1978) 233.

[23]On the "plebification" of philosophical learning, see Coleridge, *Statesman's Manual*, 47; *The Friend*, pt. 1, 447; *Church and Society*, 69.

[24]As, among others, did de Quincey, e.g., in his article on Coleridge for the *Encyclopedia Britannica* (8th ed., 1854).

[25]Coleridge, *Statesman's Manual*, 90. Coleridge came early to his formulation of the philosopher's vocation, thus, in a letter to his brother of 1798, it is described as "the seeking with patience and a slow, very slow mind . . . what our faculties are and what they are capable of becoming." Coleridge, *Collected Letters* 1:238.

[26]Schelling, *System of Transcendental Idealism*, 233.

In precisely these terms Coleridge claims that religion, "beyond all other Interests . . . is calculated to occupy the whole mind, and employ successively all the faculties of man."²⁷ The allegorical figure of "RELIGION" at the beginning of *A Lay Sermon* represents the unity of insight and passion, "deep reflection . . . animated by ardent feelings." A vital element in Coleridge's critique of contemporary religion is that it fails to mediate mind and heart. Theological reductionism, because it cannot sustain the intellectual character of religion, finally cannot sustain it as an affair of the heart either.²⁸ "The light of religion, is not that of the moon, light without heat; . . . neither is its warmth that of the stove, warmth without light."²⁹ The symbolic histories of the Bible are paradigmatic in this respect. Unlike those "unenlivened" contemporary histories, they represent "principles." These principles, however, "inevitably" elicit, to the extent that they are understood at all, an emotional as well as an intellectual response.³⁰ Religion brings "the whole soul of man into activity."³¹

---

²⁷Coleridge, *A Lay Sermon*, 196.

²⁸Coleridge, *A Lay Sermon*, 180: "It is impossible that the affections should be kept constant to an object which gives no employment to the understanding. The energies of the intellect . . . are necessary to keep alive the substantial faith in the heart."

²⁹Coleridge, *Statesman's Manual*, 48.

³⁰Coleridge, *Statesman's Manual*, 17.

³¹Coleridge, *Biographia Literaria*, pt. 2, 15-16; and see also an early letter (December 1796): "I feel strongly, and I think strongly; but I seldom feel without thinking or think without feeling. Hence tho' my poetry has in general a *hue* of tenderness or Passion over it, yet it seldom exhibits unmixed and simple tenderness or Passion." As has already been pointed out, Coleridge adopts Kant's distinction between "persons" and "things." He also came to accept the a priori, *transcendental* distinction between "duty" and "inclination" (Orsini, *Coleridge and German idealism*, 153-56). He remained, however, dissatisfied with the psychological implications of Kant's rigorism, specifically with the role accorded to the "feelings." In a letter to J. H. Green (13 December 1817), Coleridge writes, "I reject Kant's *stoic* principle, as false, unnatural, and even immoral, where in his *Critik der pratischen Vernunft* he treats the affections as indifferent in ethics, and would persuade us that a man who disliking, and without any feeling of Love for Virtue, yet *acted* virtuously, because and only because it was his *Duty*, is more worthy of our esteem, than the man whose affections were

I have argued that, in the lay sermons, the theory of imagination is taken up into an account of religion. Religion is initially introduced in *A Lay Sermon* in the form of an allegorical figure, the description of which evokes accounts of the imagination:

> Deep reflection . . . ardent feelings . . . hope . . . and a something more than all these, which I understood not; but which yet seemed to blend all these into a divine unity of expression.[32]

Coleridge, we may say, conceives religion imaginatively: as mediating universal and particular and achieving the cognitive balance between reason and understanding. Religion also brings into play the range of intellectual and affective powers, ordering and unifying the diversity of human knowledge and activity. Finally, the fullness of perception that, as I have interpreted it here, belongs to the "primary imagination" and is the end of the "secondary" is also the source and goal of religion.

Although Coleridge claims that, in the second lay sermon, he is concerned with religion simply as "any worldly object, which, as far as it employs and interests a man, leaves less room in his mind for other pursuits,"[33] it is clearly not the case that he is treating religion as Jeremy Bentham did poetry: on all fours with "pushpin." The object of religion is unique in its capacity to check and relativize all other sources of motivation. Embodying the imagination's mediatory role, religion brings together the "noblest materials" that are the gifts of reason with the objects of the understanding.[34] The limitation, and the potential danger, of commercial logic, according to Coleridge, lies in the abstraction by which, for the purposes of the market relationship, persons are considered as things. Religion, insofar as it is truly a "counterbalance" to commerce, functions to limit this abstraction to its proper sphere. Mediating the rationally based distinction between persons and things, religion is to

---

aidant [helpful] to, and congruous with his conscience." Coleridge, *Collected Letters* 4:791-92. The theory of the imagination and the account of religion that is so closely linked with it, provided Coleridge with a way of acknowledging the a priori separation of duty and inclination while allowing an account of ethical acts in which reason, will, and affections are united in a "total act of the soul."

[32]Coleridge, *A Lay Sermon*, 135-36.
[33]Coleridge, *A Lay Sermon*, 196.
[34]Coleridge, *A Lay Sermon*, 196-97.

integrate the commercial perspective, the social importance of which Coleridge does not wish to deny, within a life in which the recognition of human beings as moral agents, as personal, is preeminent. Religion, therefore, when it is not conformed to the limits of the understanding, orders and subordinates economic motivation within a larger and rationally informed context of concern. This characterization of the role of religion is anticipated in the biblical hermeneutics of *The Statesman's Manual*. There, the abstractions of present "histories and political economy" are said to render only a "shadow fight of Things and Quantities." By contrast, the Scriptures, as *"educts* of the Imagination," present us with "the history of Men" in which mere motives of expediency are seen as relativized by the formative power of ideas.

In *A Lay Sermon*, Coleridge emphasizes religion as an "interest" that, in the hearts and minds of individuals, modifies commercial acquisitiveness. However, he does not entirely ignore its institutional form. One element in that institutional form is vital to the function of religion as a "counterbalance." This is the education and maintenance of a class of professional theologians and other "learned men, as teachers and schoolmasters."[35] In the later treatise, *On the Constitution of the Church and State*, these professional scholars and educators, with the theologians at their head, form the "clerisy" as mediators of a national education, *"educing, i.e.* eliciting, the latent *man* in all the natives of the soil, *train*[ing] *them up* to citizens of the country, free subjects of the realm."[36]

The concept of education here, together with a goal that recalls the third "end of the state,"[37] discloses the persistence of theory of the imagination, though now transposed into a proposal for the social role of the clerisy. This role is that of "cultivation," informing the exercise of understanding with the energies of reason, or the "harmonious development of those qualities and faculties that characterise our *humanity*."[38]

---

[35]Coleridge, *A Lay Sermon*, 190.

[36]Coleridge, *Church and State*, 48. On the primacy of theology see "the Theologians took the lead, because the SCIENCE of Theology was the root and trunk of the knowledges that civilized man, because it gave unity and the circulating sap of life to all other sciences, by virtue of which alone they could be contemplated as forming, collectively, the living tree of knowledge" (ibid., 47).

[37]See above, 155-56.

[38]Coleridge, *Church and State*, 42-43.

The account of religion and its sociocultural function in *A Lay Sermon* thereby represents a stage in the process by which the imagination takes on social form as a professional educational order. As the imagination is subsumed into religion and as religion is sustained by an "established class of learned men," the political horizon of the theory of the imagination becomes that of the national church, "a 'traditional' structure of authority . . . polarized and insulated from the flux and fragmentation of the political world."[39] When the concept of the clerisy is further developed in *On the Constitution of the Church and State*, the cultural functioning of Coleridge's clerisy *presupposes* the existing balance of the permanent and progressive forces that constitute the state. The clerisy does not act directly within the political realm to help determine that balance. "Civilization" is, so to speak, handed over to the forces of "cultivation" that will "secure and improve" it. The clerisy is not a source of radical challenges to social structure.

Stifling the Imagination

The exhortations of *A Lay Sermon* bear down primarily upon the individual, urging his or her spiritual reform. The reader may well have expected a little more. After all, Coleridge does insist that "we must learn to act nationally as well as individually."[40] The plan of the sermon, announced at the beginning, also anticipates political and institutional proposals as well as suggestions for individual moral improvement. However, when Coleridge finally gets around to asking "What then is the remedy?" the section that follows is startlingly brief—even allowing for the pressure of his publisher to abbreviate the work—and almost derisively anticlimatic.[41] The only concrete proposal is for the abolition

---

[39]Nigel Leask, *The Politics of Imagination in Coleridge's Critical Thought*, 139. On the clerisy and its relationship to the state, see also P. Hamilton, *Coleridge's Poetics* (Oxford: Basil Blackwell, 1983) 200-208.

[40]Coleridge, *A Lay Sermon*, 228.

[41]In an annotated copy of *A Lay Sermon*, inscribed to Robert Southey, Coleridge explains, "Here I must record with a painful mixture of Shame and Indignation, that the Booksellers . . . sent back nearly four sheets and a half of MSS, and insisted on my abridging them into half a sheet—otherwise there would be no way of *covering* their expenses, they having without consulting me

of national lotteries, a longstanding Coleridgean peeve. Beyond that, a threefold summary asks that manufacturers submit to regulations, no specifying details being given; that gentry take up their educational responsibilities; and that landowners regard their ownership as an office of trust.

All very vague and rushed, this collapse of intentions is one of the most notable failures of *A Lay Sermon*. Having approached, so tentatively, the possibility of political and legislative change, Coleridge veers off in an expression of faith in the inevitable effects of moral improvement:

> Let us become a better people, and the reform of all public (real or supposed) grievances, which we use as pegs whereon to hang our own errors and defects, *will follow of itself*.[42]

I want to suggest, especially in the light of the emerging doctrine of the clerisy, that this allergic reaction to political change is not simply overcaution concerning the possibilities of government or an anxiety that the force of law might override moral responsibility.[43] Rather it is symptomatic of a larger process by which Coleridge checks the potentially radical implications of his theory of the imagination and of the epistemology that provides the rhetorical structure of the lay sermons.

On 28 July 1817, Coleridge sent copies of his two lay sermons to the then prime minister, Lord Liverpool. The letter that introduced this gift, and which left the politician somewhat bemused, argued that

---

printed an immense edition." Coleridge, *Statesman's Manual*, 215n.3.

[42]Coleridge, *A Lay Sermon*, 229-30; my emphasis.

[43]This is not to deny, of course, that Coleridge was also cautious about the possibilities of government and anxious to preserve the primacy of moral responsibility. Thus, "it is not in the power of a minister or of a cabinet to say to the current of national tendency, stay here! or flow there! The excess [of the commercial spirit] can only be remedied by the slow progress of intellect, the influences of religion, and irresistible events guided by Providence." Coleridge, *A Lay Sermon*, 169n.*. And, in connection with legislation, Coleridge warns, "all Reform or Innovation, not won from the free Agent by the presentation of juster Views and nobler Interests, and that does not leave the merit of having effected it sacred to the individual proprietor, it were folly to propose, and worse than folly to attempt." Coleridge, *A Lay Sermon*, 217.

the Taste and Character, the whole tone of Manners and Feeling, and above all the Religious (at least the Theological) and the Political tendencies of the public mind, have ever borne . . . a close correspondence, . . . [a] distinct and evident Analogy to the predominant system of speculative Philosophy.[44]

The consequence, as Coleridge reads it, of the philosophy presently most influential is political and cultural fragmentation. A "mechanic philosophy" reduces all things to the movements and collisions of atoms. Since it lacks a discourse for multileveled relationships of growth and influence, this philosophy severs past from present in the disastrous belief that states can be made and unmade at will; and it divides person from person in a crudely individualistic conception of political life. Its advocates are content to believe that, "an Atom is an Atom, neither more nor less, and by the pure Attribute of his atomy has an equal right with all other Atoms to be constituent and Demiurgic on all occasions."[45]

Coleridge attempts to provide the needed multileveled discourse: to overcome fragmentation by a system of identification and to replace the fixities of the fancy with the connections of imaginative thought. To give only one example, he proposes that an adequate exposition of the "ends of the state," requires a scheme of ascending and interrelated levels of goods from the "means of subsistence" to that needful for the development of "rational and moral Being."[46] Thinking through these levels demands that we are capable of moving from a discourse that treats of things to one that articulates the status, ends, rights, and responsibilities of persons. The rhetorical task of identification, unifying a fragmented social field, demands the transcendence, though not, within its proper sphere, the abandonment, of any discourse incapable of naming the

---

[44]Coleridge, *Collected Letters* 4:759. Liverpool commented on the rather dense argument of this letter: "[Mr. Coleridge states] that the object of his writings has been to rescue speculative philosophy from false principles of reasoning, and to place it on that basis, or give it that tendency, which would make it best suited to the interests of religion as well as of the State; at least I believe this is Mr. Coleridge's meaning, but I cannot well understand him." Coleridge, *Collected Letters* 4:757.

[45]Coleridge, *Collected Letters* 4:761.

[46]Coleridge, *A Lay Sermon*, 216-17.

proper ends of persons. Envisioning an order in which diverse social interests are coordinated is a work of such multileveled conceptual imagination.

As we've seen, the relationship of reason and understanding provides the framework whereby Coleridge orders contemporary conflicts and fragmentations and explains their genesis. Within that framework it is the imagination, or else the religion that has taken up the latter's role, that emerges as the principle of identification: the cognitive power through which dislocation may be overcome and an embracing order discerned. The "common end" of exercises of the imagination, as Coleridge says of its role in narrative and poetry, is "to convert a *series* into a *Whole*."[47] Thus, the imagination reveals the unity of past and present; finds the consubstantiality of historical particulars with truths of reason; and, as true religion, discovers the individual in the context of the universal. It is also the imagination that funds a rhetorical movement involving, as we saw in the cases of miracle, of prophecy, and of commercialism, a critique that seeks, not to reject, but to relocate its object within a comprehensive system of connections.

In Coleridge's writings, we may trace an abiding squeamishness and evasion concerning the substantial realities of political action and change. This is the case made by the authors of an essay entitled "Coleridge: Individual, Community, and Social Agency."[48] They point out, for instance, that the "Religious Musings" of 1796, a poem upon which, Coleridge then claimed, "I pin all my poetical credit,"[49] deploys abstract nouns and passive constructions in a manner that obscures issues of historical agency and offers only the vaguest of social descriptions. Alluding to the Book of Revelation, Coleridge announces a time of approaching social transformation:

---

[47]Coleridge, *Collected Letters* 4:545.

[48]David Aers, Jonathan Cook, David Punter, "Coleridge: Individual, Community, and Social Agency," in *Romanticism and Ideology: Studies in English Writing 1765–1830* (London: Routledge & Kegan Paul, 1975) 82-102.

[49]Coleridge, *Collected Letters* 1:119.

Social Criticism and the Religious Imagination 183

> ... Rest awhile!
> Children of Wretchedness! More groans must rise,
> More blood must stream, or ere your wrongs be full. ...
> Children of Wretchedness! The hour is nigh!
> And lo! the Great, the Rich, the Mighty Men,
> The Kings and the Chief Captains of the World
> ... shall be cast to earth,
> Vile and downtrodden, as the untimely fruit
> Shook from the fig tree by a sudden storm.[50]

Clearly, references to such as the "Children of Wretchedness" beg for greater precision and the natural images and passive verbs leave unanswered the entirely proper questions concerning who and by what means this epochal change is to be achieved. As Aers, Cook, and Punter extend the analysis into Coleridge's later writings, their argument suggests an important qualification to the description of an early, radical phase giving way to later reaction. Throughout Coleridge's work, the authors conclude, there is "a repeated process whereby the concrete turns back into the abstract, a process which is in itself essentially reactionary." With reference to the writings post-1800, in particular, they add that "his intellectual methods [are] continually forcing the actual and concrete back out of sight."[51]

At least with regard to their political content, these observations concerning the language and grammar of the early poems, are, I believe, correct and helpful.[52] The broader conclusion, however, is formulated in a way that demands reassessment in the light of the theory of the imagination. To give an account of the problem in terms of the opposition of "abstract" and "concrete," and of the movement from the latter to the former, obscures one of the most important features of the Coleridgean

---

[50]"Religious Musings," ll. 300-14, as in *Selected Poetry and Prose of Coleridge*, ed. Donald A. Stauffer (New York: Random House, 1951) 99.

[51]Aers, Cook, and Punter, "Coleridge: Individual, Community, and Social Agency," 87-91.

[52]They would be misleading if applied to Coleridge's treatment of the natural world, a point that, in fact, would reinforce the authors' suspicion of the political references. In poems such as "The Eolian Harp" and "Frost at Midnight" metaphysical principles are concretized in highly exact and detailed representations of nature.

imagination. The critique of false abstraction is one that Coleridge returns to in a variety of contexts. In literary theory, in his philosophy of science, in his historiography, and in his biblical hermeneutics, Coleridge opposes the imagination to the mental activity of "generalizing" or "abstracting," an opposition that he invokes in terms of the presence or absence of life.[53] As we shall see, this contrast has clear political implications and provides us with a way of approaching some of the tensions within Coleridge's political rhetoric. It also, we might add, furnishes the basis for a critique of the linguistic and political vagaries in the early poems analyzed by Aers, Cook, and Punter.

In *A Lay Sermon*, the political implications are well evidenced by the treatment of political economy. Coleridge's warnings concerning political economy refer to the abstraction involved. For the purposes of economic analysis, persons are considered as things, as in the exchange relationship itself. They therefore are abstracted from their existence as moral agents within communities that are constituted by social relations other than those of the market alone, the history of which cannot be comprised within a narrative of economic fluctuations and human expediency. Over against his account of political economy, and of the destructive consequences of absolutizing its discourse, Coleridge places anecdotes drawn from his walking tour in the Highlands. These anecdotes have, as we saw earlier, a symbolic character. They evoke a particular way of life, a concrete system of social relations, energies of mind and feeling, and moral responsibility. In contrast to economic abstractions, they insist on the irreducible individuality, the particular willing, that reveals the person. As symbols, these anecdotes stand in critical opposition to that generalization that forces "the actual and concrete back out of sight."[54] A symbol is a concrete particular through which is revealed the complex of relations that sustain it and the universal of which it is an instance. The identification that takes place in the symbolic involves a gain rather than a loss in concretion: what is lost is only an individual reality's apparent separate-

---

[53]Coleridge, *Statesman's Manual*, 28, 77-78.

[54]On the indispensability of the concrete-particular for the symbol in Romantic theory, see Todorov, *Theories of the Symbol*, 198-212. And on the eventual weakening of that insistence, see Paul de Mann, "The Rhetoric of Temporality," in *Interpretation: Theory and Practice*, ed. Charles S. Singleton (Baltimore: Johns Hopkins Press, 1969) 173-210.

ness from the system of relations through which it exists, an appearance that is the product of "transferring reality to the negations of reality, to the ever-varying framework of the uniform life." The latter is "abstract knowledge" in which "we think of ourselves as separated beings, and place nature in antithesis to mind, as object to subject, thing to thought, death to life."[55]

At this point, the political implications of the imagination, enacted rhetorically in this confrontation of economic discourse with symbolic anecdote, consist in its being the cognitive power for an apprehension of human being and human society that expands from one embracing, interpretative context to another. The discernments and representations of imagination preserve the human from abstract, reductive description. Paradigmatic among the works of the imagination, in this respect, is the "Science of *Realities*" contained in the Bible. The Scriptures, Coleridge argues, bring order into the "fleeting *chaos of facts*" without paying the price of abstraction.[56] Human beings, therefore, appear within its narratives in the particularity of portraiture with the fullness of the "one life" that unifies them, "predestinat[ing] the whole in the moral freedom of the integral parts."[57] The Bible's rendering of human individuality demands recognition of the total activity of the soul: passion, intellect, and moral will.

The exposition of the "ends of the state" in *A Lay Sermon* demonstrated how for Coleridge an understanding of society that is not reductive had to take account of hope as a necessity for a properly *human* existence. Hope is "an indispensable condition of . . . moral and intellectual progression" and that by which God has distinguished the human being "from the brute that perishes."[58] The "seminal power" of the ideas that are symbolized in Scripture find an important psychological correspondence in hope. The epistemological roots of hope lie in the

---

[55]Coleridge, *The Friend*, pt. 1, 520-21.
[56]Coleridge, *Statesman's Manual*, 18-22, 28-33.
[57]Coleridge, *Statesman's Manual*, 30-33.
[58]Coleridge, *A Lay Sermon*, 217n.*; cf. Coleridge, *The Friend*, pt. 1, 252-53; see also Coleridge, *Notebooks* 3:3564: "How aweful as Duty does not Hope become!—and what a Nurse, yea,—Mother of all other the fairest virtues.—We despair of others' goodness, and hence are ourselves bad." Cf. Coleridge, *The Friend*, pt. 1, 103.

expansiveness of the mind as Coleridge understands it: the mind as an active, progressive power that makes each new discovery a tool for further labor. A red thread through the developing theory of the imagination is the connection between imagination and this orientation of human life toward a future that is the object of intellectual and moral effort. From early in his career, still within the necessitarian philosophical frame of Priestly and Hartley, we read:

> [T]he mind must enlarge its sphere of activity, and progressive by nature, must never rest content. For this purpose our Almighty Parent hath given us Imagination that stimulates to the attainment of real excellence, by the contemplation of splendid possibilities.[59]

The "post-Kantian" imagination continues to be the engine of progression, diffusing the fixities of understanding and fancy in order to unify and idealize.

By bringing the object-world of the understanding within the universal horizon of reason, the imagination creates the possibility of moral and intellectual dissatisfaction and improvement. At precisely this point, imagination is once again brought into relation with religion:

> The grandest point of resemblance [between religion and poetry]: that both have for their object . . . the perfecting, and the pointing out to us the indefinite improvement of our nature, and fixing our attention upon that.[60]

The argumentative structure of *The Statesman's Manual* and the rifacimento *The Friend* invoke precisely this expansiveness inherent to the powers of the mind. Furthermore, the imago Dei and the differentiation of human beings from the animal creation is constituted by this capacity for progression. This capacity requires—indeed, in Coleridge's view, establishes a right to—an appropriate "sphere of action" for its exercise. The necessary sphere of action is provided by the institution of property, the protection of which, Coleridge accepts, is the originating purpose of

---

[59]Coleridge, *On Politics and Religion*, 337-38; see also the editorial comment, 109n.2: "The emphasis upon 'progression' and 'organic' in Coleridge's later writings is a significant (and uncharted) development from his ideas of 1795."

[60]Coleridge, *On Literature*, pt. 1, 325-26.

government.⁶¹ The possibilities that constitute the image of God, therefore, cannot be isolated from political existence in general or the distribution of property in particular.

This point has been stressed, perhaps even labored, because it exposes the tension between the implications of Coleridge's epistemology and his conservatism regarding the existing dispositions of political power and property. His reflections upon public education offer a clear example. The argument in favor of the universal provision of education is based upon what we have called the expansiveness of the mind. Once, Coleridge argues, "reflection and stirrings of mind, with all their restlessness" have been set in motion, then "excluding the people from all knowledge and all prospect of amelioration" is a socially destructive attempt at an impossibility.⁶² The educational die has been cast: the issue must not be whether to educate at all but what should be the content and the quality.

> The Powers, that awaken and foster the spirit of curiosity, are to be found in every village: Books are in every hovel. The Infant's cries are hushed with *picture* books: and the Cottager's child sheds its first bitter tears over pages, which render it impossible for the man to be treated or governed as a child.⁶³

Returning to the familiar account of the mind as a system of powers, Coleridge adds that reading and writing alone are insufficient as educational objectives: education "consists in *educing* the faculties and forming the habits."⁶⁴

Thus far, the educational argument, deriving as it does from the philosophical psychology, favors a universal education offering to all the widest intellectual sphere of action possible, the limits being dictated by individual ability. Such, indeed, is suggested by his remark in *The Friend* that "that Constitution is the best, under which the average sum of useful knowledge is the greatest, and the causes that awaken and encourage talent and genius, the most powerful and various."⁶⁵ The degree, however, to which Coleridge qualifies the implications of his argument is striking.

---

⁶¹Coleridge, *The Friend*, pt. 1, 199-201.
⁶²Coleridge, *Statesman's Manual*, 39.
⁶³Coleridge, *Statesman's Manual*, 39-40.
⁶⁴Coleridge, *Statesman's Manual*, 39-40.
⁶⁵Coleridge, *The Friend*, pt. 1, 353.

Education, though charged with educing the radically open-ended possibilities of the mind, is to do so only "according to the sphere in which the individuals to be educated are likely to act and become useful."[66] "It is enough," Coleridge declares, employing a quotation that is very likely of his own making, "if every one is wise in the working of his own craft: so best will they maintain the state of the world."[67] The givenness of the existing structure of power and property distribution cuts off the implications of the epistemology, even as a critical ideal. Thus, when we come to the clerisy, the term of Coleridge's educational thought, the labor of that band of educators is to conform to and instruct in "rights and duties" as presently constituted.[68] The latter are determined by the relationship of permanent and progressive forces, for the configuration of which the clerisy have no direct responsibility. The removal of the clerisy from "the state," as Coleridge defines it, and, therefore, from direct political power, may be read as a backhanded recognition of the radical possibilities of the cognitive powers they represent and of the humanity it is their task to educe.

In a previous chapter, I described the symbol as the "dynamic pole" of Coleridge's historiography and biblical hermeneutics. Within the historical and political context, ideas transcend their symbolic embodi-

---

[66]Coleridge, *Statesman's Manual*, 40; cf. Coleridge, *The Friend*, pt. 1, 540n.*. Interestingly, a similar tension appears in the political theory of later British Idealism. In Bradley's philosophy, the moral goal of the individual is said to be that of a "self-realization" that transcends social role, but at the same time conformity to one's station in life is fundamental: "[T]here is nothing better than my station and its duties, nor anything higher, nor more truly beautiful." See F. Coppleston, *A History of Philosophy*, vol. 8 (New York: Image Books, 1967) 217-23.

[67]Coleridge, *Statesman's Manual*, 7.

[68]Coleridge, *Church and State*, 44. The conservatism of Coleridge's proposals for universal education is noted by Ben Knights, *The Idea of the Clerisy in the Nineteenth Century*, 58-71. Knights emphasizes, however, that these proposals are prudentially motivated, the interest being to preserve social stability. While it is true that the references in *The Statesman's Manual* suggest this, this is a product of a rhetorical context in which political arguments against the education of the poor were still strongly urged (Altick, *The English Common Reader*, 141-72). Ultimately, Coleridge's demand for a universal system of education is a product of his theory of mind.

ments, having "an endless power of semination." The relationship between ideas and symbols, therefore, suggests a forward movement, transgressive of present limits, progressive with respect to the realization of ideas. When we also remember that, rightly understood, the Coleridgean symbol involves a turn toward rather than away from the concrete, then we have an account that invites some confidence in the capacity of historical and political reality to approach the ideal, to embody reason.[69] This is, of course, subject to the qualification that, in the realization of ideas "there will always exist disturbing forces, modifying the product, either from the imperfection of their agents, or from especial circumstance overruling them: or from the defect of the materials."[70] The approach of history to "great ideas" is asymptotic.

In terms of the philosophical psychology, the confidence in historical and political possibilities implied here corresponds to the capacity of imagination to mediate reason and understanding, to make the understanding "intuitive and a living power." In *The Friend*, however, we find another account of Coleridge's theory of mind, one which implies less confidence in the possibilities of the political realm. The first essays of the section "On the Principles of Political Knowledge" set out three different accounts of the philosophical foundations of political wisdom. These essays appeared originally in 1809 as issues 7 to 10 of the periodical edition of *The Friend* and they reappeared in the 1818 edition only slightly reordered and revised. Coleridge begins with the claim, a characteristic piece of rhetorically motivated systematizing, that "all the different philosophical systems of political justice, all the Theories on the rightful Origin of Government, are reducible in the end to three classes."[71]

These three classes are mapped according to the philosophical psychology. First, there is the "Hobbesian," that presents the mind as nothing more than "manifold modifications of passive sensation." Human beings are forced by their defenselessness into accepting the desperate refuge of government, the authority of which they accept solely through

---

[69] As Raimonda Modiano remarks, "[T]here are times when Coleridge seems to approach the Hegelian notion of a progressive realization of the absolute idea." Modiano, "Metaphysical Debate in Coleridge's Political Theory," *Studies in Romanticism* 21 (Fall 1982): 469.

[70] Coleridge, *Church and State*, 37.

[71] Coleridge, *The Friend*, pt. 1, 166.

fear. Arguing that fear alone cannot explain the acceptance of social authority, Coleridge makes short work of what is a wholly inadequate and caricatured account of Hobbes. He then turns to political institutions considered as products of "expediency," a view that "derives the origin of all government from human *prudence*." As prudential, political decisions are products of the understanding as "the faculty of suiting measures to circumstances."[72] That this does not exclude considering the demands of the moral reason is made clear in the exposition of the "third system." Coleridge's presentation of "prudential politics," despite his acknowledgement that this is the system he wishes to adopt, is extremely slight. He prefers to establish its credibility by demonstrating that the two alternatives are untenable. In consequence he is relieved of the bother of investigating the problems faced by political "prudence," such as the devising of principles to guide discrimination between rival claims to expedience. The reader is thus left quite in the dark as to whether Coleridge is capable of articulating a coherent foundation for political reasoning.

Coleridge devotes most of his attention in these essays to criticizing the claim that political institutions must be founded in the dictates of reason alone. Rousseau's *The Social Contract* is taken as the representative and most admirable exposition of this claim. The main lines of Coleridge's argument have already been described.[73] A wholly rational society is a chimera and to forget the at best only partly rational character of any existing society is to court disaster.[74] Legislation in any existing society requires judging states of affairs that originate in contingent historical circumstances and are not derivable from reason alone. The principle example of the latter is property, the institution for the protection of which, Coleridge argues, "men first formed themselves into a State."[75] The political realm originates in that which has only a minimal foothold in reason. "It is impossible to deduce the Right of Property from pure Reason," Coleridge declares in the text. This is then qualified in a

---

[72] Coleridge, *The Friend*, pt. 1, 176.
[73] See above, 125-26.
[74] Coleridge, *The Friend*, pt. 1, 193-94: "REASON itself . . . dwells in every man *potentially*, but actually and in perfect purity is found in no man and no body of men."
[75] Coleridge, *The Friend*, pt. 1, 199.

footnote in which he admits that the *idea* of property, as constituting a "sphere of action" for the exercise of the will "is deducible from the Free agency of man. If to act freely be a Right, a *sphere* of action must be so too." The kinds of property, and the means and form of its distribution, however, is an entirely contingent matter, concerning which reason alone is an inadequate guide. Political decisions regarding property are prudential ones and thus belong to the sphere of the understanding. They are not, however, simply divorced from reason: "from Reason alone can we derive the principles which our Understanding are to apply, the Ideal to which by means of our Understandings we should endeavor to approximate."[76]

Two observations need to be made about Coleridge's argument here. First, Coleridge, drawing largely upon Kant for his criticisms of Rousseau, drives a wedge between the sphere of morality and that of politics.[77] Rousseau's "sovereign will," Coleridge argues, "to which the right of universal legislation appertains," can exist nowhere as a political reality. It "applies to no one Human Being, to no Society or assemblage of Human Beings . . . but entirely and exclusively to REASON itself."[78] Reason alone, however, is an appropriate judge only of individual morality, that is, as to whether or not the "internal maxim of our actions" meets the conditions of the Kantian categorical imperative.[79] Coleridge continues:

> But with what shew of Reason can we pretend, from a principle by which we are to determine the purity of our motives, to deduce the form and matter of a rightful Government, the main office of which is to regulate the outward actions of particular bodies of men, according to their particular circumstances.[80]

---

[76] Coleridge, *The Friend*, pt. 1, 199.
[77] Deirdre Coleman, *Coleridge and the Friend (1809–1810*, 132-63.
[78] Coleridge, *The Friend*, pt. 1, 193-94.
[79] Coleridge, *The Friend*, pt. 1, 194: "So act that thou mayest be able, without involving any contradiction, to will that the maxim of thy conduct should be the law of all intelligent Beings—is the one universal and sufficient principle and guide of morality."
[80] Coleridge, *The Friend*, pt. 1, 194-95.

The disastrous failure of Rousseau, and still more of those who appealed to him during the revolutionary period in France, was to seek to employ reason as the sole criterion of those "outward actions." When that which belongs to the moral sphere, as a measure of the good will, is extended into the political realm, "we shall find little or nothing is won by it for the institutions of society; and least of all for the constitution of Governments."

The second point to be made about these essays in *The Friend* concerns the theory of mind. We have here a marked difference in emphasis compared with the account of the mind's powers found in the lay sermons and, indeed, in the *Biographia Literaria*. In the latter, the theory of the imagination plays an essential role and emphasis is placed upon the capacity of the imagination to transform the exercise of the understanding through the mediation of reason. Within this presentation, it is the imagination that "counteracts the perennial tendency of politics to vanish into its own black hole of expediency and spiritual squalor."[81] The imagination is the capacity for dissolving and diffusing the fixities of the given for the sake of orderings infused with "eternal verities." The striving of the imagination is for their representation in the aesthetic sphere; their discovery in the scientific; and, in the political, the progressive approach to their historical realization in the social reality of "Justice, Holiness, Free will, etc."[82] The theory of the imagination thereby maintains a place for the discourse of human perfectibility, at least as legitimate utopian discourse; in this case, a discourse that recognizes the mind's progressive nature as a source of critique and an impulse for political change.

By contrast, in the political section of *The Friend*, Coleridge adopts a more rigorously Kantian separation of the mental powers.[83] Reference to the imagination and its mediating activity is entirely absent,

---

[81]R. F. Storch, "The Politics of the Imagination," *Studies in Romanticism* 21 (Fall 1982): 448.

[82]Coleridge, *The Friend*, pt. 1, 177n.*.

[83]Coleridge's claims for reason here, however, as elsewhere, still go beyond Kant: "By the pure REASON, I mean the power by which we become possessed of principle, (the eternal verities of Plato and Descartes) and the ideas . . . of Justice, Holiness, Free will, etc. in Morals." Coleridge, *The Friend*, pt. 1, 177n.*.

and the emphasis falls instead upon the understanding and, distinctive of that power, prudential thought. The realm of the political is governed by the understanding, though not, it must be noted, in the complete absence of the influence of "ideas"—expedience is not *mere* expedience. The understanding, however, presupposing and working with the givens of historical contingency, judges the possible extent and manner of that influence. Coleridge represents the world of the state as resistant to rationality, employing the distinction between morality and politics to mark the distance of reason from the political sphere. There is some justification for John Colmer's claim that, in these essays, Coleridge, despite his intentions, approaches the point at which "the rule of expedience appears to be divorced from the rule of universal reason."[84]

One of the motivating forces behind Coleridge's critique of pure reason in politics is his concern with the institution of property. Government originates for the protection, not of life, but property, and property is this author's paradigm instance of the distinction between human society and a "kingdom of pure reason":

> We regard angels and glorified spirits as Beings of pure Reason: and whoever thought of property in Heaven? Even the simplest and most moral form of it, namely, Marriage . . . is excluded from the state of pure Reason.[85]

Significantly, too, Coleridge appeals, with a dangerous rhetoric, to "fears of leveling." The right to equal property, he declares, is reductio ad absurdum of rationalist argument in favor of universal suffrage: "unless he carries his system to the whole length of common labor and common possession, a right to universal suffrage cannot exist."[86]

---

[84]John Colmer, *Coleridge as Social Critic*, 103.

[85]Coleridge, *The Friend*, pt. 1, 200.

[86]Coleridge, *The Friend*, pt. 1, 202. See also at 201-202: "Again [Major Cartwright] affirms that, 'Laws to bind all must be assented to by all, and consequently every man, even the poorest, has an equal right to suffrage': and this for an additional reason, because 'all without exception are capable of feeling happiness or misery, accordingly as they are well or ill governed.' But are they not then capable of feeling happiness or misery according as they do or do not possess the means of a comfortable subsistence? And who is the judge, what is a comfortable subsistence, but the man himself? Might not then, on the

Coleridge's own political apologia is also bound up with the theme of property. Essay VI begins with the disingenuous claim that

> from my earliest manhood, it was an axiom in Politics with me, that in every country where property prevailed, property must be the grand basis of the government; and that that government was the best, in which the power or political influence of the individual was in proportion to his property.[87]

This is followed by his excusing the Pantisocracy scheme on the grounds of honest but misguided enthusiasm. It is notable, however, that in building the case for his being at no time a subscriber to truly "Jacobin" opinions, Coleridge carefully omits to mention that the critique of private property was the basis of his youthful utopia.[88]

The politically conservative thrust of the distinction between reason and understanding, as it is interpreted and employed in this section of *The Friend* is best understood in the light of Coleridge's concern to deny his early radicalism concerning property and to establish, beyond criticism, the necessity of its unequal distribution. This distribution is the primary given within which the understanding must work and which it must protect from the leveling implications of reason. What is eclipsed in this presentation, republished and thus reaffirmed in 1818, is the potential radicalism of the theory of the imagination. The emphasis upon the

---

same or equivalent principles a Leveller construct a right to equal property? . . . Here is a legal power of abolishing or equalising property."

On the "fear of levelling" and on John Reeves's "Association for Preserving Liberty and Property against Republicans and Levellers," see E. P. Thompson, *The Making of the English Working Class* (New York: Vintage Books, 1966) 102-88; Asa Briggs, *The Age of Improvement*, 129-37. On the revival of such alarms during the period in which Coleridge published the rifacimento edition of *The Friend*, see R. J. White, *Waterloo to Peterloo*, 101-13.

[87]Coleridge, *The Friend*, pt. 1, 223. Given Coleridge's exhortations earlier in *The Friend* on "speaking the truth while communicating falsehood" (introductory section, essays V–VIII), these remarks do not appear in a happy light.

[88]The climax to this argument is the supposedly vindicatory republication, at the end of the political section of *The Friend*, of the Bristol lecture of 1795. The editing of this piece, however, goes so far beyond Coleridge's claim in the introduction (Coleridge, *The Friend*, pt. 1, 326) that what we have amounts to a rather shabby fraud.

understanding, upon the distance between the political sphere and the demands of reason, blunts potential criticism of property distribution and creates a space within which radically unequal forms of that distribution may be accepted. Coleridge thus qualifies and limits radical impulses within his thought. The distinction between morality and politics he accepts in the rifacimento *Friend* contributes to the development of the clerisy ideal. The distinction foreshadows the distance of the body of educators from matters of state. The imaginative bird is belimned, prevented from flight into the political sky.

Consideration of the argument in *The Friend* raises a final caution concerning Coleridge's doctrine of "the Idea." Raimonda Modiano points out that the insistence upon the reality and actuality of ideas, an insistence maintained in the essays on "rational politics,"[89] is accompanied by a balancing stress upon their unrealizability in history.[90] Acknowledgement of the "gap between ideas and the temporal forms in which they appear" is, however, ambiguous and open to exploitation for the preservation of historically contingent forms on the grounds that they are an irreducible expression of this inevitable gap. What I have suggested here is that such exploitation depends, within the terms of Coleridge's philosophical psychology, on a stifling of the imagination: that plastic and mediatory power. Finally, we may recall the resistance, noted in an earlier chapter, of Coleridge's interpretation of history to the occurrence of the novel. That resistance, also in the name of the enduring ideas, is a similar invitation to an insufficiently self-critical conservatism.

---

[89]Coleridge, *The Friend*, pt. 1, 177n.*.

[90]"Not to comprehend the gap between ideas and the temporal forms in which they appear is as dangerous to social progress as not to possess an idea at all or to doubt its existence. Ideas have an impact on the course of historical development to the extent that they are seen as pointing to a goal in the attainment of which man and society as a whole will achieve some form of improvement. But the drive toward perfectibility is maintained as long as perfection as such remains only a point of destination, not one of arrival." Raimonda Modiano, "Metaphysical Debate in Coleridge's Political Theory," 469.

6

The Conservative Imagination: Culture, Nature, and Grace

When I heard of the death of Coleridge, it was without grief. It seemed to me that he long had been on the confines of the other world—that he had a hunger for eternity.
 —Charles Lamb, "On the Death of Coleridge"

The Secularization of Political Argument

In March 1829, the Catholic Relief Bill received its first reading in the House of Commons. Sir Robert Peel, advancing the Government's case for emancipation, committed himself to abstaining "from all discussions on the natural or social rights of man." "I shall," he promised, "enter into no disquisition upon the theories of government. My argument will turn upon a practical view of the present condition of affairs."[1] This appeal to expediency was an attempt to restrict the scope of debate, a restriction with which many members of parliament, both for and against the bill, were ready to comply. Concentration upon the pragmatic ruled political theorizing out of bounds, in particular, it represented an agreement not to

---

[1] Sir Robert Peel, quoted in Richard Hole, *Pulpits, Politics, and Public Order in England, 1760–1832* (New York: Cambridge University Press, 1989) 243-44. On the history of Catholic Emancipation, see J. C. D. Clark, *English Society*, 366-420; E. R. Norman, *Church and Society in England, 1770–1970* (Oxford: Clarendon Press, 1976) 79-86; G. I. T. Machin, *The Catholic Question in English politics, 1820–1830* (Oxford: Clarendon Press, 1964); Richard Brown, *Church and State in Modern Britain, 1700–1850* (New York: Routledge, 1991) 203-29; Owen Chadwick, *The Victorian Church*, vol. 1 (London: Adam & Charles Black, 1971) 7-23.

pose, let alone press, questions of abstract rights with their perturbing echoes of Jacobin tumult.

At the same time, such pragmatism stilled another source of division by eschewing matters of theological disagreement among Protestants and between Protestants and Catholics. Coleridge, reflecting specifically upon the 1829 bill, also noted the inappropriateness of doctrinal arguments:

> And even so, with regard to the arguments grounded on the dangerous errors and superstitions of the Romish Church. They may all be very true; but they are nothing to the purpose. . . . If the *prevention* of an evil were the point in question, *then* indeed! But the day of prevention has long passed by.[2]

The issue, Coleridge insists, is that of the practical consequences of a political fact, namely, that "three-fourths of His Majesty's Irish subjects are Roman Catholics, with a papal priesthood, while three-fourths of the sum total of his Majesty's subjects are Protestants." If this, as Coleridge puts it, "is the evil," then the question becomes "will the measures now in contemplation be likely to diminish or to aggravate it?"[3]

By 1829, exhortations to consider practical consequences as of decisive importance drew upon a well-established tradition of argument. This had received its most influential statement in Burke's *Reflections upon the Revolution in France*. Burke warned of the dangers that "abstract" political theory posed for the continuity of a social order. Especially dangerous were claims to political rights derived from nature and transcending those given or arguable from within a particular constitution. Coleridge himself had reiterated this warning in the political section of *The Friend*. After 1792, there was a change in the agenda of political discourse,[4] a shift of which Burkean suspicion of political theory, sustained by the rhetorical needs of antirevolutionary reaction, was a principal mediator. Specifically, arguments concerning the theological grounds of political authority; the relationship between those grounds and the particular form of government; and the limits of political authority and the right of rebellion, were

---

[2] Coleridge, *Church and State*, 149.

[3] Coleridge, *Church and State*, 149-50. In all likelihood this section of the treatise was not completed until mid-1829. See *Church and State*, li-lvii.

[4] Hole, *Pulpits, Politics, and Public Order*, 250; Clark, *English Society*, 97-101; 247-58.

marginalized. They were displaced in favor of a widespread interest, among statesmen, political writers and propagandists, as well as among leaders of both Establishment and Dissent, in issues of social control. The means to ensure social stability, together with the necessity of inequality and subordination and the duty of obedience: these became the focus of concern.[5] In this process, theological argument, central to the debates inherited from the Restoration and the Revolution Settlement of 1689, ceased to play a significant role in constitutional debate. Parliamentary discussions of Catholic emancipation confirm this development.[6] The arena for theological contribution shifted to the question of religion's social, stabilizing functions, an interest that transcended not only religious divisions but also that between commitment and personal indifference.

Change to the agenda, however, was not the only development in political discourse in the postrevolutionary period. Of more lasting influence, in and with the changing discursive agenda, was a shift in the character of political argument. Richard Hole has shown, in his *Pulpits, Politics, and Public Order in England, 1760–1832*, that in a "general movement away from the theoretical toward the empirical . . . [the] concept of rights was largely abandoned; constitutional reforms came for reasons of political expediency, social reforms for utilitarian or humanitarian ones."[7] Arguments that presuppose or appeal to theological commit-

---

[5]At the popular level, Evangelical tract writers, such as Sarah Trimmer and Hannah More, reached, or attempted to reach, the widest audience with these themes. Arguments for the religious duty and social necessity of inequality and obedient subordination, however, were not limited to Evangelicals or to those addressing a popular audience, rather, they were matters of common concern among church representatives of a great variety of theological persuasions. See William Reginald Ward, *Religion and Society in England, 1790–1850* (New York: Schocken Books, 1972) 21-53; Hole, *Pulpits, Politics, and Public Order*, 127-44; Marilyn Gaull, *English Romanticism: The Human Context* (New York: Norton, 1988) 47-53; Norman, *Church and Society*, 15-70.

[6]Hole, *Pulpits, Politics, and Public Order*, 229-47.

[7]Hole, *Pulpits, Politics, and Public Order*, 250. Hole also sums up his case: "[A]n essential change in political and social thinking in this period [1804–1832] was the movement from a theological concept of political and social obligation to a utilitarian one. Many men gradually ceased to believe that they had a duty to submit to government and the social order because God willed it, and instead based their allegiance on their own human perception of the usefulness of that

ments are increasingly scarce. Especially in the sphere of constitutional debate, appeals that depend for their acceptance upon recognition of some form of theologically grounded authority, whether it be that of the scriptures or the church, are avoided. Political debate, in other words, is secularized.[8] Outside Parliament, properly theological argument is, in large measure, absent from writings and speeches both for and against Parliamentary reform. This is especially so during the postwar years.[9] Even by churchmen, change is advocated or opposed on utilitarian grounds. Once again, such arguments enabled otherwise uneasy bedfellows, Anglicans and Dissenters, as well as atheists such as Bentham and Richard Carlile, to make common cause.

During the first quarter of the nineteenth century, religious argument migrated into the sphere of social concern: the grounds and means of stability and the justification of inequality. Here, too, though, secular, utilitarian arguments had an increasingly important place. The ultimate hegemony of such arguments in matters of social as well as political reform was facilitated, however, not only by the Benthamites but by the extent to which many churchmen were already influenced by, or had adopted, secularizing kinds of argument, even within the context of overtly theological discussion. The work of William Paley, a favored Coleridgean target, is representative of this.[10] Paley, of course, belongs to an earlier generation, but his influence, during the first thirty years of the nineteenth century, was at its zenith.

Paley's *The Principles of Moral and Political Philosophy* was published in 1785. The systematic principle of the work is that the moral worth of an action, or the justice of a political institution, is to be estimated according to its "tendency to promote or diminish the general

---

government and society."

[8]Cf., Hole, *Pulpits, Politics, and Public Order*, 7: "The term *secular argument* denotes one which either did not make reference to God or things divine at all, or which did so only in a cosmetic way."

[9]Major John Cartwright, a principle object of Coleridge's critique in *The Friend*, was something of an exception both in his employment of appeals to God-given rights and in his use of arguments derived from Christian doctrine. Clark, *English Society*, 362-74; White, *Waterloo to Peterloo*, 65, 130-34; Hole, *Pulpits, Politics, and Public Order*, 229-32.

[10]Richard Hole also takes Paley as a key instance.

happiness."[11] "Utility," therefore, is the measure of all things. A moral rule is binding according to whether or not its fulfillment preserves or increases the overall happiness of human beings.[12] Paley's method is empirical: he refuses to privilege on a priori grounds any particular sources of happiness, holding that pleasure, in the preponderance of which consists happiness, varies solely according to "continuance and intensity."[13] He is entirely confident that our powers of observation, comparison, and reflection are adequate to the task of judging between degrees of happiness. From such rational procedures "every question concerning human happiness must receive its decision." To be sure, the Bible is a source of guidance but Paley denies that, as far as morality is concerned, it reveals anything not derivable from the honest consideration of experience. The rules given in Scripture are, as it were, a shortcut, saving what would otherwise be a more laborious and precarious process of reflection. The secular drift of Paley's ethics is clear. The content of our moral obligations is derived empirically, it does not depend upon revelation or upon the acceptance of any theological authority.[14]

There is one point, however, at which religious commitment is crucial to this ethical scheme. Only God, Paley argues, is able to provide a sufficient motive for moral action. Wayward, self-concerned, impassioned creatures need more than the knowledge that virtue consists in promoting the general happiness, they need a reason to be virtuous. Implicitly, Paley distinguishes between what makes a moral obligation *moral* and what makes it an *obligation*. The former, as we've seen, derives from its tendency to preserve or foster the general good. As far as the latter is

---

[11]William Paley, *The Principles of Moral and Political Philosophy* (Boston: John West & Co., 1810) 65. On Paley's ethics, see Hole, *Pulpits, Politics, and Public Order*, 73-82; D. L. LeMahieu, *The Mind of William Paley*, 115-52; E. Albee, *A History of English Utilitarianism* (London: George Allen & Unwin, 1901) 165-90; Leslie Steven, *History of English Thought in the Eighteenth Century* (London: Smith, Elder, & Co., 1902) 121-26.

[12]Paley, *Principles*, 66.

[13]Paley, *Principles*, 36.

[14]There is one exception: without the divine permission given in Gen. 9:1-2, the light of nature alone would condemn us all to vegetarianism! (Paley, *Principles*, 81-82). As a vegetarian myself, this aspect of nature's illumination troubles me less than it did the archdeacon.

concerned, though, moral obligations possess the same structure as other obligations. We are obliged whenever we are presented with a command that is accompanied by an impelling motive for obeying it, when, that is, our response involves us in significant gain or loss.[15] In the case of virtue, the threat of divine judgment and the promise of divine reward provide the impelling motive. Unlike Bentham, who abandoned, along with theism, the darker side of Christian anthropology, Paley believed that only the acknowledgement of God's final judgment was sufficient to determine men and women to virtue. On this basis, Paley arrives at the distinction between prudence and duty that so offended Coleridge: "The difference, and the only difference, is this; that, in the one case [prudence] we consider what we shall gain or lose in the present world; in the other case we consider what also we shall gain or lose in the world to come."[16] Duty is prudence plus eschatology: an eternal self-interest.

It appears, then, that convictions concerning the character and activity of God only become necessary to Paley's ethics in connection with sanctions and rewards. As Hole concludes, "Paley's moral epistemology was secular, the enforcement of morality theological."[17] As it stands, however, this is an overly stark conclusion and it requires one important qualification. While the principle of utility may generate moral rules and may be applied independently of theological convictions, theology, nevertheless, grounds the principle itself. Paley needs, as it were, to secure the principle at both ends. His eschatology provides the motive for acting with regard to the general happiness but this presupposes that such an account of virtue leads us to discern the will of God correctly and, therefore, that God's will is rightly identified with the actions that

---

[15]Paley, *Principles*, 57-61. In one of his best-known discussions of "desynonymization," Coleridge comments on the consequences for ethics of successfully distinguishing the meanings of "obligation" and "compulsion." His example of the failure to do so is that of "the moral sophisms" of Hobbes. However, given that the use of "obligation" is not typical of Hobbes—indeed, it is very rare—it may well be that Coleridge is reading Hobbes in the interpretative light of Paley's discussion (Coleridge, *Philosophical Lectures*, 173-74; *Biographia Literaria*, pt. 1, 87n.* and n.1). For evidence that Coleridge was not a close or careful reader of Hobbes, see Coleridge, *The Friend*, pt. 1 166-68.

[16]Paley, *Principles*, 60.

[17]Hole, *Pulpits, Politics, and Public Order*, 78.

proceed from it. Confidence here depends upon the famous argument from design. Given that the existence of contrivance requires prior design, we are to conclude, Paley argues, from the nature of the contrivance to the intentions and character of the designer. Honest empirical reflection will convince us that had God either intended our misery or been indifferent to our happiness, the creation would have been designed very differently. "The world abounds with contrivances; and all the contrivances which we are acquainted with, are directed to beneficial purposes."[18] God's will as will for our happiness, and, therefore, the utilitarian principle it grounds, is manifest in the design of the universe. Allowing, however, for this qualification, the utilitarian principle, once established, is not dependent for its operation upon divine revelation but upon the capacity of human beings to reflect upon their experience and calculate the conditions of human happiness. In this sense, Paley, writing from within the context of belief, secularized ethical and political argument and facilitated the acceptance of "the new, profoundly secular, concept of utilitarianism, which might well otherwise have been rejected as the godless product of infidel thought."[19]

The influence of Paley's ethics upon clergy educated during the early decades of the nineteenth century makes the *Principles* more than a merely representative work. At Cambridge, where Paley had taught until 1775, the book was adopted as the primary text in moral philosophy from 1786 onwards. All students were required, for their BA, to be examined in the *Principles*, which retained this status until 1857.[20] Paley's ethics also had considerable influence at Oxford, where the *Principles* was popular as a standard textbook well into the mid-nineteenth century. The book's educational role was not lost upon its detractors. The vigor of Coleridge's wrath against Paley is, in part, to be measured against the latter's popularity. "What," he asks, "must be [the] fate of a nation that

---

[18]Paley, *Principles*, 64.
[19]Hole, *Pulpits, Politics, and Public Order*, 82.
[20]LeMahieu, *The Mind of William Paley*, 155. Furthermore, *The Principles* had no rival at Cambridge: for the vast majority of early nineteenth century undergraduates it was *the* source for any acquaintance with systematic political and moral philosophy. See Stefan Collini et al., *That Noble Science of Politics: A Study in Nineteenth-Century Intellectual History* (Cambridge UK: Cambridge University Press, 1983) 344.

substitutes . . . Paley for Morality?" The Archdeacon's ethics are "vile, cowardly, selfish, calculating," yet, Coleridge bemoans, they "do woefully influence and determine our course of action." "Our most popular Books of Morals (as Paley's for instance) are the corrupters and poisoners of all moral sense and dignity."[21]

Coleridge also notes the secularizing tendencies of the Paleyan system that

> substitutes the Lockian and Newtonian—From God we *had* our Being—for the Pauline—*In* whom we move and live and *have* our Being. The moderns take the 'Ο θεος as a hypothetical Watchmaker, and degrade the το θειον into a piece of Clock-Work—they live without God in the world.[22]

In Coleridgean terms, it is this deistic substitution that appears in the circumscribed way that the doctrine of God functions in the *Principles*. In Coleridge's own ethics, by contrast, reason appears as the active presence of the "Supersensuous," the living power of God informing the conscience, an interpretation that differentiates Coleridge from Kant as

---

[21]Coleridge, *Collected Letters* 5:138; *Anima Poetae*, 131; *Collected Letters* 3:720. See also Coleridge, *Table Talk*, pt. 2, 162: Paley's ethical philosophy is "*most* pernicious; and there is an emphatic propriety in the superlative, and in a sense which of itself would supply and exemplify the difference between *most* and *very*." A notebook entry of 1809 depicts Paley at the nadir of a brief Coleridgean history of British spiritual decline with material and educational advance, "O place before your eyes the Islands of Britain and Ireland in the reign of Alfred, its unpierced woods, its wide morasses and dreary Heaths, its blood-stained and desolated Shores, its untaught and scanty Population / —and then behold the Monarch listening now to Bede, now to Johannes Erigena— / and then behold the same Realm, a mighty Empire, full of motion, full of Books, where the Cotter's Son of 12 years old has read more <than Archbishops> and possesses the opportunity of reading more than the Monarch himself—and behold them, yea, their Rulers and their wise men, listening to Paley, and Malthus— / —O it is mournful." Coleridge, *Notebooks* 3:3560.

[22]Coleridge, *Collected Letters* 4:768. For the famous watch-maker argument, see William Paley, *Natural Theology: or, Evidences of the Existence and Attributes of the Deity*, 12th ed. (facsimile repr.: Charlottesville VA: Ibis Publishing, 1986; orig., 1809) 1-18.

well as Paley.[23] Not surprisingly, a doctrine of grace, of the "mysterious action of the moral Governor on thee" is as important to Coleridge as it is absent from Paley's *Principles*.[24] Thus, Coleridge comments that a phrase of St. Bernard of Clairvaux, "Nothing, Lord, that is Thine can suffice me without Thyself," is "a sufficient antidote to—a wagon load of Paleyan Moral and Political Philosophies!"[25]

One further feature of Paley's ethics needs to be examined before taking up the principal thesis of this chapter. The principle of utility derives much of its rhetorical force, in *The Principles*, from its capacity to simplify and to unify ethical discourse. Indeed, it was Paley's exploitation of this feature that made the work an ideal textbook. Moralists appear to answer the question, "*why* keep a moral rule?" in very different ways. Paley claims, however, that the various answers may be resolved into diverse expressions of the conviction that moral worth is measured according to the "tendency to promote or diminish the general happiness."[26] The utilitarian principle thereby exposes the ultimate coincidence of participants in moral debate, why

> moralists, from whatever principles they set out, commonly meet in their conclusions; that is, they enjoin the same conduct, prescribe the

---

[23]Cf. Coleridge, *The Friend*, pt. 1, 155-56: "I should have no objection to define reason with Jacobi . . . as an organ bearing the same relation to spiritual objects, the Universal, the Eternal, and the Necessary, as the eye bears to material and contingent phenomena. But then it must be added, that it is an organ identical with its appropriate objects. Thus, God, the Soul, eternal Truth, etc. are the objects of Reason; but they are themselves *reason*. We name God the Supreme Reason; and Milton says, 'Whence the Soul Reason receives, and Reason is her Being.' "

[24]Coleridge, *Collected Letters* 2:1189. The absence of any doctrine of grace in the *Principles* is, perhaps, most striking in Paley's treatment of prayer as one of our "duties toward God." Paley attends to the stock objections as to the efficacy of prayer but he pays little or no attention to what human beings are to pray for, and none to prayer as itself a response to God, as a "work of the Spirit." The account conforms throughout to its anthropomorphic beginning, "when one man desires to obtain anything of another. . . . " Paley, *Principles*, 260-75.

[25]Coleridge, *Notebooks* 4:4889.

[26]Paley, *Principles*, 56-57.

same rules of duty, and, with a few exceptions, deliver upon dubious cases the same determinations.[27]

Utilitarian reasoning, however, does more than reveal the common interest of moralists. The principle of utility, as Paley deploys it, discloses the common interest of all members of society, demonstrating that the realities of social inequality are, despite appearances, to everyone's benefit. Rhetorically, therefore, Paley's utilitarianism is a means of identification, of reconciling diverse social or ideological interests by achieving an acknowledgement of commonality.

The most striking example of this is the famous pigeon analogy that introduces the discussion of property:

> If you should see a flock of pigeons in a field of corn; and if (instead of each picking where, and what it liked, taking just as much as it wanted and no more) you should see ninety-nine of them gathering all they got into a heap; reserving nothing to themselves, but the chaff and refuse; keeping this heap for one, and that perhaps the weakest perhaps and worst pigeon of the flock; sitting round, and looking on all the winter, whilst this one was devouring, throwing about and wasting it; and, if a pigeon more hardy or hungry than the rest, touched a grain of the hoard, all the others instantly flying upon it, and tearing it to pieces: if you should see this, you would see nothing more, than what is every day practiced and established among men. Among men you see the ninety and nine, toiling and scraping together a heap of superfluities for one; getting nothing for themselves all the while, but a little of the coarsest of the provision, which their own labor produces; and this one, too, oftentimes the feeblest and worst of the whole set, a child, a woman, a madman, or a fool; looking quietly on, while they see the fruits of all their labor spent or spoiled; and if one of them take or touch a particle of it, the others join against him, and hang him for the theft.[28]

One might well wish that Coleridge, in his own defense of property, had maintained, at the same time, a similar awareness of its scandal but not even during his pantisocratic days did he invent so bitter an image of the savagery of unequal ownership.[29] The pigeon analogy represents a

---

[27]Paley, *Principles*, 57.

[28]Paley, *Principles*, 87-88.

[29]Paley was advised by his friend John Law that the pigeon analogy, if not removed, would cost him a bishopric. Even allowing for utilitarian reconciliation

world of violently opposed interests. There must be, Paley concludes, "some very important advantages to account for an institution, which in one view of it is so paradoxical and unnatural."[30] The justification of property that follows depends upon the principle of utility: Paley describes the contributions that the institution makes to the general happiness. Utilitarian argument, therefore, functions to identify apparently divergent interests, to show the necessity of inequality, that what appears to undermine the commonwealth in fact enables a form of it more beneficial to all.[31]

When Paley turns to the questions of established religion and toleration, the appeal to utility again operates as a principle of identification. Theological disputes over church order are undercut by the historical argument that, in the beginning, expediency, and expediency alone, determined the institutional form of the church:

> The truth seems to have been, that such offices [bishops, presbyters, and deacons] were at first erected in the Christian church, as the good order, the instruction, and the exigencies of the society at that time required, without any intention . . . of regulating the appointment, authority, or the distinction of Christian ministers under future circumstances.[32]

A religious establishment, comprising teachers from a particular Christian body whose maintenance is provided by law, is also justified by its utility. When established, Paley argues, tests designed to distinguish the teachers of the preferred body, should be minimal, no more than

---

with property distribution, Paley's suspicion of the aristocracy remains. Also, elsewhere in the *Principles* the idle rich are not kindly treated. Thus, in his account of human happiness: "I have commonly remarked in such men, a restless and inextinguishable passion for variety; a great part of their time to be vacant, and . . . irksome." Paley, *Principles*, 38.

[30]Paley, *Principles*, 88.

[31]The appeal to happiness works as a principle of identification in two ways: it provides a justification for social inequality on the basis that the latter is necessary for the greater general happiness and it also softens the harsher implications of that necessity by way of the claim that *individual* happiness is "pretty equally distributed amongst the different orders of civil society" (Paley, *Principles*, 47). The doctrine of eschatological rewards and sanctions, of course, further strengthens this claim.

[32]Paley, *Principles*, 416.

agreements to abstain from the preaching of certain doctrines injurious to the public peace. As for the matter of toleration, empirical reflection upon the conditions of human happiness demonstrates the miserable consequences of "the establishment of creeds and confessions" for free inquiry, individual liberty, and social stability. By extension of the same argument, Paley urges for "*complete* toleration," the admission of dissenters "to all the civil privileges and capacities of other citizens."[33] Only when the dissenting body professes beliefs inimical to the maintenance of the state, should there be an exception to this principle. Even in this case, however, great care must be taken to demonstrate that exclusion is based upon a political threat not religious disagreement.[34] Throughout Paley's discussion of establishment and toleration, therefore, the principle of utility serves an interest in social stability and agreement. It also relativizes theological commitments, at least insofar as those commitments differentiate one Christian tradition from another.

Beyond Utility: Church, State, and the Higher Reason

At the conclusion of *Aids to Reflection*, Coleridge returns, in a somewhat grandiose fashion, to his long-standing antipathy to Paleyan theology and ethics:

> And how gladly would I surrender all hope of contemporary praise, could I even approach to the incomparable grace, propriety, and persuasive facility of his writings. But on this very account I believe myself bound in conscience to throw the whole force of my intellect in the way of this triumphal Car, on which the tutelary Genius of modern Idolatry is borne, even at the risk of being crushed under the wheels![35]

In what follows, I want to argue that Coleridge's last work in the field of politics, *On the Constitution of the Church and State*, provides, as a rejoinder to that secularizing of political discussion of which Paley was a most influential representative, a theologically grounded rationale for the relations of state, church, and Christianity in England. In Paley's ethical and political philosophy, identification proceeds by way

---

[33]Paley, *Principles*, 434.
[34]Paley, *Principles*, 436-40.
[35]Coleridge, *Aids to Reflection*, 408.

of a single principle that operates reductively, rejecting, for instance, a distinction in kind between "prudence" and "duty." All moral actions and all political and social institutions are thus brought under the measure of the principle of utility, a principle that is secular in application. In contrast to this, Coleridge expounds the coherence of diverse social and political institutions through a system of distinctions and relations dependent upon his theological theory of symbolism and the imagination,[36] a theory that does not function reductively.

The treatise on church and state, much like the lay sermons and the revised *Friend*, presents us with a certain dissonance of intention and execution. Coleridge admitted that the work was "patchy" and incomplete, and he even drafted an advertisement apologizing for the fact. The abrupt conclusion troubled him particularly and, shortly before the work's publication, he planned a new final section, addressed "principally to the Clergy of the Establishment" and entitled "What is to be done now?" Coleridge explained to his publisher that it would "give an air of completeness" to the volume.[37] The addition still remained unwritten, however, when Coleridge completed the revisions for the work's second edition.[38] As it stands, the bulk of the treatise is framed between two references to the Catholic Relief Bill. A brief introduction declares the author's intention to offer a critical interpretation of the bill, especially with reference to the "securities," that is, guarantees that Catholic emancipation will not undermine the established position of the Church of England. This promised "Aids to an Appreciation of the Catholic Bill" is eventually taken up in a rather hurried manner at the conclusion of the

---

[36]As a further example of Paley's reductionism, see the discussion of happiness in which he rejects the primary anthropological distinctions that, for Coleridge, are essential and must condition, in advance, any theologically adequate account of human well-being, "in which enquiry [into human happiness] I will omit much usual declamation upon the dignity and capacity of our nature; the superiority of the soul to the body, of the rational to the animal part of our constitution; upon the worthiness, refinement, and delicacy of some satisfactions, or the meanness. grossness, and sensuality of others; because I hold that pleasures differ in nothing, but in continuance and intensity." Paley, *Principles*, 36.

[37]Coleridge, *Church and State*, lv-lvi.

[38]See above, 33-34, for a brief history of the composition of *On the Constitution of the Church and State*.

treatise. In a typically Coleridgean fashion, the remarks, intended as prefatory to these reflective aids, expanded to become the work's principal matter.

These "remarks" are structured into three sections and might be entitled "On the Three Possible Churches." In the first, and by far the longest, section, Coleridge expounds the "Idea" of the "National Church." He prefaces this exposition by explaining the term "idea" and outlining the ideas of the state and of the constitution: ideas upon which that of the national church depends. The second section is devoted to the Christian church, not offering a fully articulated ecclesiology but rather describing those features by which the Christian *ecclesia* is to be distinguished from the national church. Finally, Coleridge discusses the "third possible church," namely, that of which the pope, whom Coleridge identifies with the Antichrist, is the head.[39] *On the Constitution of the Church and State* concludes with an appendix consisting of a ragbag of Coleridgean forms: a glossary accompanied by extracts of marginalia introduces a dialogue inscribed within a letter to a friend, an ironic witness for the conviction that rationality is fulfilled in system. Although it is much shorter, this appendix, or so I will argue below, performs a similar interpretative role to the appended material in *The Statesman's Manual*. Its importance is in-

---

[39] As I will not discuss this third section in detail below, it is worth noting here that while the papal is a *possible* church, it is nevertheless a false one. There are for Coleridge two and only two legitimate forms of church: national, whether or not also Christian, and universal, that is, Christian. What distinguishes the Christian from the papal church is the absence of a central human authority: it is the "spiritual Christ, one and the same in all the faithful" that is "the originating and perfective focal unity" (Coleridge, *Church and State*, 120n.*). Coleridge is careful to distinguish between the Roman church as governed by the papacy, and, therefore, falsified as church, and the Roman church as containing "pious Christians" (ibid., 136). When, however, Coleridge drafted some ecumenical "articles of faith" in 1834, he recognized that they might exclude Roman Catholics on grounds other than papal allegiance: "[T]hey also hold certain opinions, partly ceremonial, partly devotional ordinances, partly speculative, which have so fatal a facility of being degraded into base, corrupting and even idolatrous practices, that if the Roman Catholic will make *them* of the essence of his religion, he must of course be excluded" (Coleridge, *Table Talk*, pt. 1, 457).

dicated in that Coleridge indulges a rhetorical habit of approaching what is crucial by way of a scurry of apparently procrastinating introductions.

Two concerns govern my discussion of the treatise on church and state. The first is to give proper attention to the theological context of Coleridge's political and social arguments. This context is not always apparent from the text of the treatise alone. Reference to other writings is necessary, especially to the drafted sections of the *Opus Maximum*. Also, in order to grasp the theological context, the treatise must be taken as a rhetorical whole, giving due weight to the discussion of the Christian church and, especially, to the appendix. Much interpretation of *On the Constitution of the Church and State* has concentrated upon the first part and the influential concepts of national church and clerisy, regarding Coleridge's reflection upon specifically Christian ecclesiology as a matter of quite distinct and marginal interest. The appendix has been all but ignored: it is the point at which Coleridge "trails off woefully [and] . . . we may decline to follow him into this polyglot twilight."[40] The path, however, to a properly theological interpretation of the whole treatise is precisely through this "twilight." Coleridge's politics, as I will show, is a distinctly theological politics: theological commitments are determinative for Coleridge's reading of the role and significance of the state and of the national church within it.[41]

My second concern involves Coleridge's system of distinctions and relations. To understand this system, and its distinctly antireductionist character, we must heed the author's insistence upon a rational method capable of "distinguishing" without "dividing." Coleridge claims that this is a vital characteristic of rationality, mediated, as we have argued above,

---

[40]Brinton, *The Political Ideas of the English Romanticists*, 80. Two of the infrequent discussions of the appendix are Elizabeth Sewell, " 'As I Was Sometime in Milan': Prospects for a Search for Giordano Bruno through Prospero, Coleridge, and the Figure of Exile," *Mosaic* 8/3 (Spring 1975): 127-37; and Anya Taylor, *Coleridge's Defense of the Human*, 183-91. Only the latter of these two works, however, considers the appendix in relation to its context, and that only in passing.

[41]Coleridge notes the "double sense" of the word "state," "a larger, in which it is equivalent to Realm and includes the Church, and a narrower, in which it is distinguished *quasi per antithesin* from the Church, as in the phrase, *Church and State*" (Coleridge, *Church and State*, 20).

by the imagination. He warrants this claim by adopting the theory, Christian in its development, Platonic in its roots, of divine "ideas." In order to understand the connection and distinction of national and the Christian churches, we must grasp Coleridge's rational method and its theological foundation. Only then may we give a proper stress to the author's very serious, though generally slighted, claim that "the perfection of each may require the union of both in the same person."[42]

When interpreters of *On the Constitution of the Church and State* no longer recognize, let alone accept, the Coleridgean theological rationality, it is hardly surprising that they read the relationship of national and Christian church as a purely fortuitous one, arguing that the idea of the former can be explicated without reference to the latter. John Stuart Mill, conceiving the relationship in utilitarian terms, denied that Coleridge vested the national church as such with any religious significance. While its religious affiliation is socially beneficial at the present stage of civilization, the idea of the national church, Mill claims, would suffer no essential distortion if, under different conditions, it were to be instituted in a purely secular form.[43] Mill's interpretation of the social role of intellectuals has other merits but as a reading of Coleridge it will not do. He ignores, for instance, Coleridge's grave warning, a warning based not on utilitarian but on theological grounds, that "fearfully great and grievous" would be the consequences of the separation of national and Christian churches.[44] David Calleo, attempting to secure Coleridge's current political relevance, argues a similar case. He proposes that the private and state educational structure of Britain and America is the contemporary embodiment of the idea of the national church: "College presidents are the bishops of the modern world."[45] This, though, misses an important point: such institutions reflect the Coleridgean idea transformed through utilitarianism and that secularization of social thought against which Coleridge set himself to write.

---

[42]Coleridge, *Church and State*, 57.

[43]John Stuart Mill, "Coleridge," 207-12. See also the letter to John Sterling, 22 October 1831, in *The Letters of J. S. Mill*, ed. Hugh S. R. Elliot, vol. 1 (London: Longmans, Green & Co, 1910) 4-7.

[44]Coleridge, *Church and State*, 57.

[45]David Calleo, *Coleridge and the Idea of the Modern State*, 117.

From time to time, as he develops his argument, Coleridge reminds his readers that he is not providing a *history* of the British constitution or of the Church of England. Rather, he is articulating the "ideas" that have their historical embodiment in the constitution and the national church. Ideas transcend the changing forms of their institutionalization and so the form of their exposition need not correspond exactly to any particular historical instance. Still less does the account of an idea refer to the earliest form in which it appears. Coleridge insists that we distinguish, for instance, between the "*idea* of an ever-originating social contract" and the "idle fancy" that by "social contract" we refer to a particular compact agreed by our ancestors when they voted for social responsibility. To arrive at the "idea" of a historical or political phenomenon is to discover its coherence over time and space and, therefore, to discern the essential from the inessential and the continuity in change. The exposition of ideas, therefore, functions as does the principle of utility for Paley: as a means of identification, unifying historical, social, and political diversity.

Human beings, as creatures of reason and not mere understanding, are capable of ideas. Hence, they are capable of rendering their political institutions intelligible. The epistemology invoked here is directed against Paleyan reductionism but it also separates Coleridge from the Burkean conservatism with which he is often associated. Burke shares with Coleridge a hostility to what the latter regarded as the abstract political theorizing of the French revolutionaries. In both cases, too, their political thought operates with a strong presumption of the goodness of things established. However, when Burke attacks the intrusion of theory into political judgment, he is serving an "antirationalist" conviction that "denies to individual reason the power to see this process [the growth of a political society] as a whole or to establish by its own efforts the principles upon which the process is based."[46] Coleridge, by contrast, wants to distinguish the political theorizing of the French constitution makers from the intelligibility attainable through the exercise of reason in the contemplation of ideas. To do so, he deploys the distinction between reason and understanding, and the corresponding distinction between ideas and "abstractions" or "generalizations." Coleridge is

---

[46]J. G. A. Pocock, "Burke and the Ancient Constitution," in *Politics, Language, and Time: Essays in Political Thought and History* (Chicago: University of Chicago Press, 1989) 203.

convinced that the knowledge of ideas allows us to gain "full and clear possession" of the inner coherence of the developing institutions that make up the British state.[47] The knowledge of that coherence provides the criteria for judging the health of political institutions, discovering "to what extent [the idea] has been frustrated by errors and diseases in the body politic."[48] In a draft speech of May 1782, Burke, without benefit of Coleridgean epistemology, rejected this claim as "a preposterous way of reasoning." It was "a perfect confusion of ideas, to take the theories which learned and speculative men have made from that government, and then, supposing it made on those theories, which were made from it, to accuse the government as not corresponding with them."[49]

In *Church and State*, Coleridge gives a teleological cast to his account of the meaning of "idea":

> By an *idea*, I mean (in this instance) that conception of a thing, which is not abstracted from any particular state, form, or mode, in which the thing may happen to exist at this or at that time; nor yet generalized from a number or succession of its forms or modes; but which is given by the knowledge of *its ultimate aim*."[50]

The definition of an idea in terms of "ultimate aim" answers to the historically developing institutions that are the subject matter of the treatise. It is also, however, consonant with Coleridge's reflections, during the 1820s, upon God as "Absolute Will" and upon causative divine ideas.[51] While "idea" is thus, at first, defined somewhat differently, its further exposition in *Church and State* is in continuity with *The Statesman's Manual* and *The Friend*. Ideas are the subjective form of that which exists in nature as law.[52] As distinct from conceptions, ideas are

---

[47]Coleridge, *Church and State*, 56.

[48]Coleridge, *Church and State*, 56.

[49]Burke, "Speech on a Committee to Enquire into the State of the Representation of the Commons in Parliament" (7 May 1782), in Burke, *Selected Writings and Speeches*, 332. See also Pocock, *Politics, Language, and Time*, 228; Miller, *Ideology and Enlightenment*, 170-73.

[50]Coleridge, *Church and State*, 12.

[51]See below, 220-31.

[52]Coleridge, *Philosophical Lectures*, 333-38; *The Friend*, pt. 1, 467n.*, 470, 478.

always a priori, "contemplated as antecedent." Grasping the idea of a thing means knowing the ultimate condition of its existence and character.[53] Ideas thus provide the essential criteria for judging the adequacy of existing social and political forms.[54] Most important, and again in contrast to conceptions, ideas are not arrived at by a process of abstracting from presenting data or by the reduction of a hierarchy to a common feature.[55] Methodologically, this last claim opposes Coleridge's thought to Paley's reductive procedure whereby happiness is identified as a desire common to all sentient things and a factor in the design of all nonsentient ones.

Ideas, then, are not arrived at by abstraction. They are possessed, rather, by the act Coleridge describes as idealizing and unifying phenomena. While he does not refer to the imagination in this context, the operation is the familiar characteristic of that mental power. The knowledge of ideas is then proved in practice, by virtue of their capacity to render complex historical phenomena intelligible and to provide effective guidance for future action:

> If you ask me how I can know that this Idea—my own invention—is the Truth, by which the phenomena of History are to be explained, I answer, in the same way exactly that you know that your eyes are made to see with—and that is—because you *do* see with them.[56]

However, what is it, exactly, that we see? When we turn to Coleridge's practice in *Church and State*, the distinction between what belongs to the ideal and what to the contingent form is unconvincing.

One example concerns the idea of the state. The state's power to achieve permanence and stability is embodied in the "possessors of land." Landholders are further divided into two subclasses. This division, Coleridge argues, is essential to the constitution. What Coleridge terms the "Major and Minor Barons" are necessary to the incarnation of the constitution's *idea*: these subclasses are required "by the nature of things common to every civilized country."[57] Despite his methodological

---

[53]Coleridge, *Church and State*, 20; *The Friend*, pt. 1, 491, 496-96; *Statesman's Manual*, 24-35.

[54]Coleridge, *Church and State*, 20, 56; *A Lay Sermon*, 156.

[55]Coleridge, *Church and State*, 20; *The Friend*, pt. 1 466-81, 493-94, 520-22.

[56]Coleridge, *Church and State*, 14.

[57]By "every civilized country," Coleridge refers to all contexts in which the

warnings, this claim is, surely, nothing more than a generalization based upon the historical experience of the British. When moving from a specific historical development such as the British Constitution to the idea of which that development is supposedly an instance, that is, the idea of the constitution, Coleridge is unable to avoid, or to show how he might avoid, attributing essential status to contingent features. Coleridge falls between the ideal and the historical stools. In the case of the landed interest, a nervous qualification indicates a sense of his precarious balance: the twofold division is required "by the nature of things common to every civilized country, at all events by the course of events in this country." The qualification, though, threatens the entire enterprise which depends upon measuring British institutions by an idea that transcends their history and upon which all bodies politic depend.

Coleridge provides his readers with a number of illustrative aids to the understanding of ideas. These examples are telling in that they disguise the special difficulties of seeking the idea in the contingent particularities of history. There is a danger, Coleridge warns, of confusing the model used to expound an idea with the forms in which that idea achieves realization. He illustrates this argument with the example of "the idea of respiration, as the copular and mediator of the vascular and the nervous systems."[58] In *The Friend*, the inductive reasoning through which ideas are achieved in the natural sciences is described as

> The striving after unity of principle through all the diversity of forms, with a feeling resembling that which accompanies our endeavours to recollect a forgotten name. . . . [the result] is the sense of a principle of connection given by the mind, and sanctioned by the correspondency of nature.[59]

---

idea of the state and therefore of the constitution has found expression to any degree.

[58]Coleridge, *Church and State*, 21. The naive naturalist, Coleridge argues, familiar only with the respiratory systems in humans and like animals might assume that the idea of respiration could only be realized in the form of lungs: "Ignorant of the functions of the spiracula in the insects, and of the gills of the fish, he would, perhaps, with great confidence degrade both to the class of nonrespirants."

[59]Coleridge, *The Friend*, pt. 1 470-71.

To explain the meaning of "idea," Coleridge also resorts to the examples of the social contract and of personality. Behind these, although Coleridge does not make this explicit, there is a process of reasoning that depends upon a transcendental argument. The idea of an "ever-originating social contract" that marks the difference between a free society and a condition of slavery is "evolved out of the yet higher idea of *person*."[60] As we know from discussions in the lay sermons, the latter, founded upon the principle that a person must never be treated without reference to his or her own interests, is itself dependent upon the idea of free agency. This, in turn, Coleridge derives, following Kant, from a transcendental reflection upon reason as it judges in matters of morality.[61]

Coleridge moves from the latter examples to the idea of the constitution with no comment as to the difference between a transcendental reflection and an attempt to identify the coherence through time of a particular historical development. He thereby implies the procedures are essentially the same and generative of the same level of certainty. Similarly, there is no acknowledgement that the verifiability of ideas in biology or chemistry differs from that of ideas in history. As we have proposed in previous chapters, Coleridge's account of ideas and of the associated theory of the imagination, attempts to present a unified account

---

[60] Coleridge, *Church and State*, 15.

[61] The argument, in a fairly Kantian form, appears in *The Friend*; the phrasing, however, reflects Coleridge's suspicion of the epistemological status of Kant's "postulates": "[The] law of conscience . . . *commands* us—from among the numerous IDEAS . . . which the reason by the necessity of its own excellence creates for itself, unconditionally *commands* us to attribute *reality*, and actual *existence*, to those ideas and to those only, without which the conscience itself would be baseless and contradictory, to the ideas of Soul, of Free will, of Immortality, and of God!" Coleridge, *The Friend*, pt. 1, 112; see also 177n.*. In *Church and State*, we find an invitation to a transcendental reflection upon human behavior with reference to a prereflective awareness of the reality of free will: "[A]ttend to their actions, their feelings, and even to their words: and you will be in ill luck, if ten minutes pass without affording you full and satisfactory proof, that the *idea* of man's moral freedom possesses and modifies their whole practical being, in all they say, in all they feel, in all they do and are done to: even as the spirit of life, which is contained in no vessel, because it permeates all." Coleridge, *Church and State*, 18.

of knowledge. The tension between the explanatory examples and the task attempted in *Church and State* indicates that, in dealing with historical particularity, the attempt overreaches itself and breaks down. The illustrations, scientific and philosophical, disclose Coleridge's own methodological reductionism. An ahistoricity of approach conforms the examination of historical material to nonhistorical procedures. A discussion of the theological context of the doctrine of ideas will illuminate both Coleridge's confidence in his method and one of the sources of its ahistoricity.

John Miller has suggested "that Coleridge's "ideas" are best interpreted as a variety of human needs."[62] This proposal attempts to explicate two essential claims Coleridge makes concerning ideas. First, that ideas, such as those of personality, the social contract, or the constitution, though possessed as objects of reflection only by a few, nevertheless exist as powerfully informing realities in the lives of the many.[63] Second, that, as truths of reason, ideas in their "own proper form [are] . . . *inconceivable*."[64] Miller interprets these claims as referring to human needs:

> The hind and the woodsman needed to be treated as persons. Citizens needed the Constitution—they needed the protection of rights and the enforcement of duties—as a precondition of social existence. The "idea" of a political institution was "given by knowledge of its ultimate aim" because the idea existed in the human mind in the form of a need which the institution was designed to satisfy. Such ideas were undeniably real, for they were integral parts of human experience.[65]

Ideas, furthermore, cannot be expressed in words and are available only to the reason because the latter "combined all the powers of the mind and took account of inexpressible feelings and instincts as well as logical

---

[62]Miller, *Ideology and Enlightenment*, 156.

[63]"It is the privilege of the few to possess an idea: of the generality of men, it might be more truly affirmed that they are possessed by it." Coleridge, *Church and State*, 13. Ideas are "the most real of all realities, and of operative powers the most *actual*." Coleridge, *Church and State*, 18n.*.

[64]Coleridge, *Aids to Reflection*, 204. Coleridge cites this passage in *Church and State*, explaining that this inconceivability "marks at once the difference between an *idea* (a *truth-power* of the reason) and a conception of the understanding; . . . the former, as expressed in words, is always, and necessarily, a *contradiction in terms*." Coleridge, *Church and State*, 17n.*.

[65]Miller, *Ideology and Enlightenment*, 156.

thoughts and tangible perceptions."[66] The inconceivability of ideas, therefore, refers to their representation of, and operation through, "feelings too deep for words."

While this interpretation implies a rather narrow view of the capacities of language, it does at least have the merit of acknowledging the unity of thought and feeling that Coleridge regards as characteristic of properly rational activity. Unfortunately, though, Miller has missed the much more radical sense in which ideas are, for Coleridge, inconceivable. Ideas are apprehensible only by reason, the "organ of the supersensuous" and cannot be expressed under the conditions of the understanding because the reality of God cannot be thus expressed. Ideas are, first and foremost, *divine ideas* and, as we shall see, an account of them is an essential part of the doctrine of the Trinity. Hence, the motto chosen for *Church and State* echoes the distinction between abstract contemporary histories and the symbolic biblical ones "characterized ... by the translucence of the Eternal through and in the Temporal":[67]

> THERE IS A MYSTERY IN THE SOUL OF STATE
> WHICH HATH AN OPERATION MORE DIVINE
> THAN OUR MERE CHRONICLERS DARE MEDDLE WITH.[68]

Among interpreters of Coleridge's politics, Miller is not untypical in failing to register the theological commitments behind the doctrine of ideas and its appearance in *Church and State*. The result is an explanation of Coleridgean ideas that oversimplifies them by secularizing them.

During the 1820s, Coleridge dictated sections of the long-planned "greater Work" that by then he was describing as written

> in assertion of the ideal truth and the *a priori* probability and a posteriori internal and external evidence of the historic truth of the Christian Religion.[69]

---

[66]Miller, *Ideology and Enlightenment*, 156-57.
[67]Coleridge, *Statesman's Manual*, 30.
[68]Coleridge, *Church and State*, 10. The passage is adapted from William Shakespeare, *Troilus and Cressida* 3.3.202-205.
[69]"Letter to Thomas Allsop," 24 September 1821, in Coleridge, *Collected Letters* 5:177. In January of that year, Coleridge had written to Allsop claiming that he had dictated at least half of the "Opus Maximum," "fit for the press," to his new pupil and amanuensis, J. H. Green (ibid.). As with many of Coleridge's

A lengthy treatment of the doctrine of the Trinity is among the parts completed. From the beginning, Coleridge makes it clear that Trinitarian theology is the essential context for understanding the doctrine of ideas. What is true of all ideas—that they are not arrived at through abstraction; that they cannot be adequately imaged; that they are the ground of the intelligibility and coherence of phenomena—all this is preeminently true of the ideas contemplated in the doctrine of the Trinity.[70] He writes, therefore, "if this [is] true of all ideas in how awful a sense must it be true of those ideas by which alone the being and attributes of the eternal Ground and Cause are revealed to us."[71]

In his Trinitarian reflections, Coleridge exposes the ontological ground for two assertions, both of which are vital to his religious philosophy. The second of these—the distinct, nondivine reality of the finite world—will be discussed later. The first, however, has a special relevance for his politics. The starting point for the development of the doctrine of the Trinity is the argument for the logical priority of "Will" over "Being."[72] The first thing that must be said about God is not that God is "Absolute Being" but that God is "Absolute Will." There can, of course, be no question here of implying any temporal priority:

> The most cloudy gnostic could not have been ignorant that the existence of a Will anterior to that of being in that sense of the term anterior in which a moment is supposed during which the one is while the other is not is a gross absurdity.[73]

The issue is rather that one can only think of God as "Absolute Will" at all, and therefore of God as *causa sui* and as creator, if one asserts the logical antecedency of the divine will over the divine being. While it is

---

claims about the progress of his work, it is difficult to judge the accuracy of this. Green's labors at dictation took place once a week, beginning in August 1820 but it is impossible to know how much of the existing manuscripts were completed by January 1821.

[70]Coleridge, *Opus Maximum*, 195-98.

[71]Coleridge, *Opus Maximum*, 198.

[72]Coleridge, *Opus Maximum*, 194-95. "Our first position therefore is that in the order of necessary thought the Will must be conceived as anterior to all, or that which supports the being" (194).

[73]Coleridge, *Opus Maximum*, 193.

absurd to think of the former without the latter, it is the divine will not the divine being that must be thought of as the coeternal condition of the other. There is, after all, no contradiction in thinking of being as a "product." The very idea of will, however, is abandoned as soon as being is regarded as the condition of will. "No other definition of Will is possible but, *verbally*, that which originates, and *really* that which is essentially causative of reality."[74] The antecedency of "Absolute Will" in God cannot, therefore, be sacrificed in favor of that of "Absolute Being" without denying the divine will through contemplating it "as a production, a generation, or procession from that being."[75]

From this argument concerning the divine will, Coleridge, derives his primary theological statement:

> An absolute will, which therefore is essentially causative of reality and therefore in origine causative of its own reality, the essential causativeness however abiding undiminished and undiminishable, this is our first idea.[76]

This affirmation of the "undiminished and undiminishable" causativeness of God initiates a theology directed against the "hypothetical Watchmaker," the God from whom "we *had* our Being."[77] It also leads us straightaway to the acknowledgement of the "personeity" of God: of God as personal and as the ground of personality. "Personeity"—and Coleridge uses the term to indicate personality freed from all limitation, dependency, and imperfection—is "necessarily contained in the idea of the perfect Will."[78] Rejecting the notion that personality is necessarily bound up with finitude, Coleridge finds the limitations of personality in exclusivity and self-concern. Personality advances toward its fulfillment with the increase of self-directedness, on the one hand, and sympathy, on the other. Considered in its perfection, then, personality involves the coincidence of absolute self-realization with unstinting directedness towards another. Such is the personeity of God.[79]

---

[74] Coleridge, *Opus Maximum*, 194.
[75] Coleridge, *Opus Maximum*, 194.
[76] Coleridge, *Opus Maximum*, 195.
[77] Coleridge, *Collected Letters* 4:768.
[78] Coleridge, *Opus Maximum*, 195.
[79] Coleridge, *Opus Maximum*, 195.

Coleridge's argument for the primacy of the divine will and for the perfection of personality that that will entails, secures a distinction that he invokes repeatedly as the basis of political and social critique: that between the human and the beast, or more generally, between the person and the thing. In the reality of the will as truly causative, in moral agency, Coleridge finds the distinctive character of the human. No political language, no ethical system, no social practice can be justified that is reductive of this distinction, that absorbs the reality of the moral will into the being that humanity shares with the rest of creation. *A Lay Sermon* inveighs against the consequences of the commercialization of agriculture precisely on the grounds that this is the character of human distinctiveness. Coleridge articulates the aims of government upon this distinction and it allows him to discriminate between mere civilization and cultivation. The social role of the national church is also developed according to this fundamental difference. The national church is charged to cultivate "those powers and instincts which constitute the man, at least separate him from the animal, and distinguish the nobler from the animal part of his own being."[80] The manner in which Coleridge sets up and employs the category of person within his political and social thought, marks that thought as a *theological* politics. As he develops his system, albeit in fragmentary moments, the affirmation of human freedom and, therefore, personality, emerges as dependent upon the argument for the priority of the will over the being of God. To put his argument in its negative form: if here, in the ground and origin of all things, being is primary and will a product, then being is primary everywhere and the notion of human free will as a causative power, that is, of practical reason, is a chimera. As *The Friend* has it,

> [Reason] unconditionally *commands* us attribute *reality*, and actual *existence*, to those ideas and to those only, without which the conscience itself would be baseless and contradictory, to the ideas of Soul, of Free will, of Immortality, and of God![81]

The *Opus Maximum* follows this imperative to its ultimate ground in the reality of God as Absolute Will.

---

[80]Coleridge, *Church and State*, 44.
[81]Coleridge, *The Friend*, pt. 1, 112.

The Conservative Imagination: Culture, Nature, and Grace 223

The concept of God's personeity marks the point at which Coleridge begins to develop his doctrine of the Trinity. Divine personeity, as we have seen, entails communicativeness, or the causativity of the Absolute Will that is eternally "undiminished and undiminishable." On the basis of this necessary causativeness, Coleridge argues:

> The causativeness hath not ceased, and what shall the product be?—All power and all reality are already present. . . . What then remains to be communicated?—It must in some high sense be other and yet it must be a Self. For there is no other than Self.[82]

Personeity requires otherness as the term of God's eternal communication but the unity of God as *actus purus* does not permit us to conceive of that communication as anything less than *self*-communication and, therefore, of the divine alterity as other than the divine self. Consequently, we are led to the idea of a second coeternal "person":

> A Self wholly and adequately repeated, yet so that the very repetition contains the distinction from the primary act, a Self which in both is self-subsistent, but which yet is not the same because the one only is self-originated.[83]

Coleridge sums up this divine self-repetition in a phrase he ascribes, somewhat strangely, to Philo, *Deus idem et alter*, the alterity being "the perfect correspondence to that infinite causality, which without this would have been retracted in itself."[84]

---

[82]Coleridge, *Opus Maximum*, 195-96.

[83]Coleridge, *Opus Maximum*, 199. Coleridge also provides the argument in the more familiar form of a reflection upon the implications of the Johannine "God is Love": "But how can there be love without communication? And how can there be a communication without presupposing some other with the communicant?—And again how can there be love without life, or communication without act, or an act divine that is not causative whether as generation or productive or creative?" (199).

[84]Coleridge, *Opus Maximum*, 206. It is not necessary for the purposes of our argument to follow Coleridge into his discussion of the Spirit as the third "person" of the Trinity. The account follows the classical lines of Western Trinitarianism: the Spirit is "the act in which the Father and the Son are One . . . the Copula by which both are one and the Copula one with them" (209-10). At one point, however, Coleridge does venture into heterodox territory. Introducing

The *Deus idem* and the *Deus alter* are, as we have seen, differentiated in that the former alone is "self-originated." In the divine self-repetition, the alterity "coeternally *becomes*." This expression provokes Coleridge to warn of the limitations of human consciousness as an analogy of the divine life, consciousness, that is, being understood in the Kantian and post-Kantian tradition as a self-reflective and self-identical activity:[85]

> I need not warn the reader to exclude all thought of succession in the term "becomes," the employment of which term objectively in the same sense in which it applies subjectively, i.e., in exclusive relation to the mechanism of the human intellect, forming one of the great errors ... in the recent writings of Schelling and his followers as often as they attempt to clothe the skeleton of the Spinozistic pantheism and breathe a life thereinto.[86]

As much as anything else, the antipantheistic thrust of the *Opus Maximum* responds to the ambiguities of Coleridge's own employment of Schelling in the *Biographia*. Initial enthusiasm for Schelling's project had given way before the recognition that the latter's system "is reduced at last to a mere pantheism."[87] In the *Biographia*, Coleridge embraced Schelling's philosophical goal: to show that our conviction of "the existence of things without us" is "not only coherent but identical, and one and the same thing with our own immediate self-consciousness." He concludes:

---

the intra-Trinitarian role of the Spirit, he describes the divine life in terms of the "venerable Tetractys of the most ancient philosophy" thus positing a primordial divine unity prior to the Trinitarian relations (209). There is no reason to suppose that Coleridge was here seeking to relativize those relations in a modalist fashion: the unity, he insists, that is the act of the Spirit is the eternal unity in distinction of Father and Son. Nevertheless, it is arguable that the suggestion of the Tetractys threatens to undermine the antinomism that is a principle concern of his account of the Trinity.

[85]The Kantian account of the structure of consciousness is analyzed in the indispensable and lavishly illustrated David S. Pacini, *The Cunning of Modern Religious Thought* (Philadelphia: Fortress Press, 1987) 106-10. See especially: "Kant means that consciousness can distinguish itself (its form of unifying) only by distinguishing itself from its states (the content it has unified)."

[86]Coleridge, *Opus Maximum*, 204-205.

[87]Coleridge, *Collected Letters* 4:874.

The Conservative Imagination: Culture, Nature, and Grace 225

The true system of natural philosophy places the sole reality of things in an ABSOLUTE . . . in the absolute identity of subject and object, which it calls nature, and which in its highest power is nothing else but self-conscious will.[88]

But as Schelling himself admitted and Coleridge soon recognized, "whoever would wish to call this system pantheism since all opposites disappear in relation to the absolute viewed as such, he should be granted this, too."[89] In the *Opus Maximum*, Coleridge attempts to establish a proper theistic dualism, avoiding any collapse into monism. By opposing the disappearance of will into being, through the affirmation of the priority of Absolute Will in God, Coleridge has already resisted one monistic possibility.[90] As he develops his Trinitarian theology further, he discovers, in the coeternity of the *Deus idem* and the *Deus alter*, the foundation of the classical doctrine of creation, of the nondivine otherness of the universe.

A distinctive feature of Coleridge's discussion of the *Deus alter* is that, at first, he avoids the traditional and most familiar terms of "Son," "Word," and "Image." His preferred analogy is provided by the Kantian account of consciousness as self-reflective, his preferred term, that of "Idea."[91] The divine other is "God's coeternal idea of himself" the

---

[88]Coleridge, *Biographia Literaria*, pt. 1, 260, 285.

[89]F. W. J. Schelling, *Philosophical Investigations into human Freedom*, 279. For Coleridge's dissatisfaction with Schelling's monism, see Thomas McFarland, *Coleridge and the Pantheistic Tradition* (Oxford: Clarendon Press, 1969) 107-90. I have found McFarland's discussion of the pantheistic implications of the principle of identity particularly helpful (ibid., 153-60).

[90]"Even the . . . Supreme Being, if it were contemplated abstractly from the Absolute WILL, whose essence is to be causative of *all* Being, would sink into a Spinozistic Deity." Coleridge, *Church and State*, 182.

[91]Having introduced the term "Idea," Coleridge then admits that it is not suitable to replace the traditional terms or even stand equally with them "inasmuch as the term, Idea, does not in itself necessarily involve relation." Coleridge, *Opus Maximum*, text fiche B_2, 264. As far as intra-Trinitarian relations are concerned it is difficult to see why "idea" is any less relational than "word": it is, however, less traditional and this is probably the more significant reason for Coleridge's terminological caution.

relationship being that of "the Supreme Mind and the adequate Idea."[92] The reality of the *Deus alter*, the complete coincidence of thought and being, is entailed in its "adequacy" as the divine Idea:

> We recollect that it is the adequate idea, and that if it be not real it cannot express the reality and therefore is not adequate. To be the adequate idea of the Father it must be first substantial as the Father and consubstantial . . . with the Father.[93]

This perfect self-correspondence is, also, the basis of the Idea's role in creation, as "being the *infinite* effect and recipient of that full power which has no other definition but that it is essentially causative, [it] is itself causative." The *Deus alter*, then, is the cornerstone of Coleridge's doctrine of ideas. The second person of the Trinity is the "Idea of ideas": supremely real and essentially causative, an infinitely seminal power.[94]

The *Deus alter*, as the perfect correspondent, is also eternally distinguished from the *Deus idem*. The acknowledgement of this coeternal otherness is Coleridge's bulwark against pantheism. Once again, we see the analogical function of the self-reflective model of consciousness: the self is self-constituted as such through becoming its own object. Without the self-repetition of the *Deus alter*, the *Deus idem*

> would be no self inasmuch as this supposes another, and therefore would be neither more nor less than the world in the scheme of Pantheism, i.e., an infinite power for ever more realized and evermore absorbed and lost in its infinite product.[95]

---

[92]Coleridge, *Opus Maximum*, 203, 211.

[93]Coleridge, *Opus Maximum*, 203-204.

[94]Cf. Coleridge, *Statesman's Manual*, 23-24: "[E]very idea is living, productive, partaketh of infinity, and . . . containeth an endless power of semination." In a marginal comment on Waterland's *Vindication of Christ's Divinity*, Coleridge refers to Christ as "that *Idea Idearum*, the one substrative truth which is the form, manner, and involvent of all truths." Coleridge, *Literary Remains* 4:227.

[95]Coleridge, *Opus Maximum*, 206-207. Thus, in his copy of Erigena's *De divisione naturae*, Coleridge noted that "Pantheism is but a painted Atheism and . . . the Doctrine of the Trinity is the great and only sure Bulwark against it." Cited in Coleridge, *Philosophical Lectures*, 433n.17.

From this eternal otherness, the unity in distinction of God and Idea, derives

> all other distinction in heaven and earth": in this other all others are included, . . . in this first substantial intelligible distinction . . . all other distinctions . . . are included.[96]

The Divine Idea is, therefore, the transcendent possibility and guarantee that those distinctions in unity, with which Coleridge is so much concerned, are real. The otherness and relation of Creator and creature; the unconfused yet united divinity and humanity in Christ; the duality of the self; the distinction and relations of finite creatures; the unity in multeity of past and present; and that focusing of the whole through the distinct part that constitutes the symbol: all these have their ground in the Divine Idea.[97] From the relationship of God and Word, all unity and difference proceeds.

Reverting to the traditional terms, Father and Son, Coleridge attempts a further exploration of the relation God and Idea. This involves the patristic doctrine of *perichoresis*. The perfect self-repetition involved requires that the relation must be conceived in terms of mutuality:

> It has been stated as the act of the Father in the generation and contemplation of the Son and directed towards the Son. But it is likewise and simultaneously as it were, the act of the Son in referring himself and in him the plenitude of the divine forms to the Father and thus directed towards the Father.[98]

Coleridge thus adopts the classical Trinitarian development of the Platonic and Neoplatonic doctrine of divine ideas.[99] According to this

---

[96]Coleridge, *Opus Maximum*, 207.

[97]Cf. "Hast thou seen, me Philip? Thou hast seen the Father—This [last] is the consummate *Symbol* [a Tautegory]," i.e., "expressing the same subject but with a difference." Coleridge, *Notebooks* 4:4832.

[98]Coleridge, *Opus Maximum*, 205-206.

[99]Albert Keller, "Universals," *Sacramentum Mundi*, ed. Karl Rahner et al. (London: Burns & Oates, 1970) 6:325-26: "The essences of created things are in the mind of God as exemplars or *rationes aeternae*. They are in created things as the *rationes seminales* which determine their development, and are known to man by virtue of an illumination given in his contemplation of the *rationes*

development, the Father contemplates in the eternal Word, the perfect, the exemplary forms of all actual and possible beings.[100] The doctrine is succinctly expressed by Aquinas:

> With God, . . . because by the one act he understands both himself and all else, his single Word expresses not only the Father but creatures as well. Moreover, even as God's knowledge is purely cognitive with respect to himself, but cognitive and causative with respect to creatures, so also the Word of God is purely expressive of what is in God the Father, but both expressive and causative with respect to creatures."[101]

Appropriating this tradition, Coleridge defines ideas as "the realizing knowledge of all the particular forms potentially involved in the absolute causativeness." In the plentitude of the ideas "contained" in the Idea, God's creative knowing contemplates everything, "whether as arising out of himself, or out of the relations which the involved realities must form and represent to each other."[102]

The Trinitarian doctrine of the divine ideas, as outlined in the *Opus Maximum*, provides us with the theological context for the account of ideas in *Church and State*. This is also the theological destination or "landing place," so to speak, of the reflections upon ideas developed earlier in the lay sermons, the *Philosophical Lectures*, and *The Friend*. The description of ideas as powers, whether as nature's laws or as moral powers expressed in historical action and embodied in political and social institutions, finds its final rationality in the causativeness of the divine ideas. The institutions of *Church and State* seek to embody the "ultimate aim" given in their idea. In discerning this, reason grasps, under the

---

aeternae."

[100]"In the adequate idea only doth the Supreme Mind behold all other forms, which can have no form if they have no being and which have no being except as they are one with that great living Idea which is one with the Father." Coleridge, *Opus Maximum*, 211.

[101]Thomas Aquinas, *Summa Theologiae* Ia.34,3. The doctrine of ideas is one context in which Aquinas's continuities with Augustine and with the Platonic tradition emerge: "It is necessary to suppose ideas in the divine mind. . . . [B]y ideas are understood the forms of things, existing apart from the things themselves" (Ia.15,1).

[102]Coleridge, *Opus Maximum*, 223.

conditions of finitude, for the divine exemplary form, the object of the creative will. Furthermore, whereas Coleridge finds, in the doctrine of the *Deus alter* the warrant for affirming the otherness of the creation, in the account of the divine ideas as contemplated in the oneness of the Father and the Son, he locates the unity of that creation with God. The world is to be affirmed, therefore, as the finite expression of the divine will and life, translucent to that life in those diverse focal moments called symbols. In every symbol, too, as the whole reveals itself through and in the part, there is the intimation of the divine plenitude: the unity of the divine ideas in the Idea, the Logos. Perceived as symbol, "every object bears witness to a mystery of infinite solution."[103]

This returns us at last to Coleridge's insistence that ideas are necessarily incomprehensible and inexpressible. Reason, as the "organ of the supersensuous," the faculty, we may say, of the *a priori*, cannot manifest itself except through the forms of the understanding, the faculty of the *a posteriori*: "the faculty by which we generalize and arrange the objects of perception."[104] That which comes forth "out of the moulds of the Understanding" cannot reproduce the unity of ideas in the divine mind. Ideas, represented under the conditions of the understanding, are subject to a necessary fragmentation. Hence the delicate balance of the mind's dynamic: the understanding is accompanied by the temptation to make its fragmentations absolute, "transferring reality to the negations of reality. . . . the science of the mere understanding."[105] Alternatively, as *The Statesman's Manual* has it, the understanding, when united to reason by imagination "becomes intuitive, and a living power." The mind is thus turned toward "the contemplation of reason, . . . that intuition of things which arises when we possess ourselves as one with the whole." The doctrine of divine ideas provides Coleridge with the ontological condition and telos of our human reaching, under the conditions of finitude, for the whole of things, for the "intellectual reunion of the all in one."[106] To say it differently: the divine ideas constitute the ontological ground of reason's systematicity, the metaphysical origin of the imperative, felt so

---

[103]Coleridge, *Statesman's Manual*, 90.
[104]Coleridge, *The Friend*, pt. 1, 156.
[105]Coleridge, *The Friend*, pt. 1, 520-21.
[106]Coleridge, *The Friend*, pt. 1, 522.

strongly, if so hopelessly, by Coleridge, for a system.[107] Coleridge's rhetoric, promising, edging towards, partially delineating the elements of a system, intimates, under the conditions of finitude, the unity of all things in the divine ideas: creation as a system of identifications in which parts find their intelligibility within encompassing wholes. To such a creation, systematic reason responds by obeying the injunction to distinguish without dividing. This, as we shall see, has implications for a reading of *Church and State*, in particular, for understanding the British relationship of national and Christian church as a "GODSEND" in a more precise and richly theological sense than Coleridge's interpreters have generally given it.

This discussion of Coleridge's Trinitarianism and his appropriation of the doctrine of divine ideas invites some immediate conclusions. First, Coleridge's appeal to ideas as the basis for an understanding of political and social institutions is a theological appeal. The coherence of the complex of institutions that make up a state and the coherence of that instrument of social education Coleridge calls the national church, are found in a correspondence to the divine intention expressed by their idea. Furthermore, for Coleridge, the ideas of society, state, and church, are implicit within a theological understanding of human beings, as moral agents: "try to conceive a *man* without the ideas of God, eternity, freedom, will, absolute truth, of the good, the true, the beautiful, the infinite. . . . [and] the *man* will have vanished."[108] In contrast to Paley's utilitarianism, the ethical and political judgement can at no point be abstracted from theological commitments.

Our second conclusion concerns the problems, described earlier, of applying the doctrine of ideas to the historically contingent. Coleridge shares an ancient anxiety about time. In *The Statesman's Manual*, the crisis of historiography and of political wisdom finds expression in the image of Heraclitan discontinuity:

---

[107]"It is the office and, as it were, the instinct of reason, to bring a unity into all our conceptions and several knowledges. On this all system depends; and without this we could reflect connectedly neither on nature nor our own minds." Coleridge, *Aids to Reflection*, 145.

[108]Coleridge, *Church and State*, 47n.*.

It is [not] possible to grasp twice any mortal substance in a permanent state, but in the suddenness and swiftness of its change it scatters and comes together again . . . it never achieves being.[109]

In the turn to the ideal, this threatening image is dispelled. Reason discloses the prephenomenal and eternal ideas that enable identification, the discovery of the consubstantialities of history. For Coleridge, as for Plato, time is "the moving image of eternity." The consequence, however, of this privileging of the changeless is the tendency, discussed above, to conform historical knowledge to the model of the discovery of scientific laws, or of the moves of transcendental argument. The framework of Coleridge's thought leads him, in the sphere of historical reflection, away from difference, from signs of discontinuity, toward, from the point of view of historiography, an inevitably distorting overemphasis upon continuity. In the French Revolution, therefore, Coleridge reads implications that are not only political but theological and metaphysical. The revolution is a countermodel of historical change. Behind the revolutionary claim to radical discontinuity hovers the suggestion of Heraclitan dissolution, the surfacing of time's appalling flux. Coleridge's doctrine of ideas is designed to save the face of time, in its bias toward the recognition of continuity, it always warrants the assumption of the meaningfulness of existing institutions. Coleridge starts from "a sympathetic scrutiny of the *status quo*."[110] Such an approach may be more reliably humane, as Burke and many conservatives since have argued. Inevitably, though, it

---

[109]Coleridge, *Statesman's Manual*, 20n.*. "The human understanding *musing on* many things, snatches at truth, but is frustrated and disheartened by the fluctuating nature of its objects; its conclusions therefore are timid and uncertain, and it hath no way of giving permanence to things but by reducing them to abstractions" (ibid., 20).

[110]Miller, *Ideology and Enlightenment*, 159. Coleridge's assumption of the innocence of the *status quo* was also noted by John Stuary Mill as a function of his choosing to ask, as his primary question to "any ancient or received opinion," "What is the meaning of it?" Mill's answer to the reactionary possibilities involved was to propose an alliance of Coleridgean historical and cultural sensibilities with Benthamite criticism (Mill, "Coleridge," 177, 206). The price, of course, was the sacrifice of Coleridge's philosophical psychology and its associated metaphysics and theology (ibid., 187-90).

is also slower to acknowledge the arbitrariness of what exists; more resistant to radical political critique; and, as we saw earlier, prone to elevate the contingent to the status of ideality.

Finally, Coleridge's account of divine ideas in the *Opus Maximum* invokes a synthetic vision, a knowing that transcends the fragmentations of the understanding. This knowing is the burden of the dialogue appended to *Church and State*. Mystes the Allocosmite addresses the representative man of understanding, Demosius of Toutoscosmos.[111] The former describes an unfragmented knowledge, the capacity for which is present in all human beings and waits only upon the will. Knowledge, here, is knowledge of the ideal world. Yet this ideal world is not divided from the phenomenal world of the understanding, rather the latter is recognized and known in its translucence to the ideal. The "Allo cosmos" that Mystes expounds, "the other World that *now is*," is intimately present in "this world" as that through which its coherence appears:

> The Allokosmite [*sic*], therefore . . . possesses the same world with the Toutoscosmites; and has, besides, in *present* possession *another* and *better* world, to which he can transport himself by a swifter vehicle than Fortunatus's Wishing Cap.

The Allocosmite is positioned at the point of mediation between reason and understanding, a cognition that is, as it were, stereoscopic.[112] He knows symbols, not fragmented images: "he does not bark at the image in the glass, because he knows what it is." The *Opus Maximum* and the appendix to *Church and State* describe knowing as finite participation in the divine ideas. These accounts recall the "original vision" of the *Biographia*'s "primary imagination," the vision in which

---

[111] By all accounts, the "dialogue" is thoroughly Coleridgean in a biographical sense: Demosius cannot get a word in once Mystes starts expounding!

[112] The term "stereoscopic" comes from Stephen Prickett's discussion of the Coleridgean imagination: "[O]ver and over again we find Coleridge describing the 'Imagination' in terms of bringing into a single focus two separate levels of experience, and seeing them as a coherent whole. His concept of the Imagination is essentially 'stereoscopic'; it stands at the intersection of two different perspectives, and so enables us to see 'in depth.'" Stephen Prickett, *Romanticism and Religion: The Tradition of Coleridge and Wordsworth in the Victorian Church* (Cambridge UK: Cambridge University Press, 1976) 19.

the world appears in its divinely given fullness. As is commonly pointed out, Coleridge's later writings draw back from "the exalted view of the imagination" found in the *Biographia* and in *The Statesman's Manual*.[113] References to the imagination become rarer and more modest, the emphasis falling instead upon participation in reason through the moral will.[114] Despite this, however, what these later writings offer us is not an abandonment of the theme of the imagination and its promise but rather a reconfiguration of that promise in terms of the doctrine of divine ideas and a more fully worked out Trinitarianism.

Prophetic Relations: The Ordering of Nature and Culture

We now turn to a more detailed consideration of the appendix to *Church and State*, beginning by examining its rhetorical place in relation to the rest of the treatise. The appended glossary and dialogue take the reader from political matters into considerations of the philosophy of nature, religious language, rationality, epistemology, and the relationship of will and reason. Though anything but uniform in terms of literary genre, the appendix is unified by a concern with the grounds and method of a systematic knowledge, grounds that are ultimately those of a Trinitarian religion. The system of true knowledge thus derives from our participation in "Reason ('Ο Λογος) . . . the supreme reality, the only true *being* in all things visible and invisible! the Pleroma, in whom alone God loveth the world!"[115]

The evocation of system at the end of *Church and State* connects this treatise with Coleridge's oft promised *magnum opus* in which he would provide his comprehensive account of "Revelation and Christianity, the

---

[113] James Boulger, *Coleridge as Religious Thinker*, 106.

[114] "The Creator has given us spiritual senses, and sense organs—ideas I mean. . . . Another and answerable world there is; and if man discern it not, let him not, whether sincerely or in contemptuous irony, pretend a defect of faculty as the cause. The sense, the light, and the conformed objects are all there and for all men. The difference between man and man in relation thereto, results from no difference in their several gifts and powers of *intellect*, but in the will. . . . I repeat it again and again—the cause is altogether in the WILL." Coleridge, *Church and Society*, 176-77.

[115] Coleridge, *Church and Society*, 182.

Reservoir of my Reflections and Reading for 25 years past."[116] In 1821, this hoped-for "Reservoir," on which Coleridge was "advancing regularly and steadily," was taking the form of the *Opus Maximum* manuscripts dictated to J. H. Green. The *magnum opus*, however, was an even larger, more ambitious, indeed unfulfillable, project than appears from the existing pages of the *Opus Maximum*.[117] The *magnum opus*, would "reduce all knowledges into harmony": it was the project for a final, great, and unitive work, and it persisted as an ideal throughout Coleridge's career.[118] This proposed systematic fulfillment, to which Coleridge's literary life was the fragmentary and asymptotic approach, informed the meaning and structure of his published prose works. He described it to Thomas Allsop as "my GREAT WORK . . . to which all my other writings (unless I except my poems, and these I can exclude in part only) are introductory and preparative."[119] As Thomas McFarland has argued, the chaotic structure of the *Biographia Literaria* in general, and the abruptly severed deduction of the imagination in particular, reflect the constitution of that work as "a kind of antechamber," developed preparations, for the *magnum opus*.[120]

Coleridge's prose works, then, need to be seen in relation to the "omnipresent reality" of his systematic ambitions, as they are expressed

---

[116]Coleridge, *Collected Letters* 5:160.

[117]"So uncloseable is the gap between the ideal and the real entities indicated by the term *magnum opus* . . . that scholars by mutual agreement now call only the ideal entity *magnum opus*; by the same agreement, the manuscript fragments in the libraries in New York, California, and Ontario are called by the name *Opus Maximum*. By a further paradox, there is no particular reason for thinking that these fragments deserve even that name; though written with the idea of the larger whole in view, they are actually merely the residuum of Coleridge's conception." McFarland, "Coleridge's Magnum Opus," in *Romanticism and the Forms of Ruin* (Princeton NJ: Princeton University Press, 1981) 355.

[118]Coleridge, *Table Talk*, pt. 1, 248: "I have endeavoured to unite the insulated fragments of truth and frame a perfect mirror (September 11th, 1831)."

[119]Coleridge, *Collected Letters* 5:27-28.

[120]McFarland, "Coleridge's Magnum Opus," 350-53. In the letter to himself in chap. 13, Coleridge draws on the capital of the promised *magnum opus* to justify the abandonment of the deduction, "Be assured, however, that I look forward anxiously to your great book on the CONSTRUCTIVE PHILOSOPHY, which you have promised and announced." Coleridge, *Biographia Literaria*, pt. 1, 302.

in the various plans for the *magnum opus*.[121] In these writings, elements of the ideal project are crystallized into a penultimate literary existence. Friedrich Schlegel's reference to a dialogue as "a garland of fragments" may also be applied to Coleridge's prose works in relation to the *magnum opus*.[122] The garland of fragments constituted by those works traces outlines of the never-realized system. The appendix to *Church and State*, like the essays attached to *The Statesman's Manual*, open up the arguments in the body of the work, indicating the systematic completeness that their central concepts demand and towards which they point. It discloses, albeit in a fragmentary way, the system of identifications within which the constitutional, economic, and educational institutions treated in *Church and State* receive their context of intelligibility. The appendix thereby issues a warning against the narrowly political reading that *Church and State* has, in fact, often received. It is a plea, therefore, for a reading in which its distinguishable themes are not divided from the embracing desire for a theological system. Due to their relationship with the *magnum opus*, these few appended pages bear a rhetorically greater weight than their brevity would suggest. Our dependence, and Coleridge's, upon fragments for some purchase upon the unfulfilled system finds its ironic representation in the form of the appendix. As the reflections of *Church and State* turn toward the system, they fragment into a variety of forms, indeed, of fragmentary forms: glossary, marginalia, letter, and dialogue. Here, the ideal project has its concrete representative in "a sere and ragged half-sheet" whisked and caught upon a rose bush by a gust of wind.[123]

---

[121]McFarland, *Coleridge and the Pantheist Tradition*, 194. For a survey of the changing lists of contents, see McFarland, "Coleridge's Magnum Opus," 356-63.

[122]Friedrich Schlegel, *Friedrich Schlegel's Lucinde and the Fragments*, trans. with an introduction by Peter Firchow (Minneapolis: University of Minnesota Press, 1971) 170.

[123]Coleridge gives this account of his recovery of the dialogue: "In emptying a drawer of understockings, rose-leaf bags, or brain fritters, I had my attention directed to a sere and ragged half-sheet by a gust of wind, which had separated it from its companions, and whisked it out of the window into the garden—Not that I went after it. I have too much respect for the numerous tribe, to which it belonged, to lay any restraint on their movements, or to put the Vagrant Act in

A culture that absolutizes the divisions of "an unenlivened generalizing Understanding" is desperately in need of reason, specifically of the rationality that strives for system. In its form, Coleridge's garland of fragments intimates the cultural problem; in its substance, it expresses the need for, as we have termed it here, a philosophy and a rhetoric of "identification." Identification involves discerning the unity within which the multiplicity of things is articulated. For Coleridge, it depends, therefore, upon that primary act of identification in which the understanding becomes translucent to reason and thus discloses humanity, the imago Dei. As identification, reason's task is both philosophical, in the discovery and practice of principles of method, and rhetorical, in the development of educational and literary strategies and in the deployment of the symbolic.

In the dialogue that concludes *Church and State*, the Coleridgean Allocosmite conducts a brief pedagogy in intellectual method. This requires that we break the habits of a fragmenting understanding and acclimatize ourselves to the ideal air of the present, other world. The pedagogy is summarized in four rules

> by which you may *educate* in yourself that state of mind which is most favourable to a true knowledge of both the worlds that *now are*, and to a right faith in the *world to come*.[124]

The rules are not all of a kind: two concern the practice of thinking in terms of relations, the others are principles summarizing the nature of the relations among living things. All four, however, aim at a unitary knowledge in terms of ideas. The Allocosmite urges that we learn to distinguish permanent from impermanent relations. First, we must recognize that which belongs essentially to a thing as opposed to any feature deriving from the transitory relations in which it stands. Next, we have to begin thinking of things themselves in terms of the relations of ideas, or "productive *powers*." All that is real must be thought of as the product of ideas, "living words." This is the basis of Coleridge's rejection

---

force against them. But it so chanced that some afterbreeze had stuck it on a standard rose tree, and there I found it, as I was pacing my evening walk." Coleridge, *Church and State*, 173. The letter containing the dialogue fragment was originally sent to Edward Coleridge. Coleridge, *Collected Letters* 6:593-601.

[124]Coleridge, *Church and State*, 183.

of the dualism of organic and inorganic, expressed in the "rule": "whatever *is, lives.*" "A thing absolutely lifeless is inconceivable, except as a thought, image, or fancy, in some other being." It remains, however, to give the organizing principle of the relations of living things, both with reference to each other and as themselves "products" of the relations of "productive *powers.*" This is provided in the rule:

> In every living form, the conditions of its *existence* are to be sought for in that which is *below* it; the grounds of its *intelligibility* in that which is *above* it.[125]

As this latter rule is central to my argument concerning the institutional relations of *Church and State*, it is necessary to discuss it in some detail.

Coleridge's hierarchical principle refers, in the first instance, to prephenomenal powers, that is, to ideas. Living entities, in their "several classes and orders," are, to use Coleridge's term, the "exponents" of these ideal powers. This relationship is another instance of the symbolic, of the "translucence" of the "universal in the particular."[126] The principle orders the hierarchy of powers and, in consequence, the relations among living beings, remembering, of course, the unitive maxim, "whatever *is, lives.*" Within this ordering, the lower is related to the higher in a twofold way. The idea of a lower power provides the condition for the manifestation of a higher but, on the other hand, that same power cannot be understood without recourse to the concept of the higher power.

To explain the notion of living entities as "exponents" of ideas, Coleridge provides the example of the orders of plant and animal life. The argument is not one of his most lucid but he appears to be proposing the following. The distinctive thing about the growth of a plant, as distinct from the development of a crystal, for instance, is that organization takes place from within, the plant integrating material from its environment. In a primitive sense, therefore, the plant exists "for itself" whereas the crystal's development is merely additive, *ab extra*. To talk of the plant being "for itself," however, is to appeal to the higher idea of "sensibility." Sensibility, characteristic of animal life and physiologically mediated in the development of the nervous system, is the "self-finding"

---

[125]Coleridge, *Church and State*, 183.
[126]Coleridge, *Statesman's Manual*, 30.

power, the capacity for sensation as "what I *find in* me *as* in me."[127] The growth of the plant therefore, is distinguished by a level of individuation that requires language distinctive of sensibility. "Vegetative life" is differentiated from the crystalline and, therefore, understood at all only by drawing upon the capital of the higher concept of sensibility, although the latter is precisely what is distinctive of the higher *animal* life. The concept of sensibility renders the idea of growth intelligible, and reveals it as an anticipation of sensibility: the "self-seeking" that has the "self-finding" latent within it.[128] Coleridge terms this anticipation, "prophetic." This anticipatory relationship binds together the levels of the natural hierarchy and, as Coleridge insists, embraces the relations of life to mind and mind to self-consciousness, consequently, nature is "prophetic up the whole vast pyramid of organic being."[129]

As we saw in our earlier discussion of biblical and historical narrative, the recognition and interpretation of prophecy depends upon knowledge of ideas as the unitive principles of history. This is also true of the discernment of the prophetic in nature. Nature's prophecies are founded upon its orders being united and related as "exponents" of prephenomenal powers. Their relations are the unfolding of the relations of preexistent ideas, a claim that indicates the distance between Coleridge's natural philosophy and Darwin's theory of evolution. As the discernment of the ideal, prophecy in nature is manifest only to the proper functioning of reason. The movement of reason, characteristically distinguishing without dividing, is the movement of identification: discovering the necessary links by which the diversity of creation comes into unity as a many-leveled hierarchy.

The hierarchical principle provided in the appendix *Church and State* has wide-ranging methodological and rhetorical implications. First, the act of distinguishing depends upon, and takes place within, an act of identification.[130] This is form by which plant is distinguished from animal,

---

[127]Coleridge, *Notebooks* 3:4443. Coleridge, following Fichte and Schelling here, appeals to "the German word for sensation or feeling . . . Empfindung, i.e., an *inward finding*." Coleridge, *Church and State*, 180.
[128]Coleridge, *Church and State*, 180-81.
[129]Coleridge, *Church and State*, 176.
[130]As in the *Logic*, where Coleridge emphasizes the priority in the development of the mind of the perception of likeness over that of difference. Coleridge,

understanding from reason, fancy from imagination, the lower from higher aims of government, and, as we shall see, national from Christian church. The lower is differentiated as an anticipation of the higher latent within it. Coleridge's system is directed against the absolutization of difference, whether it be that of the inorganic as distinguished from the organic, or the novelty of the present set over against the past.[131] Similarly, Coleridge's hierarchical principal is antireductionist. Since no form of life is intelligible without reference to a higher form, reality eludes a reductive account even of the level upon which that account seeks to base itself. Finally, this relationship of lower to higher constitutes an important form of symbolic relations, enabling human beings to discover themselves as integral parts of that seamless system of identifications which is the creation. In their anticipatory relationship, lower forms of life serve as symbols of the higher. Reason is thus latent within nature and the "book of nature" confronts us with the power and dynamism of the mind present "in a lower dignity." According to Coleridge, of course, such symbolism is a matter of discernment and not projection, imagination and not fancy. They are "symbols established in the truth of things," that is, in the hierarchical relations of prephenomenal and eternal ideas: in the Logos.

Coleridge's natural philosophy frames the order of creation as a mirror for human self-recognition. The social, intellectual, moral, and religious life of human beings is not alien to nature but rather its hermeneut. What we have here is a countermetaphysic to the "mechanic and corpuscular" philosophy; epistemologically, to the absolutizing of the categories of the understanding. As Coleridge explains in the conclusion to *Aids to Reflection*:

> In order to submit the various phenomena of moving bodies to geometrical construction, we are under the necessity of abstracting from corporeal substance all its *positive* properties, and obliged to consider

---

Logic, 11-12.

[131]See Coleridge, *Statesman's Manual*, 25-26; and above, 86-88. An early letter criticizes empiricism in terms of a failure to move beyond the recognition of difference: "They contemplate nothing but *parts*—and all *parts* are necessarily little—and the Universe to them is but a mass of *little things*." Coleridge, *Collected Letters* 1:209.

Bodies as differing from equal portions of Space only by figure and mobility.[132]

The mechanical philosophy took this "Fiction of Science," by which body is defined as "Space or Extension with the attribute of visibility," and literalized it into fact. Thus,

> Instead of a World *created* and filled with productive forces by the Almighty Fiat, left a lifeless Machine whirled about by the dust of its own Grinding: as if Death could come from the living Fountain of Life; Nothingness and Phantom from the Plenitude of Reality! the Absoluteness of creative Will![133]

Within this reductionist metaphysic, the activity of the human mind is either left alienated from nature or given a materialist explanation. In Coleridge's reading, Descartes's philosophy is the paradigm case of the former, Hartleyan or Godwinian necessitarianism of the latter. His countermetaphysic sets itself against both alienation and reduction, finding a natural home for humanity's ultimately supernatural identity: nature is prophetic of history, of the moral and religious life of human beings. In a nature so understood, that life has a sustaining home. Thus, Coleridge construes the mind's life as providing the hermeneutical key to nature, disclosing it as a system of identifications, "all the subordinate gradations" of which recur, and are reordained *in more abundant honor*, in the human mind.[134] Furthermore, nature's hermeneut, human rationality, itself demands, as Coleridge has the Allocosmite argue, intelligibility through a higher life. The "*self-containing* power" of the mind "supposes a self-*causing* power," the Absolute Will, of which it is the prophetic image.[135] The principle that discovers the creation as a system of prophetic relations grounds both the symbolic language in which we acknowledge our home in the natural world and, also, the symbolism by which both nature and history provide us with a language for the divine.

---

[132] Coleridge, *Aids to Reflection*, 399-400.
[133] Coleridge, *Aids to Reflection*, 400-401.
[134] Coleridge, *Statesman's Manual*, 72.
[135] Coleridge, *Church and State*, 182.

The World's "Befriending Opposite"

Others have argued that Coleridge's natural philosophy is important to his account of symbolism.[136] What has not been noticed, given the lack of interest in the appendix to *Church and State*, is that the principle of prophetic relations provides a hermeneutical key to Coleridge's ordering of political and social institutions.

The role of the national church is an educative one. In terms of historical institutions, the national church may be, and as an idea it should be, distinguished from the Christian church. In Coleridge's account, the primary concern of the latter is with the individual's ultimate destiny.[137] The educative task of the national church is "the communication of that degree and kind of knowledge to all, the possession of which is necessary for all in order to their CIVILITY."[138] To fulfill this charge, the national church needs to be socially omnipresent, the pastor and schoolmaster forming "in the remotest villages . . . a nucleus, round which the capabilities of the place may crystallize and brighten."[139] The work of the clerisy constitutes an enlightening power that is supposed to inform all society's other institutions—family, commerce, communication, arts, law, government. Under the guidance of the national church, they are constituted as spheres for the development, maintenance, and expression of moral agency. The gospel parable of the leaven is never far from Coleridge's description of the national church. This is the institution that secures a proper national unity, that is, the unity of the state as a moral entity, the only kind of unity adequate to a *human* society. The rhetorical task, prosecuted through teaching and example, is to secure morally responsible agreement to society's duties, responsibilities, and rights.[140]

---

[136]M. H. Abrams, "Coleridge's 'A Light in Sound': Science, Metascience, and Poetic Imagination" and "Coleridge and the Romantic Vision of the World," in *The Correspondent Breeze*, 158-91 and 192-224; Owen Barfield, *What Coleridge Thought*, passim; Thomas McFarland, *Romanticism and the Forms of Ruin*, 289-343.

[137]Coleridge, *Church and State*, 45.

[138]Coleridge, *Church and State*, 54.

[139]Coleridge, *Church and State*, 75.

[140]"The objects and final intention of the whole order being these—to

By formulating the task of the national church in this way, Coleridge also accords that church the role of bearing witness to the moral limits of economic and political inequality. Inequality may be the inevitable, indeed, necessary condition of society, but inequalities must remain compatible with the nature of the state as a union of persons, moral agents. In sum, the national church is concerned with educing those capacities that constitute the human as opposed to the brute.[141] Apart from this educative presence, the civil state collapses toward barbarism, its very "civilization"—the economic and social forces that stabilize and enlarge it—turning into the means of its corruption.[142]

A careful look at the structure of the relations Coleridge proposes between state and national church, will show that it corresponds to the hierarchical principle announced in the appendix. Clearly, in terms of its existence, the national church depends upon the state, upon the operation of those forces that make for its "permanence," the land and its ownership, and its "progression," the "mercantile, the manufacturing, the distributive and the professional" classes.[143] The "nationality," the wealth by means of which the national church is sustained, is taken from the sphere of private property, the "propriety," and reserved for the benefit of the nation. By means of this "nationality," the church maintains itself as relatively independent from the state and is preserved from becoming the vulnerable creature of government.

While dependent upon the state for its existence, however, the national church proves essential to an understanding of the idea of the state. Any attempt to understand the state in abstraction from the idea of a national church is doomed to failure. To consider the state entirely without reference to the educative role of the church is to lose the idea

---

preserve the stores, to guard the treasures of past civilization, and thus to bind the present with the past; to perfect and add to the same and thus to connect the present with the future; but especially to diffuse through the whole community, and to every native entitled to its laws and rights, that quantity and quality of knowledge which was indispensable both for the understanding of those rights, and for the performance of the duties correspondent." Coleridge, *Church and State*, 43-44.

[141] Coleridge, *Church and State*, 42-3, 48, 54, 72-73.
[142] Coleridge, *Church and State*, 42-43, 48-49.
[143] Coleridge, *Church and State*, 25-26.

of the state as a *human* institution: as a moral order arising out of an "ever-originating social contract." The intelligibility of the idea of the state, therefore, depends upon the idea of the national church as the institutional means of educing and sustaining moral agency. The state, as a balance of progressive and permanent forces, in itself looks toward, anticipates, the *nisus formativus* of a national church. In the latter, the body politic finds its security and the manifestation and fulfillment of the moral nature latent within it and its institutions. Thus Coleridge argues, its role is

> To secure for the nation, if not a superiority over the neighbouring states, yet an equality at least, in that character of general civilization, which equally with, or rather more than, fleets, armies, and revenue, forms the ground of its defensive and offensive power. . . . [and] to secure and improve that civilization, without which the nation could be neither permanent nor progressive.[144]

The idea of a national church is indispensable to the idea of the state. Remove from the state the educative forces provided by that church and the result is barbarism, the collapse of the state as an implicitly moral union.

It is now possible to appreciate the way Coleridge, in *Church and State*, reformulates the social problem addressed in *A Lay Sermon*. In the earlier work, agriculture appeared as an essentially moral sphere opposed to, and threatened by, the sphere of commerce as one of nonmoral relations. The destructive inroads of the commercial spirit into the ownership and use of the land was blamed largely on the failure of religion as a counterweight to commercialism. *A Lay Sermon* does not provide much substance in terms of the institutional form of this counterweight but the clerisy of *Church and State* is at least anticipated. The sermon articulated the social problem upon the structure of Coleridge's philosophical psychology. The agricultural world embodied rational relations undermined by a one-sided development of commerce. The latter was interpreted as a paradigmatic expression of the understanding while the failure of religion represented a breakdown in the power of imagination. In *Church and State*, the social order is differently configured. The state consists in a balance of permanent and progressive forces. These,

---

[144] Coleridge, *Church and State*, 44.

however, do not confront each other in terms of moral and nonmoral relations. Commerce is included among the forces of progression along with the arts and the professions.[145] Furthermore, Coleridge is now at pains to point out the historical links between the expansion of political freedoms and the increased practice of trade.[146] None of the forces that make up the state, whether permanent or progressive, can be adequately understood apart from the idea of moral agency. The epistemological framework is still present though its elements are differently distributed. The role of the national church is, through education, to preserve and extend human society as a rational order. It does so through its influence upon the institutions of the state. Apart from this influence, such institutions lose their integrity as embodiments of the moral idea that is human society. They do so in the same way that the understanding and its productions are dehumanized, become "*mere* understanding," insofar as the influence of reason is eclipsed. In *Church and State*, therefore, the social problem is framed more broadly and more radically. Commercialism is no longer singled out as *the* threatening force. On the one hand, that suggests a less one-sided appreciation of that particular social sphere, on the other, all social institutions are now seen as dependent upon the continuing mediation, through the national church, of understanding and reason. Finally, what is at stake in the work of the national church is the continued existence of the state itself.

The burden of the national church, then, is the survival of the state as a moral order. Its end is thereby distinguished from that of the specifically *Christian* church, with which it may or may not institutionally coincide. The concern of the Christian church is with the individual's ultimate destiny, with the spiritual and eternal rather than the temporal survival of human beings, a distinction recalling that between the Old and New Testaments in *The Statesman's Manual*.[147]

---

[145] Coleridge, *Church and State*, 25-26.

[146] "It was the profound policy of the Austrian and the Spanish courts, by every possible means to degrade the profession of trade; and even in Pisa and Florence themselves to introduce the feudal pride and prejudice of less happy, less enlightened countries. Agriculture, meanwhile, with its attendant population and plenty, was cultivated with increasing success; but from the Alps to the Straits of Messina, the Italians are slaves." Coleridge, *Church and State*, 26.

[147] "You will indeed have directed your *main* attention to the promises and

In the second part of his treatise, "The Idea of the Christian Church," Coleridge offers a brief ecclesiology with the intention of clarifying the distinctive character of the church as *Christian* church. The idea of the Christian church, he proposes, is that of a visible community but not one holding political power within the state. Nor does it have allegiance to a power outside the state, such as the papacy, that could conflict with its members duties as citizens. The Christian church addresses itself to all forms of that moral unity which is a state. In principle, therefore, it does not represent or favor any particular political form: it does not seek to extend the virtues of democracy, aristocracy, or monarchy, nor is it, as Christian, antidemocratic, aristocratic, or monarchical. Rather, the task of the Christian church, with reference to the state, is to advance the "beneficent and humanizing" aims that belong to the idea of a political community as such. Coleridge declares:

> The Christian Church, I say, is no state, kingdom, or realm of this world; nor is it an Estate of any such realm, kingdom, or state; but it is the appointed Opposite to them all *collectively*—the *sustaining, correcting, befriending* Opposite of the world![148]

The principle, here, is an important one insofar as it preserves the church's freedom, indeed vocation, to exist within any and every form of the state and to do so, moreover, without securing special privileges for any particular political allegiance.

There are, however, ambiguities regarding the nature and extent of the political role compatible with such a vocation. Why should the work of influencing for further good "whatever is beneficent and humanizing in the aims, tendencies, and proper objects of the state" stop short of criticism, where necessary, of particular political institutions? Coleridge

---

the information conveyed in the records of the evangelists and apostles: promises, that need only a lively trust in them . . . to be the means as well as the pledges of our *eternal* welfare! information that opens out to our knowledge a kingdom that is not of this world, thrones that cannot be shaken, and scepters that can neither be broken or transferred! Yet not the less on this account will you have looked back with a proportionate interest on the *temporal* destinies of men and nations, sorted up for our instruction in the archives of the Old Testament." Coleridge, *Statesman's Manual*, 8.

[148]Coleridge, *Church and State*, 114.

is characteristically nervous about such criticism. The "correcting" role of the church, he insists, is directed at the evils inherent in any and every political community, "without reference to its better or worse construction as a particular state." As all social evils are institutionally mediated, it is difficult to see how this distinction could be maintained in practice. Later, Coleridge introduces a different distinction: the church's counterforce, he says, is directed against the evil *results* of particular political institutions rather than against the institutions themselves. It remains unclear, though, why the idea of the Christian church requires that, with respect to the criticism of institutions, the exercise of the Church's moral force should be so circumscribed.

This distinction between the educational presence of the national church as an "estate of the realm" and the Christian church as a community with no special political status, addresses thorny and persistent issues in debates over establishment. The ecclesiological arguments of *Church and State* are aimed at demonstrating the falsity of claims, frequently made by dissenters, that establishment represents *in principle* the confusion of the political power of the state with the spiritual power of the Christian religion. Coleridge's distinction of national and Christian church provides him with a theoretical basis for resisting attempts by the state to interfere in matters of specifically Christian doctrine and practice. It also articulates his long-standing conviction that employing secular power for religious ends imperils both social concord and the religious task of the Christian community. Cromwell, Coleridge noted, had understood this. Showing his "attachment to the best interests of human nature," he resisted the civil enforcement of articles of belief or the practice of Christian piety: "in all but true Xtnty Priests are Magistrates, Powers, Agents—in Xtnty only Teachers, Persuaders, Comforters."[149]

The national church is the crucial institution for maintaining both liberty of conscience and social peace. The national church fulfills that role most adequately, though, when it is combined with the Christian church in a unity founded on the understanding that *only* with respect to

---

[149] Coleridge, *Marginalia*, ed. George Whalley, vol. 12, pt. 1 of 2 of *The Collected Works of Samuel Taylor Coleridge* (Princeton NJ: Princeton University Press, 1980) 248; Coleridge, *Coleridge on the Seventeenth Century*, 270; see also, Morrow, *Coleridge's Political Thought*, 149-55.

its role as national and *not* as Christian does it have legal status as an "estate of the realm." Explaining this rather bold claim, requires us to piece together and make some inferences from comments Coleridge made in contexts other than that of *Church and State*. Given that the existence of a national church, a "church by law established," is a social necessity, its absence or its vulnerability to political change creates a social vacuum. Such a vacuum invites two dire consequences. On the one hand, part of the Christian church might succeed in establishing itself as a secular power, intruding law into matters of conscience. The Papacy, of course, is Coleridge's principal instance. On the other hand, as in the seventeenth century interregnum, society may fracture under the pressure of sectarian disputation:

> If there were no National Church, the mere spiritual Church would either become like the Papacy a dreadful tyranny over mind and body— or else fall abroad into a multitude of enthusiastic sects as in England in the seventeenth century.[150]

Where national and Christian church coincide as another example of unity in distinction, however, it is possible, within a single institution, to realize the conditions of a general toleration. As mediator of national education, the established church possesses legal powers but in its vocation as spiritual guide and teacher it must maintain that vocation, most strictly, as a moral one. In its role as national, the church may call upon the power of the law for maintenance and protection. As far, though, as its specifically Christian duty is concerned it must exercise its power as a purely spiritual one, a power of moral influence. To ensure and preserve this distinction, the clergy of the established church are to "infuse into the minds of their flock juster and *more spiritual* conceptions of the *Christian* Church."[151] The existence and beliefs of dissenting Christian communities are thereby protected, their integrity as spiritual bodies secured, in the internal practice of the established church: an internal practice to which they may appeal as the warrant for their own independent existence. The relationship of established church as national and established church as the body of Christ articulates the proper and necessary distinction between law and religion: that distinction is the

---

[150]Coleridge, *Table Talk*, pt. 1, 482.

[151]Coleridge, *Marginalia*, pt. 1, 530; my emphasis.

condition of toleration and social peace. So, at the risk of supposing a bench of perfect bishops, Coleridge concludes, "I do not believe that in a country of any religion, liberty of conscience can be preserved except by means and under the shadow of a National Church—a political establishment connected with, but *distinct* from, the spiritual Church."[152]

Coleridge's interpreters have not always appreciated the emphasis that he places upon the existing unity of Christian and national church in England. This coincidence within a single institution is nothing less than an act of providential grace, a "GODSEND" of which we should be in awe.[153] This is not merely a contingent practical arrangement with certain notable advantages, it is the historical expression of relations that belong to the ideas of the national and the Christian church. For this reason, the confounding of the two is the source of social conflict and loss of liberty. Furthermore, if "great and grievous errors" attend their confusion, "fearfully great and grievous" evils await the mistaken reaction that attempts their separation by disestablishment.[154] Though Coleridge does not specify the harm he has in mind here, an examination of the relational structure of these ideas, in the light of our discussion of prophetic relations in nature, will guide us to the source of his concern.

The legal separation of national and Christian churches, of the educational task from the specifically religious vocation, will not benefit the mission of either one. Rather it is the case that the "perfection of each," the fullest embodiment of their ideas, requires "the union of both in the same person." As we have seen, Coleridge found in the threatening alternatives of papacy and sectarianism a demonstration that the Christian church is able to exercise its life most perfectly when the national church provides the institutional context and basis of its manifestation. It remains to show how Coleridge's argument relates national and Christian churches in such a way that the idea of the national church looks toward and anticipates the Christian as its fulfillment.

---

[152]Coleridge, *Table Talk*, pt. 1, 483.

[153]Coleridge, *Church and State*, 55n.*.

[154]Coleridge, *Church and State*, 57: "And in the instance now in question, great and grievous errors have arisen from confounding the functions; and fearfully great and grievous will be the evils from the success of an attempt to separate them."

The only power that the Christian Church is mandated to exert in the pursuit of its calling is "*spiritual* power."[155] Coleridge defines "spiritual power" in terms of its object: it is exercised upon the "intelligent Will." An entirely moral power, it corresponds to the human capacity to will in accordance with the ultimate ends, "moral *Ideas*," presented by the reason. There are motivations that draw their power from the senses and bear down upon those "appetites and passions, which we possess in common with the beasts."[156] Spiritual power, however, must be radically differentiated from such motives.

This argument implicates William Paley's very different account of moral obligation. The latter's claim that "to be *obliged* is to be urged by a violent motive, resulting from the command of another" and, in the case of moral obligation, by the promise of reward or the threat of hellfire, turns virtue into a means to another end. In Coleridge's terms, Paley's ethics eclipses reason and, therefore, *spiritual* power, by conforming morality to the categories of the understanding. All that is left is that form of motivation we share with the beasts:

> Whether the man expects the *auto de fe*, the fire and the faggots with which he is threatened, to take place at Lisbon or Smithfield, or in some dungeon in the centre of the earth, makes no difference in the *kind* of motive by which he is influenced; nor of course in the nature of the power, which acts on his passions by means of it.[157]

For Coleridge, what is at stake in the presence or absence of a power that "acts on the *spirits* of men," is the possibility of *human* action and moral community.

The idea of the Christian church, in Coleridge's ecclesiology, is that of a community, the essential vocation of which is to exercise spiritual power. This calling is to manifest and extend the rule of Ideas and, therefore, to represent the Logos, the Divine Idea. The Christian church is thus the social presence of that world invoked in the appendix: the other world that now is "Her paramount aim and object, indeed, is

---

[155]Coleridge, *Church and State*, 118-24.
[156]Coleridge, *Church and State*, 124.
[157]Coleridge, *Church and State*, 124.

another world, not a world *to come* exclusively, but likewise *another world that now is.*"[158]

A Christian community represents that present, other world both by speaking of its eternal completeness in the vision of God, the "spiritual sunrise" that is the horizon of human hope, *and* in being the social symbol of the Logos which is the source of the Church's unity and life.[159] While it must be distinguished, the Body of Christ, as the symbolic presence of the Divine Idea, is not divided from the bodies politic in which it finds itself. In the Logos, there is continuity between the Body of Christ and the corporation of the state. The Christian church thus takes up "whatever is beneficent and humanizing in the aims, tendencies, and proper objects of the state" and reflects them back "in a higher quality," that is, as manifestations of the originating Divine Idea.

The national church, as we've seen, is charged with the task of communicating that "quantity and quality of knowledge" which will enable citizens, in their various stations, to understand their social rights and fulfill the obligations the state lays upon them. Coleridge will not, however, allow this to be understood reductively: a "popular ethics," he notes scornfully, that offers a "Digest of the Criminal Laws, and the evidence requisite for conviction under the same."[160] Proper citizenship requires "*cultivation* . . . the harmonious development of those qualities

---

[158] Coleridge, *Church and State*, 117.

[159] On the Matthean saying, "Where two or three are gathered together in my name, there am I in the midst of them," Coleridge notes that "this promise is not confined to houses of worship and prayer meetings exclusively." He goes on to point out that the presence of Christ is that of a "*spiritual immanence* . . . [not] of an individual coming in or down, and taking *a place*, as soon as the required number of petitioners [is] completed!" The spiritual presence is, therefore, "the total act itself, of which the spiritual Christ, one and the same in all the faithful, is the originating and perfective focal unity. Even as the physical life *is* in each limb and organ of the body, 'all in every part'; but is *manifested* as life, by being one in all and thus making all *one*: even so with Christ, our Spiritual Life! He *is* in each true believer . . . no less than in the congregation of the faithful; but he *manifests* his indwelling presence more characteristically . . . when many, convened in his name, whether for prayer or for council, do through him become ONE." Coleridge, *Church and State*, 120n.*.

[160] Coleridge, *Church and State*, 62.

The Conservative Imagination: Culture, Nature, and Grace 251

and faculties that characterise our *humanity*." "We must be men," he adds, "in order to be citizens."[161] The clerisy, as guides and instructors, have to *educe* moral agency. It is in this sense, that the national church anticipates, in fulfilling its temporal and social role, the "spiritual power" of the Christian community. According to Coleridge, of course, the idea of a national church has found embodiment in pre-Christian societies and also in societies in which the national and Christian churches did not coincide. However, while the idea of the national church is necessarily distinguishable from that of the Christian, it is not divisible from it. The educational task of the national church is only intelligible in the light of those moral ideas, the unity and possibility of which lies in the Logos. The work of the national church thus looks forward, beyond itself, to the freedom and moral life of the Church: the community that is the symbolic presence of the Divine Idea, the body of Christ. In turn, this continuity, this "prophetic relation" between national and Christian church, grounds Coleridge's assertion of the benefits that should accrue to the national from the copresence of the Christian church, as in the case of the established church in England. He presents these advantages in the metaphor of the olive and the vine:

> As the olive tree is said in its growth to fertilize the surrounding soil; to invigorate the roots of the vines in its immediate neighborhood, and to improve the strength and flavour of the wines—such is the relation of the Christian and the National church.[162]

The underlying relationship, however, somewhat disguised by the metaphor, is the symbolic one that belongs to creation's prophetic hierarchy, the lower symbolizing the higher to which it points. Even in its national aspect, in which its clergy act as schoolmasters or Justices of the Peace, the Church of England, is the more or less adequate symbol of the Christian church that is both within it yet distinct from it.

Despite the continuities Coleridge discloses between the national and the Christian church, the latter, he emphasizes, is not and could never be the product of any state.[163] Where it exists in coincidence with a national

---

[161]Coleridge, *Church and State*, 43.
[162]Coleridge, *Church and State*, 56.
[163]Coleridge, *Church and State*, 55: "Christianity is an aid and instrument, which no State or realm could have produced out of its own elements—which

church, its presence is to be welcomed as "most awfully, a GODSEND!" The providential character that Coleridge ascribes to the constitution of church and state in Britain appears most tellingly when he warns his readers of the perils of disestablishment. The relation of national and Christian church, he claims, exemplifies that the perfect fulfillment of two different roles "may require the union of both in the same person." Consequently, the attempt to "confound," or to "separate" them will only produce evils. As with the term "consubstantial," which Coleridge uses in connection with the symbol, the language here is Christological. More precisely, it is an echo of the Chalcedonian definition, in which "one and the same Christ," is "recognized IN TWO NATURES, WITHOUT CONFUSION, WITHOUT CHANGE, WITHOUT DIVISION, WITHOUT SEPARATION."[164] Coleridge interprets the union of national and Christian church, of the temporal state and the spiritual community, as a symbol of the incarnate Christ, of the perfect presence of the Idea in history.[165] Political theory rises into soteriology: the political order is fulfilled in the presence of the church as "godsend," gift and representative of the Logos that takes flesh. Coleridge's principle of prophetic relations enables him to achieve a complex identification of the order of politics and the history of salvation. Properly understood, that is, according to the idea, *homo politicus* is prophetic of *homo Christianus*.

Enquiry into the grave and grievous evils courted by those who advocate disestablishment returns us to Coleridge's persistent cultural anxiety. As he reads the present, the cultural conditions for disestablishment already exist. For him, the "moral history of the last 130 years" is one of the advancing hegemony of the understanding; the eclipse, therefore, of those conditions that nurture the moral capacities proper to humanity. Motivation according to those ultimate ends that only the reason can provide makes way for lesser inspirations. Significantly for my argument here, Coleridge names the revealing cultural symptom as the adoption of Paley's *Principles* for a Cambridge textbook. The separation of Christian and national church, of social education and spiritual

---

no State had a right to expect."

[164]*Documents of the Christian Church*, ed. Henry Bettenson (New York and London: Oxford University Press, 1943; ²1963) 73 (51 in 2nd ed.).

[165]I am using "state" here, of course, in Coleridge's "larger sense," as inclusive of the national church. See Coleridge, *Church and State*, 22.

community, is the unhappy but logical telos of conditions in which an "Idea-less" philosophy prevails. He outlines this reductive end as follows.

> National Education to be finally sundered from all religion, but speedily and decisively emancipated from the superintendence of the National Clergy. Education reformed. Defined as synonymous with Instruction. *Axiom of Education so defined.* Knowledge being power, those attainments, which give a man the power of doing what he wishes in order to obtain what he desires, are alone to be considered as knowledge.... Subjects to be taught in the National Schools. Reading, writing, arithmetic, the mechanic arts, elements and results of physical science, but to be taught as much as possible, empirically.[166]

In terms of Coleridge's theological politics, then, disestablishment is the denial of the Logos in history and humanity. When *Church and State* is read in the wider context of his thought, the author's trinitarianism emerges as providing him the underpinning of any account of society and politics that is not, like Paley's, anthropologically reductionist.

"The moderns," Coleridge bemoans, follow Paley's lead and "take the Ὁ Λογος as a hypothetical Watchmaker, and degrade the το θειον into a piece of Clockwork—they live without God in the world." St. Paul's "*in* whom we move and live and *have* our Being" is replaced by the "Lockian and Newtonian—From God we *had* our Being."[167] In the sphere of Paleyan ethics, this substitution is found in the circumscribed role of God: as source of the creation's design and as wielder of eschatological sanctions. Coleridge responds to the secularizing tendencies of Paley's theology and ethics with his doctrine of ideas and his application of that doctrine to the institutional relations expounded in *Church and State*. He attempts to recover for political thought the Pauline "*in* whom we move and *have* our being." Thus, political institutions, Coleridge argues, exist as the embodiments of divine ideas: "truth powers" that exercise their seminal pressure upon the minds and hearts of those who possess them or who are unconsciously influenced by them.[168] Ideas such as those of

---

[166]Coleridge, *Church and State*, 62.
[167]Coleridge, *Collected Letters* 4:768.
[168]For the expression "truth powers," see Coleridge, *Church and State*, 20. Also, "we speak, and have a right to speak, of the idea itself, as actually existing, i.e., as a *principle*, existing in the only way in which a principle can exist—in

the constitution and the national church depend upon, are ideal developments of, the idea of the person as moral agent, as capable of willing in accordance with reason. It is in moral agency, in the practical reason, that Coleridge finds the *imago Dei*:

> As the identity or coinherence of the absolute will and the reason is the peculiar character of God; so is the *synthesis* of the individual will and the common reason, by the subordination of the former to the latter, the only possible likeness or image of [God], and therefore the required character of man.[169]

The cultural hegemony of a philosophy that judges the ideas of reason by the categories of the understanding reduces history to the shifts of expedience, poetics to the mechanics of fancy, and nature to a cog-and-wheel system in which the mind can find no self-anticipation. And what of virtue? Virtue is the common sense of the eschatologically prudent. The dominating influence of such a philosophy alienates human beings from themselves: from that being "in God" which is the "synthesis" of will and reason.[170] The "philosophy of mechanism" is an ideology for the "voluntary ABSENTEE" and the hapless exile from the other, yet present world of the Logos.[171] From such an alienating philosophy, so Coleridge suggests, come blind "reforms," changes that miss the meaning of society's institutions. The result is political fragmentation. Disestablishment, whether as the separation of the Christian and national church or as the progressive "spoliation of the nationality," involves the separation of institutions from the system of relations in which they receive their intelligibility and without which they are reduced to the status of prudent

---

the minds and consciences of the persons, whose duties it prescribes, and whose rights it determines" (ibid., 19) and "knowledge [of an idea] may very well exist, aye, and powerfully influence a man's thoughts and actions, without his being distinctly conscious of the same, much more without his being competent to express it in definite words. . . . it is the privilege of the few to possess an idea: of the generality of men, it might be more truly affirmed, that they are possessed by it" (ibid., 12-13).

[169]"Essay on Faith," in Coleridge, *Literary Remains* 4:431.

[170]Cf., *Literary Remains* 4:437-38: "Faith subsists in the *synthesis* of the reason and the individual will."

[171]Coleridge, *Church and State*, 177.

The Conservative Imagination: Culture, Nature, and Grace 255

means to "proximate ends."[172] Political change directed by the categories of the understanding, we may say, fails "to discern the body."[173] St. Paul's phrase is a peculiarly appropriate one here. As we have interpreted it, Coleridge's political thought takes the classical metaphor of the body politic and coadunates it, via the doctrine of ideas, with the Pauline ecclesiology of being "in Christ."[174]

The Imagination

At the end of *The Friend*'s spiral climb, the reader finally arrives at the point from which he or she may view the principles that have accompanied and guided the reflections from the start. Here, too, as we complete our ascent through Coleridge's political writings, we gain our perspective from which to view the theory of the imagination that was our beginning. The imagination is the power by which we indwell our environment: an environment that includes both the created and the uncreated, the divine. Through imagination, we find ourselves imaged and anticipated in nature and, through imagination, we know ourselves as made in the image of God. This power, as we've seen, proceeds by dissolution and recombination. Out of the mute fixities of the fancy it raises vocal symbols. As Coleridge presents it, this is not only an epistemological theory, it is a historical one. Thus, he interprets both British history since 1688 and the French Revolution as involving the eclipse of the imagination and the absolutizing of the understanding and the fancy. It is noteworthy that Coleridge, sensitive both to what language discloses and to its formative power, rejects what he regards as the corrupting misdescription of the events of 1688 and 1689 as the "glorious *revolution*."[175] The very notion of a "revolution" carries, for Coleridge, the suggestion of discontinuity

---

[172]Coleridge, *Statesman's Manual*, 61n.2.

[173]First Cor. 11:29.

[174]"With, perhaps, one exception, it would be difficult in the whole compass of language, to find a metaphor so commensurate, so pregnant, or suggesting so many points of elucidation, as that of *Body Politic*, as the exponent of a State or Realm." Significantly, the one exception is that of the "Logos." Coleridge, *Church and State*, 84-85.

[175]For the "erroneously entitled . . . REVOLUTION OF 1688," see Coleridge, *Church and State*, 64.

incompatible with his account of history as a system of symbols: its enthusiastic use betrays a cast of mind fatal to imagination.[176]

"All true science," Coleridge writes, "is contained in the Lore of Symbols and Correspondences."[177] The historical and political task of the imagination lies in what I have described as identification: the disclosure and presentation of human beings as indwelling a system of symbols. The task, therefore, is to educe "a love of 'the Great,' and 'the Whole,' " to liberate the mind and the passions from fixation upon the "Universe [as] a mass of *little things*."[178] For Coleridge, social and political responsibility, the preservation of human dignity, depends upon such liberation because, without it, persons are not recognized as symbols of the transcendent personeity of God. Against a utilitarian account of ethics and social order, Coleridge's treatise on Church and State effects a renewal of the symbol of the "body politic." State, national church, and Christian church are here disclosed as mutually necessary parts, parts, however, of a whole that is both anticipated in nature and that points beyond itself to the life of the Triune creator.

During the final decade of his life, Coleridge, as we've noted, provided little by way of further treatment of the imagination. References to this power drop out of his accounts of philosophical theology and such references as there are tend to be modest in the role they assign to the imagination.[179] It is easy, however, to exaggerate the significance of this. The shift away from discussion of the imagination is a function of his strenuous concern, in the 1820s, to avoid any suggestion of Schellingite pantheism.[180] Theologically, Coleridge's emphasis, in these years, falls upon the doctrine of God as "Absolute Will" and upon the role of the

---

[176]This understanding of history, as I have argued above, leads, in the context of Coleridge's biblical hermeneutics, to a sapientializing of prophecy.

[177]Coleridge, *Collected Letters* 5:19.

[178]Coleridge, *Collected Letters* 5:354.

[179]See, for instance, the expositions of the distinction between reason and understanding in Coleridge, *Aids to Reflection*, 189-206. For a later reference to the imagination, see Coleridge, *Literary Remains* 4:433.

[180]James D. Boulger, *Coleridge as Religious Thinker*, 106-107. Boulger suggests a radical turning away on Coleridge's part from the concerns of the theory of the imagination. In my opinion, this fails to recognize the enduring importance of the theory to Coleridge's later thought.

will in faith; faith being the love that unites with the divine reason.[181] The earlier developments in the theory of the imagination, remain, however, determinative for Coleridge's method in *Church and State*. Thus, Coleridge's doctrine of ideas and of their "prophetic relations" still appeals to the human capacity for disclosing and deploying symbols: to that "vehicle," unnamed by the Allocosmite, that brings the mind, "swifter than Fortunatus's Wishing Cap," into the 'present, other world.'[182] In his later writings, and especially in the *Opus Maximum*, Coleridge provided a Trinitarian foundation for his account of the symbol. The theory of the imagination finds its final "landing place" here, in an account of nature and society as a system of symbols that has its ultimate referent in the divine ideas; and thus in the Logos, the Idea Idearum, whose incarnation is the paradigm case of the symbolic, the "translucence of the Eternal through and in the Temporal."

---

[181] Coleridge, *Literary Remains* 4:433-34.
[182] Coleridge, *Church and State*, 184.

7

Conclusion

And whatever the world may opine, he who hath not much meditated upon God, the Human Mind, and the Summum Bonum, may possibly make a thriving Earthworm, but will most indubitably make a blundering Patriot and a sorry statesman.

—Coleridge, *The Friend*[1]

I began this book noting that an initial attraction of Coleridge's work was his opposition to "reductionism," specifically to the reductionist tendencies of British political, philosophical, and theological thinking after the "Glorious Revolution"—"the Epoch of the Understanding and the Senses."[2] By way of a conclusion, I want to revisit that theme as one dependent upon certain theological commitments. This will take us from the political concept of a subject to the "mystery" of personality.

To explain what is meant by the "idea" of the constitution, Coleridge recycles some material from *The Friend* dealing with the social contract.[3] The latter, considered as referring to "an actual occurrence in the first ages of the world," is in fact a complete fiction.[4] For that matter, even were it not an "idle fancy" it would still be useless as a theory of political obligation. A particular agreement between individuals can never be absolutely binding on their successors: its authority ceases as soon as the agreement no longer serves the common good. As Coleridge is attacking a rather crude version of social contract theory, his argument is not a very arresting example of his antireductionist flair. The proposal he makes in the stead of a "theory of an original social contract" is, however, more suggestive:

---

[1] Coleridge, *The Friend*, pt. 1, 113. Coleridge is quoting, with alterations, Bishop Berkeley.
[2] Coleridge, *The Friend*, pt. 1, 203.
[3] Coleridge, *Church and State*, 12-16; cf. Coleridge, *The Friend*, pt. 1, 173.
[4] Coleridge, *Church and State*, 14.

If instead of the *conception* or *theory* of an original social contract, you say the *idea* of an ever-originating social contract, this is so certain and indispensable, that it constitutes the whole ground of the difference between subject and serf, between a commonwealth and a slave plantation.[5]

To describe oneself as a "subject" as opposed to a "slave" is an act of self-interpretation, one mediated by a particular cultural and linguistic context. Underlying that self-interpretation, according to Coleridge, is the "idea of an ever-originating social contract." To put it differently, talk of the "idea of an ever-originating social contract" identifies certain political and social realities as constituting the conditions whereby self-interpretation as "subject" is intelligible.

If we consider being a "subject" in terms of the self-interpretation involved, then claiming this status entails what Charles Taylor has termed "strong evaluation," a phrase he applies to judgments concerning desire.[6] We evaluate "strongly" when we assess our motivations in terms of their worth, when we measure them according to their compatibility or otherwise with a way of life we regard as worthy.[7] Our discussion of Coleridge's politics has suggested that to be a "subject," in his account, is not only a matter of politically accorded status. Rather, this is a status we may or may not live up to, that we may betray in our actions or contradict in our ideologies, and that involves us in a cause we should

---

[5]Coleridge, *Church and State*, 15.

[6]Charles Taylor, "What Is Human Agency?," *Human Agency and Language: Philosophical Papers 1* (Cambridge UK: Cambridge University Press, 1985) 15-44; see also *Sources of the Self: The Making of Modern Identity* (Cambridge MA: Harvard University Press, 1989) 14-24.

[7]A choice of entertainment provides a simple example of Taylor's distinction between "strong" and "weak" evaluation. I turn up at a theater showing two different movies. As one appears to be preferred by a large and noisy crowd, I choose the other. My choice is purely contingent, based on the fall of circumstances. This is, in Taylor's terms, "weak evaluation." Alternatively, one movie, to my mind, glorifies sadomasochism and I consider it an affront to human dignity. On that basis, because I judge a desire to attend this performance as incompatible with my moral vision and, therefore, as unworthy, I opt for the other movie, even though I may find myself with the rambunctious crowd. Such is the cost of strong evaluation.

further. Rightly understood, it is both status and vocation: a self-interpretation involving responsibilities. We may specify, therefore, a range of desires that are incompatible, compatible, or specifically worthy with regard to being a subject.[8] Economic decisions sound as to political economy but heedless as to human cost are incompatible, for instance. Securing education for oneself or others, on the other hand, is a proper fulfillment of the responsibility to *live* as a subject. By what "*moral right*" Coleridge asks, do you enjoy the benefits of subjects if, ignoring the "living landscape of good and evil . . . you continue to gaze only on the sod beneath your feet?"[9]

Certain human beings acknowledge one another as subjects as opposed to slaves. This reciprocal understanding arises within specific cultural and linguistic histories. "Subjectivity," with its benefits and duties, is formed within a particular complex of institutions, beliefs and practices: a complex that "originates" the mutuality of subjects, not once upon a time but presently. According to Coleridge's argument, of course, this complex is a realization of that divine intention which is the *idea* of an ever-originating social contract.[10] We are thus brought back to a central claim of both Burke's and Coleridge's conservatism. Political existence, as Burke put it, is "an entailed inheritance" and pursuit of radical remakings only an illusory flight from history and the given conditions within which we understand ourselves and the character of our freedom.[11] On the other hand, these same institutions, beliefs, and practices also enable processes by which political life becomes the object of reflection and, therefore, critique. They are, in this sense, too, "ever-originating," inciting comparison with their "idea." Coleridge, given his doctrine of ideas, is more confident than Burke as to the degree to which

---

[8]"Motivations or desires do not only count in virtue of the attractions of the consummations but also in virtue of the kind of life and kind of subject that these desires properly belong to. . . . Strong evaluation is not just a condition of articulacy about preferences, but also about the quality of life, the kind of beings we are or want to be." Taylor, "What Is Human Agency?" 25-26.

[9]Coleridge, *A Lay Sermon*, 124.

[10]Interpreting "idea" as divine intention indicates both the centrality of "will" in Coleridge's theology and the need to consider his doctrine of ideas within the context of expressivist accounts of the symbol rather than that of Platonic forms.

[11]Burke, *Reflections*, 189.

we may secure reflective purchase upon political reality. Coleridge's "conservative imagination," therefore, looks both to the concrete and originating conditions of responsible political reflection and, against the temptation to idealize the existent, to the "seminal power" of the "ideas," the divine intention only ever partially realized in the political conditions for "subjectivity."

Coming to reflective grips with our self-interpretation as subjects, articulating that self-interpretation, involves us, then, in those formative ideas which, in relation to particular contexts, urge questions, stimulate critique, and indicate change. When we engage with these seminal ideas we come upon ourselves, find ourselves in the eye of a creative power that exceeds the present without the excesses of "novelty":

> At the annunciation of *principles*, of *ideas*, the soul of man awakes, and starts up, as an exile in a far distant land at the unexpected sounds of his native language, when after long years of absence, and almost of oblivion, he is suddenly addressed in his own mother tongue.

As I have argued above, Coleridge's doctrine of ideas as having "an endless power of semination" opens up an element of utopian pressure within the conservative imagination, a pressure to be applied to present political conditions. That being said, we have, of course, noted sufficient examples of Coleridge, in this respect, stifling the imagination.[12]

Existing political institutions and social practices provide the context within which the interpretation of ourselves as subjects is both possible and plausible. For Coleridge, however, these institutions and practices, being, after all, expressions of divine intent, are not the ultimate ground of such vital self-interpretations. The difference between a subject and slave is the political form of the distinction between persons and things. That distinction finds its possibility in the being and "personeity" of God, specifically in the priority of Absolute Will over Absolute Being.[13] If being were prior to will, Coleridge argues, then we could not consistently affirm God's freedom and "absolute causativeness." Neither, in that event, could we defend the image of God's freedom constituted by the moral life of human beings. The distinction in thought and action of persons from things depends upon our faithfulness to finite moral freedom. This

---

[12]See above, 187-90.
[13]See above, 220-22.

is the point of leverage from which Coleridge resists discourse that reduces human life, thought, and action to "products," to the interaction of impersonal forces.

Within the order of being, divine personeity is the ground of human personality and the political reality of subjects. As to the order of knowing, divine personeity is, in part, at least, reached by way of striving to "know thyself," an injunction to which Coleridge frequently appeals.[14] "We begin with I KNOW MYSELF, in order to end with the absolute I AM."[15] A full articulation of one's self-interpretation as "person" or political subject leads, by way of a transcendental argument, to the personeity of God. That is not the whole picture, though. Coleridge's use of transcendental argument for theological purposes differs from that of Kant, more, indeed, than Coleridge at times admits.[16] For a start, the argument from practical reason is only one element in a complex of reflections, supportive of Christian belief. Within this complex of reflections, biblical revelation has a central place.[17] Coleridge appeals to an audience for whom theological language is the language of Christian tradition and history, a history which, when read in the synthesizing power of imagination, provides its own form of witness.[18] Neither does Coleridge's

---

[14]Often in allusion to Juvenal, *Satires* 11.27: *E caelo descendit gnôthi seautón* ("[This precept] descends from heaven: *Know thyself!*").

[15]Coleridge, *Biographia Literaria*, pt. 1, 283. The following sentence reads: "We proceed from the SELF in order to lose and find all self in GOD."

[16]This is one reason for accusations, such as those of Rene Wellek, that Coleridge failed to grasp Kant's work even at a fairly rudimentary level. See Rene Welleck, *Immanuel Kant in England: 1793-1838* (Princeton NJ: Princeton University press, 1931) 65-135.

[17]See, for instance, the discussion of immortality in Coleridge's *Aids to Reflection* (348-59). After attending to arguments from "the frequent, not to say ordinary disproportion between moral worth and worldly prosperity"; from the "universality" of the belief and the "instinctive and practical Anticipation" of persistence beyond death, Coleridge rests the weight of argument upon, not biblical proof texts, but the scriptural logic of salvation.

[18]See above, chap. 3. Reading history within the biblical system of prophetic symbols establishes itself practically. As Coleridge insists to those skeptical of "ideas": you know their truth as that "by which the phenomena of History are to be explained . . . in the same way exactly that you know that your eyes are made to see with—and that is—because you *do* see with them." Coleridge, *Church and*

account of theological knowing abstract from the experience of biblical authority. This authority, though, is not secured by objectivizing arguments from "evidences" but known in the experience of the Spirit that "finds me," an experience that reveals both self and Other.[19] Finally, the anthropological context of Coleridge's account of theological knowing—and Coleridge insists that "knowing" is the proper term—is broader than Kant's: not the practical reason alone, but the motivating passions, the speculative reason, and the cravings of spiritual hope.[20]

Following the command "know thyself" in the context of Christian revelation and with that self-sympathy in which the heart's yearnings are acknowledged, one is led to affirm the irreducible "mystery" of personality. This is the discovery that:

> Try to conceive a *man* without the ideas of God, eternity, freedom, will, absolute truth, of the good, the true, the beautiful, the infinite. . . . [and] the *man* will have vanished."[21]

In Coleridge's early work, "mystery" is a term charged with associations of mystification, manipulative obscurity, and mitres.[22] Within the later theology and politics, however, "mystery" names that by which humanity and nature elude all reductionist explanation. Coleridge's rhetoric—the *Biographia*'s theologically charged announcement of the

---

State, 47.

[19]"[In Scripture] I have met everywhere more or less copious sources of truth, and power, and purifying impulses;—that I have found words for my inmost thoughts, songs for my joy, utterances for my hidden griefs, and pleadings for my shame and my feebleness. . . . In short, whatever *finds* me, bears witness for itself that it has proceeded from a Holy Spirit, even from the same Spirit, *which remaining in itself, yet regenerateth all other powers, and in all ages entering into holy souls maketh them friends of God, and prophets.*" Coleridge, *Confessions of an Inquiring Spirit* (Philadelphia: Fortress Press, 1988) 26.

[20]On "religious feelings" see, for instance, Coleridge, *Statesman's Manual*, 73n.1; *Biographia Literaria*, pt. 1, 80-81. As regards the speculative reason, see Coleridge's insistence that ideas are constitutive and not "regulative only," e.g., in *Statesman's Manual*, 114; *Aids to Reflection*, 286.

[21]Coleridge, *Church and State*, 47n.*.

[22]"I enter my protest! Ere yet our laws as well as our religion be muffled up in mysteries," Coleridge, *On Politics and Religion*, 285; see also, 30, 66-67, 206-208, 337.

primary and secondary imagination; the account of the symbol and the vision of Ezekiel's chariot; the exposition of "prophetic relations"—issues in the recognition of mystery. We have here a pedagogy that consists of strategies for educing—in the Coleridgean sense—a recognition that, if creation is to be thought and moral community fostered, mystery is inescapable. As mysterious, finite reality cannot, to use Coleridge's terms, be brought within the coordinates of the understanding.[23] Put differently, it cannot be fully objectified. Unable to be comprehended, the finite may be apprehended truly, only in the context of that infinite and transcendent reality, for which, in the readings of imagination, it provides a "system of symbols."[24] "Mystery," therefore, transcends the distinction between persons and things:

> Are we struck with admiration at beholding the Cope of Heaven imaged in a Dew drop? The least of the animacula to which that drop would be an Ocean contains in itself an infinite problem of which God Onmipresent is the only solution.[25]

Put in the hierarchical terms of nature's "prophetic relations," no level of nature is explicable without recourse to that above it, a process that is

---

[23] For twentieth-century discussion of "mystery," see John Macquarrie, *Mystery and Truth* (Milwaukee: Marquette University Press, 1985); Karl Rahner, "The Concept of Mystery in Catholic Theology," in *Theological Investigations*, vol. 4: *More Recent Writings*, trans. Kevin Smyth (London: Darton, Longman & Todd, 1974) 36-73. The latter is especially intriguing in relation to Coleridge as Rahner is questioning a reductionist understanding of mystery in Catholic theology, especially in that of Vatican I. Consider: "As long as we measure the loftiness of knowledge by its perspicuity, and think that we know what clarity and insight are, though we do not really know them as they truly are; as long as we imagine that analytical, coordinating, deductive and masterful reason is more and not less than experience of the divine incomprehensibility; as long as we think that comprehension is greater than being overwhelmed by light inaccessible, which shows itself as inaccessible in the very moment of giving itself: we have understood nothing of the mystery and of the true nature of grace and glory." Rahner, *Theological Investigations* 4:56.

[24] On the distinction between "comprehension" and "apprehension," see Coleridge, *Notes, Theological, Political, and Miscellaneous*, ed. Derwent Coleridge (London: Edward Moxon, 1853) 169-70.

[25] Coleridge, *Statesman's Manual*, 50.

only completed in that radical incompletion when the "self-containing power" of the mind finds its solution in the "self-causing" reality of God.[26] And so we reach, from another point, that structure of relations according to which, as I have argued above, the national and Christian church are to be distinguished but not divided. The condition of humanity is spirit and action in the midst of mystery.

---

[26]See above, and Coleridge, *Church and State*, 182. Again, Coleridge concludes that "Will is either the first . . . or it is not WILL at all."

Bibliography

Abrams, M. H. *The Correspondent Breeze*. New York: Norton, 1984.
―――. *The Mirror and the Lamp*. Oxford: Oxford University Press, 1953.
―――. *Natural Supernaturalism: Tradition and Revolution in Romantic Literature*. New York: Norton, 1973.
Aers, David, Jonathan Cook, and David Punter. "Coleridge: Individual, Community, and Social Agency." In *Romanticism and Ideology: Studies in English Writing 1765–1830*. London: Routledge & Kegan Paul, 1975.
Albee, E. *A History of English Utilitarianism*. London: George Allen & Unwin, 1901.
Altick, Robert. *The English Common Reader: a Social History of the Mass Reading Public, 1800–1900*. Chicago: University of Chicago Press, 1957.
Aquinas, Thomas. *Summa Theologiae*. Volumes 7 and 9. Blackfriars edition. New York: McGraw-Hill, 1976.
Aristotle, *Rhetoric*. Translated by W. Rhys Roberts. New York: Random House, Inc., 1954.
Ashton, Rosemary. *The German Idea: Four English Writers and the Reception of German Thought, 1800–1860*. Cambridge UK: Cambridge University Press, 1980.
―――. *The Life of Samuel Taylor Coleridge*. Oxford: Blackwell Publishers, 1996.
Augustine. *On Christian Doctrine*. Translated by D. W. Robertson. New York: Macmillan, 1958.
Bacon, Francis. *The Advancement of Learning and New Atlantis*. Oxford: Clarendon Press, 1974.
Barfield, Owen. *What Coleridge Thought*. Connecticut: Wesleyan University Press, 1971.
Barth, J. Robert. *Coleridge and Christian Doctrine*. Cambridge MA: Harvard University Press, 1969.
―――. "Coleridge's Scriptural Imagination." In *Coleridge, Keats, and the Imagination: Romanticism and Adam's Dream. Essays in Honor of Walter Jackson Bate*. Edited by J. Robert Barth and John Mahoney. Columbia: University of Missouri Press, 1990.

_____. *The Symbolic Imagination: Coleridge and the Romantic Tradition.* Princeton NJ: Princeton University Press, 1977.

_____. "Theological Implications of Coleridge's Theory of Imagination." In *Coleridge's Theory of Imagination Today*, edited by C. Gallant. New York: AMS Press, 1989.

Beer, John, editor. *Coleridge's Variety.* Pittsburg PA: Pittsburg University Press, 1974.

Bentham, Jeremy. *An Introduction to the Principles of Morals and Legislation.* Oxford: Clarendon Press, 1876.

Bettenson, Henry, editor. *Documents of the Christian Church.* The World's Classics. London: Oxford University Press, 1943. Second edition: New York and London: Oxford University Press, 1963.

Blake, William. *Blake: Complete Writings.* Edited by Geoffrey Keynes. London: Oxford University Press, 1972.

Blair, Hugh. *Lectures on Rhetoric and Belles Lettres.* Philadelphia: Zell, 1833.

Bloom, Harold, editor. *Romanticism and Consciousness.* New York: Norton, 1970.

Boulger, James D. *Coleridge as Religious Thinker.* New Haven CT: Yale University Press, 1961.

Brett, Richard, editor. *S. T. Coleridge.* London: G. Bell & Sons, 1971.

Briggs, Asa. *The Making of Modern England: 1783–1867.* New York: Harper & Row, 1965.

Brinton, Crane. *The Political Ideas of the English Romanticists.* New York: Russell & Russell, 1962.

Brown, Richard. *Church and State in Modern Britain, 1700–1850.* New York: Routledge, 1991.

Brown, Marshall. *The Shape of German Romanticism.* Ithaca NY: Cornell University Press, 1979.

Burke, Edmund. *An Appeal from the New to the Old Whigs.* Edited by James M. Robson. New York: Bobbs-Merrill, 1962.

_____. "Letters on a Regicide Peace," In volume 2 of *The Works of the Right Honorable Edmund Burke.* London: Henry G. Bohn, 1854.

Burke, Edmund. *A Philosophical Enquiry into the Origin of Our Ideas of the Sublime and Beautiful and Other Pre-Revolutionary Writings.* Edited by David Womersley. London: Penguin Books, 1998.

_____. *Reflections on the Revolution in France.* Edited by Connor Cruise O'Brien. London: Penguin Books, 1968.

_____. "Speech on the Petition of the Unitarians." In volume 6 of *The Works of the Right Honourable Edmund Burke.* London: George Bell & Sons, 1890.

---. "Speech on the Representation of the Commons in Parliament." In *Selected Writings and Speeches*, edited by Peter J. Stanlis. New York: Anchor Books, 1963.
Burke, Kenneth. *A Rhetoric of Motives*. New York: Prentice-Hall, 1950.
Butler, Marilyn. *Romantic, Rebels, and Reactionaries*. Oxford: Oxford University Press, 1982.
Calleo, David. *Coleridge and the Idea of the Modern State*. New Haven CT: Yale University Press, 1966.
Chadwick, Owen. *The Victorian Church*. Volume 1. London: A. & C. Black, 1971.
Christensen, Jerome. *Coleridge's Blessed Machine of Language*. Ithaca NY: Cornell University Press, 1981.
Cicero, Marcus Tullius. *De Inventione*. Translated by J. Hubbell. New York: Putnam's Sons, 1949.
---. *De Oratore*. Translated by P. Sutton and T. Rackham. New York: Putnam's Sons, 1942.
Clark, J. C. D. *English Society 1688–1832: Ideology, Social Structure, and Political Practice during the Ancien Regime*. New York: Cambridge University Press, 1985.
Cobban, Alfred. *Edmund Burke and the Revolt against the Eighteenth Century: A Study of the Political and Social Thinking of Burke, Wordsworth, Coleridge, and Southey*. New York: Barnes & Noble, 1960.
Cobbett, William. *The Last Hundred Days of English Freedom*. London: Allen & Unwin, 1921.
---. *Rural Rides*. New York: Penguin, 1985.
Coburn, Kathleen, editor. *Coleridge: A Collection of Critical Essays*. Twentieth-Century Views, Maynard Mack, series editor. A Spectrum Book. Englewood Cliffs NJ: Prentice-Hall, 1967.
Coleman, Deidre. *Coleridge and the Friend: 1809–1810*. Oxford: Clarendon Press, 1988.
Coleridge, Samuel Taylor. *Aids to Reflection* (1825). Edited by John Beer. Volume 9 of *The Collected Works of Samuel Taylor Coleridge*, Kathleen Coburn, general editor. Princeton NJ: Princeton University Press, 1993.
---. *Anima Poetae: From the Unpublished Notebooks of Samuel Taylor Coleridge*. Edited by Ernest Hartley Coleridge. Boston and New York: Houghton, Mifflin, 1895.
---. *Biographia Literaria* (1815). Edited by James Engell and W. Jackson Bate. Volume 7 of *The Collected Works of Samuel Taylor Coleridge*, Kathleen Coburn, general editor. Princeton NJ: Princeton University Press, 1983.

_____. *Biographia Literaria, with His Aesthetical Essays.* Edited by John Shawcross. Two volumes. London: Oxford University Press, 1907.

_____. *Coleridge on the Seventeenth Century.* Edited by Roberta Florence Brinkley. Cambridge UK: Cambridge University Press, 1955.

_____. *Coleridge's Miscellaneous Criticism.* Edited by Thomas Middleton Raysor. Cambridge UK: Cambridge University Press, 1936.

_____. *Coleridge's Shakesperian Criticism.* Edited by Thomas Middleton Raysor. Two volumes. Cambridge MA: Harvard University Press, 1930.

_____. *Coleridge's Treatise on Method as Published in the Encyclopaedia Metropolitana.* Edited by Alice D. Snyder. London: Constable & Co., 1934.

_____. *Collected Letters of Samuel Taylor Coleridge.* Edited by Earl Leslie Griggs. Six volumes. Oxford: Clarendon Press, 1956–1971.

_____. *Collected Works of Samuel Taylor Coleridge.* Sixteen titles ("volumes") in twenty-three volumes ("parts"). Kathleen Coburn, general editor. Princeton NJ: Princeton University Press, 1970–2002. These sixteen titles are cited by individual title, individual editor or editors, and series volume number (and part number where appropriate).

_____. *Essays on His Times.* Edited by David V. Erdman. Volume 3 (in three parts) of *The Collected Works of Samuel Taylor Coleridge*, Kathleen Coburn, general editor. Princeton NJ: Princeton University Press, 1978.

_____. *The Friend.* Edited by Barbara E. Rooke. Volume 4 (in two parts) of *The Collected Works of Samuel Taylor Coleridge*, Kathleen Coburn, general editor. Princeton NJ: Princeton University Press, 1969.

_____. *Hints towards the Formation of a More Comprehensive Theory of Life.* Edited by Seth B. Watson. London: John Churchill, 1848.

_____. *Imagination in Coleridge.* Edited by John Spencer Hill. Totowa, New Jersey: Rowman & Littlefield, 1978.

_____. *Inquiring Spirit: A New Presentation of Coleridge from His Published and Unpublished Prose Writings.* Edited by Kathleen Coburn. London: Routledge & Kegan Paul, 1951.

_____. *Lay Sermons.* Edited by Reginald James White. Volume 6 of *The Collected Works of Samuel Taylor Coleridge*, Kathleen Coburn, general editor. Princeton NJ: Princeton University Press, 1972.

_____. *Lectures 1808–1819: On Literature.* Edited by Reginald A. Foakes. Volume 5 (in two parts) of *The Collected Works of Samuel Taylor Coleridge*, Kathleen Coburn, general editor. Princeton NJ: Princeton University Press, 1987.

_____. *Lectures 1795: On Politics and Religion.* Edited by Lewis Patton and Peter Mann. Volume 1 of *The Collected Works of Samuel Taylor Coleridge*, Kathleen Coburn, general editor. Princeton NJ: Princeton University Press, 1971.

---. *The Literary Remains of Samuel Taylor Coleridge*. Edited by Henry Nelson Coleridge. Four volumes. London: William Pickering, 1836.

---. *Logic*. Edited by James Robert de Jager Jackson. Volume 13 of *The Collected Works of Samuel Taylor Coleridge*, Kathleen Coburn, general editor. Princeton NJ: Princeton University Press, 1981.

---. *Marginalia*. Edited by George Whalley and H. J. Jackson. Volume 12 (in six parts) of *The Collected Works of Samuel Taylor Coleridge*, Kathleen Coburn, general editor. Princeton NJ: Princeton University Press, 1980, 1985, 1992, 1998, 1999, 2001.

---. (1) *The Notebooks of Samuel Taylor Coleridge*. Edited by Kathleen Coburn and Merton Christensen. Four volumes thus far. New York: Pantheon Books, 1957–1990.

---. (2) *The Notebooks of Samuel Taylor Coleridge*. Edited by Kathleen Coburn, Merton Christensen, and Anthony John Harding. Five volumes. Princeton NJ: Princeton University Press, 1957–2002.

---. *Notes, Theological, Political, and Miscellaneous*. Edited by the Rev. Derwent Coleridge. London: Edward Moxon, 1853.

---. *On the Constitution of the Church and State in Accordance with the Idea of Each* (1829). Edited by John Colmer. Volume 10 of *The Collected Works of Samuel Taylor Coleridge*, Kathleen Coburn, general editor. Princeton NJ: Princeton University Press, 1976.

---. *Opus Maximum*. Edited by Thomas McFarland and Nicholas Halmi. Volume 15 of *The Collected Works of Samuel Taylor Coleridge*, Kathleen Coburn, general editor. Princton NJ: Princeton University Press, 2002.

---. *The Philosophical Lectures of Samuel Taylor Coleridge [1818–1819]: Hitherto Unpublished*. Edited by Kathleen Coburn. New York: Philosophical Library; London: Pilot Press, 1949.

---. "Religious Musings." In *Selected Poetry and Prose of Coleridge*, edited by Donald A. Stauffer. New York: Random House, Inc., 1951.

---. *Table Talk*. Edited by Carl Woodring. Volume 14 (in two parts) of *The Collected Works of Samuel Taylor Coleridge*, Kathleen Coburn, general editor. Princeton NJ: Princeton University Press, 1990.

---. *The Watchman* (1796). Edited by Lewis Patton. Volume 2 of *The Collected Works of Samuel Taylor Coleridge*, Kathleen Coburn, general editor. Princeton NJ: Princeton University Press, 1970.

Collini, Stefan, Donald Winch, and John Wyon Burrow. *That Noble Science of Politics: A Study in Nineteenth-Century Intellectual History*. Cambridge UK: Cambridge University Press, 1983.

Collins, Arthus Simons. *The Profession of Letters: A Study of the Relation of Author to Patron, Publisher, and Public, 1780–1832*. London: E. P. Dutton, 1929.

Colmer, John. *Coleridge: Critic of Society.* Oxford: Oxford University Press, 1959.

———. *Coleridge to Catch 22: Images of Society.* New York: St. Martin's Press, 1978.

Corrigan, Timothy. *Coleridge, Language, and Criticism.* Athens GA: University of Georgia Press, 1982.

Coulson, John. *Newman and the Common Tradition: A Study in the Language of Church and Society.* Oxford: Clarendon Press, 1970.

Courtney, C. F. "Edmund Burke and the Enlightenment." In *England in the Eighteenth Century.* Edited by Roy Porter. Revised second edition. London: Folio Society, 1998.

Cragg, Gerald R. *Reason and Authority in the Eighteenth Century.* Cambridge UK: Cambridge University Press, 1964.

Cutsinger, James. *The Form of Transformed Vision.* Macon GA: Mercer University Press, 1987.

Davidson, Geoffrey. *Coleridge's Career.* New York: St. Martin's Press, 1990.

de Mann, Paul. "The Rhetoric of Temporality." In *Interpretation: Theory and Practice*, edited by. Charles S. Singleton, 173-210. Baltimore: Johns Hopkins Press, 1969.

Droz, Jaques. *Europe between Revolutions: 1815–1848.* London: Fontana, 1967.

Duffy, Edward. *Rousseau in England: The Context for Shelley's Critique of the Enlightenment.* Berkeley CA: University of California Press, 1979.

Eatwell, Roger, and Noel O'Sullivan, editors. *The Nature of the Right: European and American Politics and Political Thought since 1789.* London: Pinter Publishers, 1989.

Engell, James. *The Creative Imagination: Enlightenment to Romanticism.* Cambridge MA: Harvard University Press, 1981.

Fruman, Norman. *Coleridge, the Damaged Archangel.* New York: George Braziller, 1971.

Gaull, Marilyn. *English Romanticism.* New York: Norton, 1988.

Godwin, William. *Enquiry Concerning Political Justice.* Edited by I. Kramnick. New York: Penguin, 1985.

Gravil, Richard, and Molly Lefebure, editors. *The Coleridge Connection.* London: Macmillan, 1990.

Gray, Malcolm. *The Highland Economy: 1750–1850.* Westport: Greenwood Press, 1957.

Griggs, Earl Leslie. "*The Friend*: 1809 and 1818 Editions." *Modern Philology* (May 1938): 369-73.

Gross, John J. *The Rise and Fall of the Man of Letters: Aspects os English Literary Life since 1800.* London: Weidenfeld & Nicholson, 1969. Paperback reprint: Chicago: I. R. Dee, 1992.

Habermas, Jurgen. *The Structural Transformation of the Public Sphere.* Translated by Thomas Burger. Cambridge MA: MIT Press, 1989.
Halevy, Elie. *The Growth of Philosophic Radicalism.* London: Faber & Faber, 1934.
_____. *A History of the English People in the Nineteenth Century.* Two volumes. New York: Peter Smith, 1949, 1951.
Hamilton, Paul. *Coleridge's Poetics.* Oxford: Basil Blackwell, 1983.
Harding, Anthony John. *Coleridge and the Idea of Love.* Cambridge UK: Cambridge University Press, 1974.
Hartley, David. *Observations on Man, His Frame, His Duty, and His Expectations.* Sixth edition, corrected and revised. Facsimile reprint: Charlottesville VA: Ibis Publishers, 1980–1989? = London: T. Legg and Son, 1834.
Hegel, Georg Wilhelm Friedrich. *Hegel's Logic. Being Part One of the Encyclopaedia of the Philosophical Sciences (1830).* Translated by William Wallace. Oxford: Clarendon Press, 1975.
Hobsbawm, Eric John. *The Age of Revolution: 1789–1848.* London: Weidenfeld & Nicolson; New York: Mentor; New York: New American Library, 1962.
_____. *Industry and Empire: From 1750 to the Present Day.* The Pelican Economic History of Britain 3. London: Penguin Books, 1969. Earlier editions published under the titles *Industry and Empire: The Making of Modern English Society, 1750 to the Present Day* and *Industry and Empire: An Economic History of Britain since 1750* (London: Weidenfeld & Nicolson, 1969).
Hodgson, William. *The Commonwealth of Reason.* London: printed and distributed by the author and by H. D. Symonds, 1795. Herein cited as "The Commonwealth of Reason." In *Utopias of the British Enlightenment*, edited by Gregory Claeys. Cambridge UK: Cambridge University Press, 1994.
Hole, Richard. *Pulpits, Politics, and Public Order in England, 1760–1832.* New York: Cambridge University Press, 1989.
Holmes, Richard. *Coleridge: Early Visions.* London: Hodder & Stoughton, 1989.
Hulme, Thomas Ernest. "Romanticism and Classicism" and "A Tory Philosophy." In *Selected Writings*, edited by Patrick McGuinness. Flyfield Books. Manchester UK: Carcenet Press, 1998.
Jack, Ian. *English Literature: 1815–1832.* Oxford: Clarendon Press, 1964.
Jackson, James Robert de Jager. *Method and Imagination in Coleridge's Criticism.* London: Routledge & Kegan Paul, 1969. Cambridge MA: Harvard University Press, 1969.
Kant, Immanuel. *Critique of Practical Reason.* Translated by Lewis White Beck. New York: Macmillan Publishing Company, 1985.
_____. *Critique of Pure Reason.* Translated by J. M. D. Meiklejohn. London: J. M. Dent & Sons, 1934.

_____. *Groundwork of the Metaphysic of Morals*. Translated by H. J. Paton. New York: Harper, 1956.

_____. *Kant's Political Writings*. Edited by Hans Reiss. Cambridge UK: Cambridge University Press, 1977.

_____. *Lectures on Ethics*. Translated by Louis Infield. Indianapolis: Hackett Publishing, 1963.

Keller, Albert. "Universals." In *Sacramentum Mundi*, edited by Karl Rahner et al. London: Burns & Oates, 1970.

Kennedy, George. *Classical Rhetoric and Its Christian and Secular Tradition from Ancient to Modern Times*. Chapel Hill: North Carolina University Press, 1980.

_____. *The Art of Persuasion in Greece*. Princeton NJ: Princeton University Press, 1963.

Kennedy, William F. "Coleridge's Economic Views on Postwar Depression: 1817." In *Coleridge: A Collection of Critical Essays*, edited by Kathleen Coburn, 142-51. Englewood Cliffs NJ: Prentice-Hall, 1967.

_____. *Humanist versus Economist: the Economic Thought of Samuel Taylor Coleridge*. Berkeley: University of California Press, 1958.

Kirk, Russell. *The Conservative Mind: From Burke to Santayana*. Chicago: Henry Regnery Company, 1953.

Klancher, Jon. "Reading the Social Text: Power, Signs, and the Audience in Early Nineteenth-Century Prose." *Studies in Romanticism* 23/2 (Summer 1984): 183-204.

Knights, Ben. *The Idea of the Clerisy in the Nineteenth Century*. London: Cambridge University Press, 1978.

LeMahieu, D. L. *The Mind of William Paley: A Philosopher and His Age*. Lincoln NE and London: University of Nebraska Press, 1976.

Leask, Nigel. *The Politics of Imagination in Coleridge's Critical Thought*. London: Macmillan, 1988.

Link, A. S. "Coleridge and the Crisis in Great Britain, 1816–1820." *Journal of the History of Ideas* 9 (1948): 323-38.

MacFarland, Thomas. *Coleridge and the Pantheist Tradition*. Oxford: Clarendon Press, 1969.

Machin, G. I. T. *The Catholic Question in English Politics, 1820–1830*. Oxford: Clarendon Press, 1964.

Macquarrie, John. *Mystery and Truth*. Milwaukee: Marquette University Press, 1985.

Malthus, Thomas. *An Essay on Principle of Population*. Edited by Anthony Flew. New York: Penguin, 1985.

McFarland, Thomas. *Coleridge and the Pantheistic Tradition*. Oxford: The Clarendon Press, 1969.

———. "Coleridge's Magnum Opus." In *Romanticism and the Forms of Ruin*. Princeton NJ: Princeton University Press, 1981.
McGann, Jerome, editor. *The New Oxford Book of Romantic Period Verse*. Oxford: Oxford University Press, 1993.
McGann, Jerome. *The Romantic Ideology: a Critical Investigation*. Chicago: Chicago University Press, 1983.
McKensie, Gordon. *Organic Unity in Coleridge*. Berkeley: University of California Press, 1939.
McKinnon, Donald M. "Coleridge and Kant." In *Coleridge's Variety, Bicentenary Studies*, edited by John Beer. Pittsburgh: University of Pittsburgh Press, 1974.
McManners, John. *The French Revolution and the Church*. London: SPCK, 1969.
Mill, John Stuart. *The Letters of J. S. Mill*. Edited by Hugh S. R. Elliot. London: Longmans, Green and Co, 1910.
Mill, John Stuart, and Jeremy Bentham. *Utilitarianism and Other Essays*. Edited by Alan Ryan. New York: Penguin, 1987.
Miller, John T. *Ideology and Enlightenment: the Political and Social Thought of Samuel Taylor Coleridge*. New York: Garland Publishing, 1987.
Milton, John. *Milton: Poetical Works*. Edited by Douglas Bush. London: Oxford University Press. 1966.
———. *Paradise Lost. An Authoritative Text. Backgrounds and Sources. Criticism*. Second edition. Edited by Scott Elledge. A Norton Critical Edition. New York/London: W. W. Norton, 1993, [1]1975.
Modiano, Raimonda. "Metaphysical Debate in Coleridge's Political Theory." *Studies in Romanticism* 21 (Fall 1982): 465-74.
More, Hannah. "Village Politics, Addressed to All the Mechanics, Journeymen, and Laborers in Great Britain. By Will Chip, a Country Carpenter." In volume 1 of *The Complete Works of Hannah More*. New York: Harper & Brothers, 1855.
Morrow, John. *Coleridge's Political Thought: Property, Morality, and the Limits of Traditional Discourse*. London: Macmillan, 1990.
Muirhead, John. *Coleridge the Philosopher*. London: Allen & Unwin, 1930.
Newsome, David. *Two Classes of Men: Platonism and English Romantic Thought*. London: James Murray, 1974.
Nisbet, Robert Nisbet. *Conservatism: Dream and Reality*. Milton Keynes UK: Open University Press, 1986.
Norman, Edward R. *Church and Society in England, 1770–1970. A Historical Study*. Oxford: Clarendon Press, 1976.
O'Gorman, Frank. *British Conservatism: Conservative Thought from Burke to Thatcher*. London: Longman Group, 1986.

_____. *The Long Eighteenth Century: British Political and Social History, 1688–1832*. London: Arnold Books, 1997.
Orsini, Gian Napoleone Giordano. *Coleridge and German Idealism: A Study in the History of Philosophy with Unpublished Materials from Coleridge's Manuscripts*. Carbondale: Southern Illinois University Press, 1969.
O'Sullivan, Noel. *Conservatism*. New York: St. Martin's Press, 1976.
Pacini, David S. *The Cunning of Modern Religious Thought*. Philadelphia: Fortress Press, 1987.
Paley, William. *Natural Theology: or, Evidences of the Existence and Attributes of the Deity: Collected from the Appearances of Nature*. Twelfth edition. London: printed for J. Faulder, 1809. Facsimile reprint: Charlottesville VA: Ibis Publishing, 1986.
_____. *The Principles of Moral and Political Philosophy*. Boston: John West, 1810.
_____. *A View of the Evidences of Christianity, in Three Parts; and the Horae Paulinae*. Edited by Richard Potts. Cambridge UK: Cambridge University Press, 1849.
Perkin, Harold. *Origins of Modern English Society*. London: Routledge & Kegan Paul, 1969.
Plato. *Plato: The Collected Dialogues*. Edited by Edith Hamilton and Huntingdon Cairns. Princeton NJ: Princeton University Press, 1961.
Pocock, John Greville Agard. "Burke and the Ancient Constitution." In *Politics, Language, and Time: Essays on Political Thought and History*. Reprint with new preface: Chicago: University of Chicago Press, 1989 (1971).
Porter, Roy. *English Society in the Eighteenth Century*. New York: Penguin, 1990.
Prebble, John. *The Highland Clearances*. London: Secker and Warburg, 1963.
Preyer, Robert O. "Coleridge's Historical Thought." In *Coleridge: A Collection of Critical Essays*, edited by Kathleen Coburn, 152-60. New Jersey: Prentice Hall, 1967. (See at Coburn, above.)
Price, Richard. *A Discourse on the Love of our Country, delivered on Nov. 4th 1789 at the Meetinghouse in Old Jewry, to the Society for the Revolution in Great Britain*. London: Edward E. Powars, 1790.
Prickett, Stephen. *Romanticism and Religion: The Tradition of Coleridge and Wordsworth in the Victorian Church*. Cambridge UK: Cambridge University Press, 1976.
_____. *The Romantics*. New York: Holmes & Meier, 1981.
Rahner, Karl. "The Concept of Mystery in Catholic Theology." In *Theological Investigations*, volume 4: *More Recent Writings*, translated by Kevin Smyth. London: Darton, Longman & Todd, 1974.

Reardon, Bernard M. G. *From Coleridge to Gore: A History of Religious Thought in England*. London: Longmann, 1971.
Ricardo, David. *The Principles of Political Economy and Taxation*. London: Dent, 1973.
Richards, Ivor Armstrong. *Coleridge on Imagination*. Third edition with a new foreword. London: Routledge and Kegan Paul, 1962.
Rist, John M. *Plotinus: The Road to Reality*. Cambridge UK: Cambridge University Press, 1967.
Robinson, James M., and Helmut Koester. *Trajectories through Early Christianity*. Philadelphia: Fortress Press, 1971.
Roe, Nicholas. *Wordsworth and Coleridge: The Radical Years*. Oxford: Clarendon Press, 1988.
Rousseau, Jean-Jaques. *The Social Contract and Discourses*. Translated by G. D. H. Cole. London: J. M. Dent & Sons, 1973.
Schelling, Friedrich Wilhelm Joseph von. *Ideas for a Philosophy of Nature*. Translated by Errol E. Harris and Peter Heath. Cambridge UK: Cambridge University Press, 1988.
———. "Philosophical Investigations into the Essence of Human Freedom and Related Matters." In *Philosophy of German Idealism*, edited by Ernst Behler. Translated by Priscilla Hayden-Roy. New York: Continuum, 1987.
———. *System of Transcendental Idealism (1800)*. Translated by P. Heath. Charlottesville: University Press of Virginia, 1978.
Schlegel, Friedrich. *Friedrich Schlegel's* Lucinde *and the Fragments*. Translated by Peter Firchow. Minneapolis: University of Minnesota Press, 1971.
Schofield, P. "Conservatism in the Late-Eighteenth Century." *Historical Journal* 39 (1986).
Scruton, Roger. *The Meaning of Conservatism*. Second edition. London: Macmillan, 1984.
Sewell, Elizabeth. " 'As I Was Sometime in Milan': Prospects for a Search for Giordano Bruno through Prospero, Coleridge, and the Figure of Exile." *Mosaic* 8/3 (Spring 1975): 127-37.
Simmons, Eva, editor. *Augustan Literature: From 1660 to 1789*. London: Bloomsbury Publishing, 1994.
Smart, Ninian, et al., editors. *Nineteenth Century Religious Thought in the West*. Volume 2. Cambridge UK: Cambridge University Press, 1985.
Smith, Adam. *An Enquiry into the Nature and Causes of the Wealth of Nations*. Chicago: University of Chicago Press, 1976. Great Books of the Western World 39. Chicago: Encyclopaedia Britannica, 1952.
Snyder, Alice. *Coleridge on Logic and Learning*. New Haven CT: Yale University Press, 1929.

Soloway, R. A. *Prelates and People: Ecclesiastical Social Thought in England, 1783–1852*. London: Routledge & Kegan Paul, 1969.
Southey, Robert, and Samuel Taylor Coleridge, *Omniana*. Edited by Robert Gittings. Sussex: Fontewell Press, 1969.
Steven, Leslie. *History of English Thought in the Eighteenth Century*. London: Smith, Elder, & Co., 1902.
Stevenson, John. "Popular Radicalism and Popular Protest, 1789–1815." In *Britain and the French Revolution, 1789–1815*, edited by H. T. Dickinson. London: Macmillan Education, 1989.
Storch, R. F. "The Politics of the Imagination." *Studies in Romanticism* 21 (Fall 1982): 448-56.
Suvanto, Pekka. *Conservatism from the French Revolution to the 1990s*. New York: St. Martin's Press, 1997.
Talmor, Sascha. *The Rhetoric of Criticism: From Hobbes to Coleridge*. New York: Pergamon Press, 1984.
Taylor, Anya. *Coleridge's Defense of the Human*. Columbus: Ohio State University Press, 1981.
Taylor, Charles. "Atomism." In *Philosophy and the Human Sciences: Philosophical Papers 2*. Cambridge UK: Cambridge University Press, 1985.
_____. *Sources of the Self: The Making of Modern Identity*. Cambridge MA: Harvard University Press, 1989.
_____. "What is Human Agency?" In *Philosophy and the Human Sciences: Philosophical Papers 1*. Cambridge UK: Cambridge University Press, 1985.
Thompson, Edward Palmer. *The Making of the English Working Class*. New York: Random House, 1966.
Todorov, Tzvetan. *Theories of the Symbol*. Translated by Catherine Porter. Ithaca NY: Cornell University Press, 1982.
Torrance, Alan. "Introductory Essay." *In Christ, Justice, and Peace* by Eberhard Jungel. Translated by Alan J. Torrance and D. Bruce Hamill. Edinburgh: T. & T. Clark, 1992.
Trevelyan, George Macaulay. *British History in the Nineteenth Century (1782–1901)*. London: Longmans, 1922.
Vickers, Brian. *In Defence of Rhetoric*. Oxford: Clarendon Press, 1988.
Ward, William Reginald. *Religion and Society in England, 1790–1850*. New York: Schocken Books, 1972.
Waterman, A. M. C. "The Ideological Alliance of Political Economy and Christian Theology, 1798–1833." *Journal of Ecclesiastical History* 34/2 (April 1983): 231-44.
Welleck, Rene. *Immanuel Kant in England: 1793–1838*. Princeton NJ: Princeton University Press, 1931.

White, Reginald James, editor. *Political Tracts of Coleridge, Wordsworth, and Shelley.* Cambridge UK: Cambridge University Press, 1953.
⎯⎯⎯⎯. *Waterloo to Peterloo.* London: Heinemann, 1957.
Willey, Basil. "Coleridge on Imagination and Fancy." Warton Lecture on English Poetry, May 1946. *Proceedings of the British Academy* 32.
⎯⎯⎯⎯. *Samuel Taylor Coleridge.* New York: W. W. Norton, 1972.
Williams, Raymond. *Culture and Society.* New York: Columbia University Press, 1953.
⎯⎯⎯⎯. *Marxism and Literature.* Oxford: Oxford University Press, 1977.
⎯⎯⎯⎯. *Problems in Materialism and Culture.* London: NLB, 1980.
Wollstonecraft, Mary. *The Vindications: The Rights of Men; The Rights of Women.* Edited by D. L. Macdonald and Kathleen Scherf. New York: Broadview Press, 1997.
Woodring, Colin. *Politics in the Poetry of Coleridge.* Madison: Wisconsin University Press, 1961.
Wordsworth, Jonathan. "The Infinite I AM: Coleridge and the Ascent of Being." In *Coleridge's Imagination*, edited by Richard Gravil, Lucy Newlyn, and Nicholas Roe. Cambridge UK: Cambridge University, Press, 1985.

Indexes

Name Index

Archimedes, 73
Aristotle, 42, 76, 77
Ashton, Rosemary, 47
Augustine of Hippo, St., 42, 43, 228

Bacon, Sir Francis, 77, 94, 110
Ball, Sir Alexander, 39, 49
Bede, The Venerable, St., 204
Bentham, Jeremy, 40, 177, 200, 202
Bernard of Clairvaux, St., 205
Bonaparte, Napoleon, 126
Bradley, F. H., 188
Brougham, Henry, 143
Burdett, Sir. Francis, 29, 33, 143
Burke, Edmund, viii, ix, 1, 9, 10-20, 21, 22, 23, 24, 25, 26, 27, 33, 107-108, 125, 135, 198, 213-14, 231, 262
Burke, Kenneth, 43, 48

Calleo, David, 212
Carlile, Richard, 200
Cartwright, Major John, 29, 110, 137, 143, 144, 200
Charlemagne, 91
Cobbett, William, 29, 35, 92, 110, 143, 144, 157, 160
Coleridge, Edward, 236
Colmer, John, 193

Cooper, Anthony Ashley. *See* Shaftesbury, Earl of.

Darwin, Charles, 238
Davy, Humphrey, 31
De Quincey, Thomas, 47
Descartes, Rene, 240
Diderot, Denis, 128
Donne, John, 174

Queen Elizabeth I, 51
Erigena, Johannes, 204, 226

Ferguson, Adam, 149
Fichte, Johann Gottlieb, 238
Foster, John, 90

Gillman, James, 88
Gillray, James, 135
Godwin, William, 3, 4, 7, 20, 35, 240
Green, J. H., 176, 219, 227, 234

Harrington, James, 51, 110
Hartley, David, 79, 80, 186, 240
Hazlitt, William, 90
Hegel, G. W. F. 47, 119, 154
Heraclitus, 82, 105, 109, 230-31
Hobbes, Thomas, 16, 130, 189-90, 202
Hodgson, William, 1-3, 5, 6, 11, 19
Holcroft, Thomas, 3

Hole, Richard, 199, 200,
Holmes, Richard, 47, 174
Hume, David, 83
Hunt, Henry, 143, 157
Hunt, John, 29, 143
Hunt, Leigh, 29, 143

James II (king), 10
Jenkinson, Robert Banks. *See* Liverpool, Earl of.
Justinian, 76

Kant, Immanuel, 77, 94, 124, 129, 154, 176, 191, 192, 204, 217, 224, 263, 264

Lamb, Charles, 34, 135, 197
Leibnitz, Baron Gottfried Wilhelm von, 81
Liverpool, Robert Banks Jenkinson, Earl of, 181
Locke, John, 204, 253
Lockhart, John Gibson, 29

Machiaveli, Niccolo, 110
Malthus, Thomas, 149, 150, 204
McFarland, Thomas, 225, 234, 235
Mill, John Stuart, viii, 40, 148, 212, 231
Millar, John, 149
Miller, John, 218-19, 231
Milton, John, 51, 55, 148, 205
Modiano, Raimonda, 189, 195
More, Hannah, 9-10, 199
Morrow, John, 147, 149, 160
Mudford, William, 153

Napoleon. *See* Bonaparte.
Newton, Sir Isaac, 80, 104, 204, 253
Northmore, Thomas, 4, 7, 11

Paine, Thomas, 8, 9, 20
Paley, William, 37, 91, 97-98, 106, 132, 133, 170, 200-208, 209, 213, 215, 230, 249, 252, 253
Paul, St., 204, 253, 255
Peel, Sir Robert, 197
Percival, Spencer, 71, 96
Philo of Alexandria, 223
Pitt, William, 135, 136
Plato, 76, 77, 79, 90, 91, 92, 94, 212, 228, 231
Poole, Thomas, 39, 5
Pope, Alexander, 15 2
Preyer, Robert, 117-18
Price, Richard, 10-11, 15,
Prickett, Stephen, 232
Priestly, Joseph, 79, 186
Pythagoras, 73-79, 82, 112

Richards, I. A., 53-56, 63
Rousseau, Jean-Jacques, 125, 130, 191-92

Schelling, F. W. J. von, 68, 174-75, 224, 225, 238, 256
Schlegel, Friedrich, 71, 118, 235
Sewell, Elizabeth, 211
Shaftesbury, Anthony Ashley Cooper, Earl of, 7, 51
Smith, Adam, 149, 150, 151, 153
Southey, Robert, viii, 135, 179
Sterling, John, 212
Sterne, Laurence, 25
Steuart, Sir James, 149, 150
Sydney, Sir Philip, 51

Tacitus, 110
Tawney, Richard Henry, 173
Taylor, Anya, 211
Taylor, Charles, 260
Taylor, Jeremy 70, 174

Tetens, Johann Nicolaus, 68
Thales, 73, 78
Thucydides, 110
Tillich, Paul, 173
Torrance, Alan 37
Trimmer, Sarah, 199

Voltaire, Francois-Marie Arouet de, 128

Weber, Max, 173
Whitbread, Samuel, 143
Willey, Basil, 63
Wollstonecraft, Mary, 2, 6, 20-21, 23-26
Wordsworth, Jonathan, 63-64
Wordsworth, William, viii

Subject Index

agriculture, 144, 159, 164, 222, 243
anthropology, 6, 19, 174, 202, 253
aristocracy, 134, 135, 137
art, 22, 51, 66, 104, 105, 174-75
Associationism, 79, 80, 81, 83, 120, 172
atheism, 66, 120, 121, 122, 123, 125, 126, 129, 171

Bible, 8, 27, 68, 72, 74, 82, 88, 96-117, 119, 120, 131, 141, 174, 176, 185, 200, 201, 218
Bill for Catholic Emancipation, 32, 33
botany, 55
Britain, 212, 213, 214, 215-16, 230, 252, 255

Cambridge University, 203, 252
catechism, 169
Catholic Emancipation, 197-98, 199, 209
Catholicism, 197-98
Chalcedonian Definition, 252
Chemistry, 53, 55
Christ, 100, 101, 103, 113, 227, 247, 250, 251, 252, 255
Christianity, 97, 98, 106, 129, 130, 157, 161, 165, 169-72, 174, 263, 266

Christology, 100, 101, 103, 107, 108
Church, 120, 123, 125, 132, 134, 141, 179
Church, Christian, 210, 211, 212, 230, 239, 241-55
Church, national, 207-208, 210, 211, 212, 213, 223, 230, 239, 241-44, 245-48, 250-54
civilization, 50, 66
clerisy, 178-79, 180, 188, 195, 211, 241, 243, 247, 251
cognition, 139, 154, 156, 163
commerce, commercialism, 7, 27, 44, 45, 69, 128, 143, 144, 145, 146, 147, 152, 155, 159, 161-65, 167-74, 177, 178, 182,
commonwealth, 1, 3, 5, 11, 19,
consciousness, 224, 225, 226, 238
Conservatism, 1, 2, 10, 11, 12, 15, 17, 18, 26, 27, 39, 42, 48, 86, 111, 112, 114, 134, 136, 137, 165, 168, 187, 194, 195, 213, 231, 261-62
constitution, 3, 4, 5, 6, 7, 8, 9, 11, 13, 14, 15, 21, 32, 33, 34, 94, 115, 125, 131, 136, 144, 145, 187, 192, 198, 199-200, 213, 215-16, 217
consubstantiality, 52, 53, 55, 56, 66, 70, 74, 79, 85, 92, 96, 101, 111, 118, 226, 252

The Courier, 33
creation, 43, 46, 50, 52, 62, 65, 66, 68
culture, 45, 51, 69, 70

Democracy, 3,
desynonymization, 46
Deus alter, 223-26, 229
Deus idem, 223-26,
disestablishment, 248-53
Dissenters, 200, 208, 246-48
Divine Ideas, 213, 226-32

ecclesiology, 210-11, 245, 249, 255
education, 2, 3, 34, 35, 74, 75, 91, 92, 93, 94, 95, 100, 173, 175, 178-79, 180, 187-88, 241-44, 246, 252-53
empiricism, 73, 78, 79, 83, 86
Enlightenment, 116, 121, 128
epistemology, 79, 81, 87, 92, 123, 129, 130, 138, 142, 151, 164, 165, 180, 187, 188, 213, 233, 239, 244, 255
eschatology, 202, 253-54
extremism, 134, 135, 136, 137, 139, 141

faith, 127, 129, 169, 171, 172, 174, 176, 256-57
Fall, 65, 69, 70
fancy, 55, 56, 57, 58, 59, 60, 61, 65, 66, 67, 75, 81, 99, 102, 130, 132, 134, 162, 173, 181, 186, 239, 254, 255
France, 1, 8, 9, 10, 11, 14
French National Assembly, 1, 2, 10, 12, 14, 17, 20, 21
French Revolution, 1, 9, 10, 11, 21, 76, 84, 100, 107, 116, 123-30, 134, 135, 140, 142, 192

Glorious Revolution, 10, 15, 255

God, 4, 6, 23, 37, 52, 64, 65, 69, 86, 101, 102, 103, 105-13, 131, 132, 133, 139, 140, 142, 148, 171, 174, 185, 187, 201-204, 214, 219, 220-29, 233, 250, 253, 254, 255, 256, 264-66
government, 2, 7, 11, 12, 13, 20, 144, 147, 155, 156, 157, 180, 187, 189-90, 192, 197-200, 214, 222, 238, 242
grace, 205

hermeneutics, 35, 72, 96, 101, 102, 112, 114, 117, 178, 184, 188
historiography, 74, 79, 82, 86, 88, 96, 101, 117
history, 3, 9, 12, 13, 14, 16, 17, 18, 25, 26, 27, 35, 71-88, 95, 96, 97, 100, 101, 103, 104, 107-18, 120, 125, 126, 129, 132, 141, 142, 154, 161
homoousios, 52
hope, 122, 137, 149, 155, 156, 157, 158, 159, 163, 177, 185-86

identification, 42, 43, 44, 45, 46, 48, 49, 51, 52, 53, 70, 74, 75, 108, 111, 116, 117, 118, 120, 142, 153, 181, 184-85, 206-207, 208, 213, 230, 235, 236, 238, 239, 240, 252, 256
imagination, 21, 22, 23, 24, 25, 26, 27, 34, 42, 45, 47, 51, 52, 53, 54, 55, 56, 57, 58, 59, 60, 61, 62, 63, 64, 65, 66, 67, 68, 69, 70, 71, 75, 79, 81-83, 87, 88, 92, 95, 99, 102-105, 109, 111, 114-17, 119, 120, 122, 130-34, 139, 140, 154, 172, 173, 174, 177, 178, 179, 181, 182, 184-85, 186, 189, 192-93, 194-95, 209, 211-12, 215, 217, 229, 232-33, 234, 239, 243, 255-57, 262, 263, 265

Index

imago Dei, 45, 62, 64, 67 103, 134, 156, 174, 186-87, 236, 254
individual, 2, 3, 5, 12, 14, 16, 17, 18, 19, 20, 24, 25, 30, 35
Israel, 4, 5, 6

Jacobinism, 6, 124, 125, 126, 131, 135-39, 142, 173, 194
Jewish Constitution, 4, 5, 6, 7

labor, 194
liberty, 3, 6, 8, 9, 10, 20, 25
Logos, 44, 223-39
Loyalism, 10

mind, 172-73, 174, 176, 177, 185, 186, 187, 188, 189, 192
miracle, 98, 99, 100, 101, 106, 115
monarchy, 11, 15
monism, 225
Morning Post, 33
mystery, 264-66

Napoleonic Wars, 28
nationality. *See* church, national.
nature, 2, 6, 13, 14, 15, 19, 21, 22, 35, 73, 83, 84, 85, 86, 93, 94, 99, 106-109, 115, 116, 120-22, 126, 128, 130, 131, 134, 142, 153, 154, 156, 157, 162, 175, 185, 233-41
Necessitarianism, 186, 240

original sin, 2, 6

Painites, 6
pantheism, 224, 226, 256
Pantisocracy, 194
Papacy, 210, 245, 247, 248
Parliamentary reform, 8, 9, 15
patriotism, 32, 22
perichoresis, 227

personeity, 221-23, 263
philosophy, 71-90, 92, 95, 105-109, 114-18, 120, 123, 128, 130, 132, 133, 134, 140, 141, 142, 156, 157, 163, 167-68, 173, 174, 175
poetry, 167, 182, 183-84, 186
prejudice, 14, 18, 22, 23, 24
property, 2, 5, 6, 7, 9, 17, 125, 137, 138, 139, 158, 159, 160, 165, 186-87, 188, 190-91, 193-95
prophecy, 71, 85, 96, 100, 102, 105-10, 115, 118, 233-41, 265

Quakers. *See* Society of Friends.

Radicalism, 1, 2, 3, 6, 7, 8, 9, 11, 12, 13, 15, 18, 20, 33, 183, 194
rationalism, 123, 124, 126, 130, 137, 138, 142, 145, 146, 150, 155, 158, 164
reason, 1, 2, 3, 11, 13, 14, 15, 17, 18, 21, 22, 23, 24, 25, 26, 28, 33, 73, 75, 79, 80-84, 87, 102, 103, 104, 107-109, 114, 115, 120, 121, 122, 123, 125, 126, 127, 128, 129, 130, 131, 133, 134, 135, 136, 138, 139, 142, 143, 147, 151, 152, 154, 155, 158, 163, 164, 171-72, 174, 177, 179, 182, 186, 189, 190, 191, 192, 193, 194, 195, 204, 213, 217, 218, 219, 222, 228-29, 230, 231, 232, 233, 236, 238, 239, 244, 249, 252, 254, 257
reductionism, 6, 20, 72, 83, 84, 92, 95, 106, 116, 132, 133, 134, 139, 150, 154, 155, 162, 169, 171, 176, 213, 218, 259, 263
reform, 8, 9, 15
religion, 3, 4, 6, 12, 13, 20, 26, 27, 28, 29, 31, 32, 35, 83, 84, 86, 96, 97, 98, 99, 104, 105, 116, 120, 122,

123, 126, 128, 129, 132, 134, 139, 140, 141, 142, 158, 167-79, 182, 186
republicanism, 6, 8, 11
rhetoric, 40-43, 45, 46, 48, 49, 50, 51, 64, 70, 180, 182, 184 189, 193
Rights of Man, 1, 2, 8, 9, 11, 13, 14, 17, 19, 20, 23, 24

sacrament, 57, 58, 59
science, 39, 45, 48, 51, 53, 54, 55, 56, 66, 67, 70, 77, 82, 88, 96, 97, 102-105, 107-109, 111, 112, 115, 118, 122, 126, 128, 132, 153
secularism, 197-208
sense, 39, 45, 53, 56, 59, 60, 61, 63, 64, 65, 66, 68, 70
Sensibility, 24
Society of Friends (Quakers), 168-73
Socinianism, 169, 174
soul, 57, 58, 65, 67, 84, 91, 94, 95, 96, 99, 100, 121, 128, 139, 140, 152, 162
subjectivity, 57, 62
suffrage, 32
superstition, 120, 121, 122, 123, 124, 125, 127, 134, 141, 171
symbol, 24, 43, 44, 47, 52, 53, 55, 56, 57, 58, 61, 66, 67, 69, 70, 73-75, 79, 81, 82, 85, 88, 99, 100, 103, 106, 107, 109, 110, 111-15, 117, 124, 126, 133, 134, 139, 140, 152, 161, 162, 175, 176, 184-85, 188-89, 265

theocracy, 5
theological politics, 4, 17, 37
theology, 3, 17, 36, 37, 44, 52, 53, 56, 57, 58, 63, 70, 86, 102, 105, 106, 169, 171-72, 176, 178
toleration, 246-49
Trinity, 44, 70, 219, 220, 223-30, 253, 257

understanding, 42, 43, 44, 45, 46, 59, 60, 61, 62, 64, 65, 66, 67, 68, 69, 70, 73, 78, 79, 81-84, 88, 95, 97, 99, 101-104, 107, 109, 114-16, 123-25, 127-34, 138, 139, 142, 146, 147, 148, 150, 153-55, 158, 162-64, 171, 172, 177, 178, 182, 186, 189, 191, 192, 193, 194, 213, 219, 232, 229, 232, 236 238-39, 243, 244, 246, 249, 252-54, 255, 259, 265
Unitarianism, 168-79
Utilitarianism, 27, 42, 46, 199-203, 205-208
utopia, 3, 5, 6, 7, 9

virtue, 132, 133, 137, 140, 141, 164, 201-202, 249, 254
vocation, 44, 49

wealth, 2, 5, 7, 24